The Book of *Ecclesiastes* (*Qohelet*) and the Path to Joyous Living

This is the first full-length study of Ecclesiastes using methods of philosophical exegesis, specifically those of the modern French philosophers Levinas and Blanchot. T. A. Perry opens up new horizons in the philosophical understanding of the Hebrew Bible, offering a series of meditations on its general spiritual outlook. Perry breaks down Ecclesiastes's motto "all is vanity" and returns "vanity" to its original concrete meaning of "breath," the breath *of life*. This central and forgotten teaching of Ecclesiastes leads to new areas of breath research related both to environmentalism and breath control.

T. A. Perry is Professor of Comparative Literature (Emeritus) at the University of Connecticut. He has previously taught at Williams College, Smith College, Loyola University, Hebrew University, Boston College, and Ben-Gurion University of the Negev. He is the author of numerous books, including *Wisdom Literature and the Structure of Proverbs*, *Erotic Spirituality: The Integrative Tradition from Leone Ebreo to John Donne*, *The Moral Proverbs of Santob de Carrion: Jewish Wisdom in Christian Spain*, *Wisdom in the Hebrew Bible: God's Twilight Zone*, and *Jonah's Arguments with God: The Honeymoon Is Over*.

The Book of *Ecclesiastes* (*Qohelet*) and the Path to Joyous Living

T. A. PERRY
University of Connecticut

CAMBRIDGE
UNIVERSITY PRESS

Shaftesbury Road, Cambridge CB2 8EA, United Kingdom

One Liberty Plaza, 20th Floor, New York, NY 10006, USA

477 Williamstown Road, Port Melbourne, VIC 3207, Australia

314–321, 3rd Floor, Plot 3, Splendor Forum, Jasola District Centre, New Delhi – 110025, India

103 Penang Road, #05–06/07, Visioncrest Commercial, Singapore 238467

Cambridge University Press is part of Cambridge University Press & Assessment,
a department of the University of Cambridge.

We share the University's mission to contribute to society through the pursuit of
education, learning and research at the highest international levels of excellence.

www.cambridge.org
Information on this title: www.cambridge.org/9781107458444

First published 2015
First paperback edition 2024

A catalogue record for this publication is available from the British Library

Library of Congress Cataloging-in-Publication data
Perry, T. Anthony (Theodore Anthony)
The book of Ecclesiastes (Qohelet) and the path to joyous living / T. A. Perry.
pages   cm
Includes bibliographical references.
ISBN 978-1-107-08804-7 (hardback)
1. Bible. Ecclesiastes – Criticism, interpretation, etc.   I. Title.
BS1475.52.P47   2015
2232´.806–dc23   2014047369

ISBN   978-1-107-08804-7   Hardback
ISBN   978-1-107-45844-4   Paperback

To my beloved grandchildren, Esther, Eli, Isaac, Isaiah, Jonah,

Maya, Miriam, and Sacha
"Grandchildren are the crown of the aged."

Proverbs 17:6

Contents

Preface

The dominant and defining theme of Qohelet is *hebel*, ritually and almost exclusively translated as "vanity." It is emphatically announced at the very start as Qohelet's motto:

VANITY OF VANITIES, VANITY OF VANITIES, IT IS ALL VANITY (*hebel*).

Thereupon it spreads its pessimism through the entire book, occurring thirty-seven times as a refrain, typically in the formula "this too is *hebel*."

"Vanity" is only an interpretation, however, since the *peshat* or literal meaning of *hebel* is "breath," yielding different and more complex valences:[1]

A BREATH OF BREATHS, A BREATH OF BREATHS, IT IS ALL BREATH.

In my title I retain the traditional motto dear to generations as the book's calling card, but I attach and advertise Qohelet's root meaning in order to stress crucial differences between the *peshat* and its many possible interpretations.

Further, given the synonymy of *hebel* with "wind" in the Qohelet text, an expanded literal rendering of the opening motto would be:

BREATH OF WINDS, WIND OF BREATHS: IT IS ALL WIND-BREATH.

---

[1] R. B. Y. Scott's Anchor Bible translation clings to the *peshat* or simple meaning in much the same way: "Breath of a breath! (says Qoheleth). The slightest breath! All is a breath" *Proverbs, Ecclesiastes*, AB 18 (New York: Doubleday, 1965), 209. Similarly, Iain Provan suggests (but not in his translation), "The merest of breath, everything is a breath." *Ecclesiastes/ Song of Songs*. Application Commentary (Grand Rapids, MI: Zondervan, 2001), 52. "The goal of these tiresome repetitions is not pessimism but lucidity, the concrete rather than the abstract.... And we must keep to the original word, the literal sense, the breath which dissolves into nothing in the air and which is an eternal point of departure because it is concrete, whereas 'vanity of vanity' to which habit has attached us is an abstract point of arrival." Henri Meschonnic, *Les Cinq rouleaux* (Paris: Gallimard, 1970), 132.

This neologism wind-breath further challenges the vanity interpretation, stressing Qohelet's argument of a *continuity* between outer and inner, macrocosm and microcosm, as against the widespread view of a disjunction between the two and the implied "absurdity" of the human condition. It is a welcome surprise, therefore, to encounter the German translation (the *EinheitsÜbersetzung*) of *hebel* as *Windhauch*, wind-breath. Such a perspective renews the discussion of the resistant pessimism of popular readings, enabling Qohelet's spiritual message to resurface: to joy!

> The light is sweet,
> And the eyes enjoy the sunlight....
> Even if a person lives many years,
> That person should take joy in every single one.
>
> Qohelet 11:7–8

> Do this before all else, my Lucilius: learn joy.
>
> Seneca[2]

> Many endeavored in vain joyfully to speak profoundest joy;
> Here at last, in the tragic, I see it expressed.
>
> Hölderlin[3]

The poet Goethe once characterized as self-defeating the use of dissection to understand the phenomenon of life:

> You have all the parts in hand.
> You missed just one thing: the living band![4]

Such is the situation of one of humankind's greatest moral teachers: all the words and parts of Qohelet's book (Ecclesiastes) have been scrutinized to exhaustion, but the life message has vanished. We now know well enough (well, almost) what the words mean; but even the work's literary genre is still a mystery, and understanding of its spirituality – of its project to live livingly, joyously[5] – remains mired in that despair that

---

[2] Seneca, *Ad Lucilium Epistulae Morales*, 3 vols. (trans. Richard M. Gummere: Loeb Classical Library, 1971), Letter 23 (I:161). All quotations from Seneca are from this translation unless noted otherwise.

[3] "Viele versuchten umsonst, das freudigste freudig zu sagen, / Hier spricht endlich es mir, hier in der Trauer sich aus." Hölderlin, "Sophokles," trans. Michael Hamburger. In Hölderlin, *Poems* (New York: Pantheon, 1942), "Sophocles," 103.

[4] "... hat er die Teile in seiner Hand, / Fehlt leider nur das geistige Band." *Faust*, Part 1, vv. 1938–39.

[5] Similarly, the goal of love, in the words of a great teacher (Ananda K. Coomaraswamy), is to "love *lovingly*." For why do we spend our lives wishing to be alive after we are dead, while tolerating being dead even while we are alive?

we have so desperately foisted upon Qohelet. The goal of this essay is to find a way to put the pieces of the puzzle together again, to get back to a wisdom that brings relief from what Emerson called our lives of exaggeration, to recover Qohelet's sense of balance and tranquility and joyous living.

Qohelet summarized his entire message in a single sentence:

> I know that a person's only good is to be joyous and to enjoy his/her life.
>
> Qoh 3:12

How curious, then, that this potentially strong appeal to modern sensitivities continues to be countered by a few catchwords wrenched out of context and poorly understood! Here are a few, along with the typical, tired reactions:

> "Vanity of vanities" (1:2) – *Oy vey! What a world!*
> "What profit from one's toil?" (1:3) – *I'm calling in sick tomorrow!*
> "There is a time for this and a time for that" (3:2–8) – *God has us in a straitjacket!*
> "Fear God and keep the Commandments" (12:13) – *Go to Sunday school and behave yourself!*

Our understanding of the Book in fact abounds in paradox. Despite Qohelet's popularity, did you ever hear it quoted at a wedding? Too gloomy! At a funeral? Not gloomy enough! At a religious service? Look out: it's awfully secular! At a secular gathering? Too religious! There is no book of the Hebrew Bible that has aroused such deep suspicion from religious establishments. Is he not, after all, "upper class" and "too interested in money"? Unsystematic? Anti-activist? Anti-God? Perhaps – even worse – not even canonical! And what of his theology? No covenant! No cult or prayers or revelation! No religion, really – "purely secular man," ventures one prominent critic.[6] Not that these matters divert anyone from reading Qohelet, our most philosophical book in Hebrew Scripture. At least, all sides of the atheistic divide may concur that God has more serious things to worry about than His mere existence!

In other words, Qohelet's is a good theology for modern people, for when religion itself has been put in a straitjacket or, worse, become a mere commodity, Qohelet's discrete about-face seems a fine way to save spirituality itself. Qohelet surely does have a theology and existential commitment (otherwise, what is it doing in the Bible?), but it sidesteps those radical intensities ("down on your knees!") and absolutist

---

[6] Emmanuel Levinas was pleased to quote Rosenzweig's remark that "God did not create religion, he created the world."

pronouncements that we have come to identify as the total content of the religious life. Qohelet a "preacher"?! Surely not in the sense of those featured on American television, which look more like circuses and Hollywood extravaganzas.

To be sure, Qohelet has little to offer those who derive enjoyment from getting – co(he)llecting! – and spending and overworking. Until, that is, either the money runs out or they find themselves out of a job; or, at the other extreme, they just never do, despite objective needs and reasonable standards, seem to have enough. But for those who aspire to be rid of the great addictions of the day – workaholism, violence, affluenza, gambling, consumerism (including religion) especially – Qohelet offers moral support and a sensible guide. As for those recurrent idolatries – senseless quest for permanence and power and absolute knowledge and heaven on earth – his calm and concrete sense of contentment recalls a perennial alternative.

My focus on Qohelet's spirituality can thus be taken as a reaction to the thesis, nurtured by generations of both academic and even clerical scholarship, that it does not have one. Except for a face-saving conclusion ("fear God and keep the commandments") and a few so-called pious glosses, which, according to this view, have kept it in the canon, scholars have focused, sometimes with shuddering delight, on its pessimism.[7] This strikes me as having too easy a time of it – not that Qohelet disallows yelling out when the pain is intense. However, as Euripides put it, "The easiest thing is to accuse the gods."[8] For what remains unnoticed is both Qohelet's own rejection of such complaints and his insistence (11:8) that humans, with all our woes, must take enjoyment in every single day. And responsibility, too, when we do not.

I offer these exegetical reflections as a contribution to the sea change that is taking place in Qohelet criticism, passing from a mood of brooding pessimism against life and God that in some circles has become so ingrained as to have taken on the semblance of pieties.[9] At the center

---

[7] Or, on a somewhat more positive tone, its epicureanism – hardly a canonical criterion, even though, as Montaigne loved to observe, the master Epicurus was anything but easygoing.

[8] "Le plus facile c'est d'accuser les dieux." Quoted in Charles Mopsik, *La Sagesse de ben Sira* (Paris: Verdier, 2003), 157.

[9] In this context, how refreshing Jim Limburg's book, inspired by Luther; Marie Maussion's careful dissertation; Thomas Krüger's balanced and inspiring commentary; Rami Shapiro's quietist approach, to name only a few. Jewish exegesis is often more upbeat. As an early and virtually unstudied example, I like Gershon Lange's *Sefer Kohelet: übersetz und erklärt* (Frankfurt am Main, 1910); translated and annotated by Yosef B. Fagin

of my endeavor is a rethinking of his central notion of *hebel* ("vanity"), without the privileged help of clergy or even Albert Camus. While not so systematic as some might wish, Qohelet has clear notions of the *human* sources of misery and happiness, and he offers concrete and extensive techniques for passing from one to the other. Of particular interest is his dense meditation on the polysemy of *hebel*, its many levels of meaning, occasioning a spiritual transformation that leads through withdrawal to concrete engagement with the world: if not with the world we would like, at least with the only one available to us, as our human and spiritual birthright.

One fruitful approach would be to meditate on the paradox – in a book that multiplies this mode of perception – at the book's very center: if Qohelet is mainly about universal "vanity," then it should be read on days of abstinence and withdrawal from things earthly. At least in traditional Jewish observance, however, the book is read when all of that is over and done with and "the time of our joy" has arrived. Doesn't this seem to suggest that "vanity," properly understood, can sponsor spiritual celebration? At the very least, we would do well to downshift from high despair to a sober acknowledgment that allows life to go on *without* all the stress. For, after considering the proposition that our lives are utterly vain and absurd and meaningless, we still wouldn't mind knowing what's for supper.

King Qohelet addresses us from the royal perspective of someone who "has it all" and makes all the mistakes common to that kind of person. Why and how does this speak to simpler folk like most of us would like to be? Because we too "want it ALL." But his repetitive conclusion that "ALL is vanity" may not imply that *everything* is, at least not to the same degree. What then is this ALL that we all want and why is it important, according to Qohelet, that we NOT get it? Perhaps it was important to experience the emptiness of it all, not only to then be able to turn from its pursuit but also to discover, beneath the rubble, the seeds of rebirth into a better wisdom.

The broad trajectory of Qohelet's curriculum vitae, on his own testimony, is characteristic of many of us humans. Laboring to pursue and acquire the goods of life, at some point we change direction in order to

(Lakewood, NJ: Gilayon, 2007). Lange concludes that Qohelet's "optimistic approach is the thread that runs through the entire book and ties the whole work together" (p. xxi). New generic possibilities are also emerging. Daniel Harrington has put forth the idea that Ben Sira is a biblical guide for living wisely. Years ago I proposed that Qohelet be read as intended, as a guide for living well – *bene vivere*, the equivalent of living wisely.

pursue the good life.[10] The similarity of formulas accentuates the reversal of intention, for life's goods are nothing like the good life. At the base is perhaps the wisdom conviction, sometimes taught through tradition or acquired through life experience, that life's goodness is occluded by goods and that the real and elusive goal is, indeed, life itself, a given that is repeatedly given and yet perpetually pursued under different forms because it is never the same, elusive by its own nature, as obvious as the nose on another's face and the breath of cosmic air that circulates through me as I breathe in and out, and the inspiration that enlivens my imagination and instinct with every breath. In a word – Qohelet's favorite – life is a *hebel,* an empty or "vanity" breath, and we are its breathers. And the "almost nothing" that is life's breath, the one unrecognized and despised by the builders, has become the cornerstone of Qohelet's teaching of joyous living.

And, oh, my opening quip about dissection…. All the parts may indeed make a countable sum, but not a living whole. For this to occur in a literary text, it is the connections that count, and these are basically the work of imagination and philosophy. Those authors of greatest assistance in interpreting Qohelet are those who cleave closest to his perennial moral and pedagogical vision, whether deliberately (Montaigne takes the lead here) or accidentally (Seneca).[11] When the text is also a sacred one, a smidgen of spiritual imagination would also help. Among moderns, Emerson and Annie Dillard seem to me exciting guides and companions. When, additionally, the goal is to think greater perspectives yet – from "out of the box," as we currently say, then Rabbinic midrash and, yes, Maurice Blanchot can be trusted to open things up a bit further. However, for understanding this most philosophical of our biblical books and rendering it into modern intellectual parlance, my greatest debt is to Emmanuel Levinas, most notably in the literary meditations as outlined in his recently published

---

[10] Richard A. Lanham quotes Lewis Mumford's pun "the goods of life rather than the good life" as a form of *antanaclasis: A Handlist of Rhetorical Terms* (Berkeley: University of California Press, 1991), 12, article "*antanaclasis.*" See Appendix 6, "Antanaclasis."

[11] For Montaigne I use the edition of Pierre Villey, *Les Essais de Michel de Montaigne* (Paris: Presses Universitaires de France, 1965) and attach, after the page number, the book and chapter; thus, II:1 refers to book 2, chapter 1. For a complete English translation, Donald Frame's is highly recommended: *The Complete Essays of Montaigne* (Palo Alto, CA: Stanford University Press, 1976). There is no better warm-up text for Qohelet than Montaigne's essay "On Vanity" (*Les Essais* III:9). For abundant parallels on both cosmology and moral philosophy, Santob de Carrión's (Spain, fourteenth century) medieval autobiography is hard to beat. See T. A. Perry, *The Moral Proverbs of Santob de Carrión* (Princeton, NJ: Princeton University Press, 1987).

Carnets de Captivité. It is Levinas's acute moral sensitivity that has furnished an appropriate philosophical vocabulary, innovative exegetical principles, and to my mind stunning parallels to Qohelet's own moral and philosophical quest.[12] My method is thus adventurous in that it combines standard biblical exegesis (with a dash of Midrash) with those modes of thinking most appropriate to rendering Qohelet's ethical spirituality in terms of being both traditional and modern. Jewish sages quipped that if there can be no learning without bread, they were also persuaded that there can be no bread without learning. Applied to our task at hand, if there can be no philosophy without philology, the inverse is equally true, and for Qohelet Levinas may be a reliable guide. Among modern critics there have always been those who have gone beyond the totalizing pessimistic suggestion that *all* is vanity and readily admit another side to Qohelet's teaching, if not altogether joyous, at least balanced. Leading the rising tendency is, again, Michael V. Fox in his second phase, the perennials such as Ogden, Whybray, Lohfink, and more recent studies such as those of Eunny P. Lee, Alison Lo, and Martin Shuster, who in his astonishing philosophical essay senses that *hebel* "is a philosophical concept that must be unpacked philosophically." His title, "Being as Breath, Vapor as Joy..." approximates my own orientation, with slight changes: "Life as Breath, Breath as Joy."[13] Shuster goes on to express his common purpose with Douglas B. Miller in his conviction that "Qohelet pondered just what image might best represent *life* as he has experienced and deliberated upon it" (Shuster 2008, 230; italics added). He concludes that "once the translation of *hebel* as 'vanity' is dropped, it becomes difficult to maintain a pessimistic reading" of Qohelet, opting rather, like Johnston, for a "qualified optimism."[14]

---

[12] Although Levinas has been primarily known as a philosopher and Talmudic exegete, his influence is now extending to ever newer fields, such as social action, humor, literature, and linguistics. In the field of biblical exegesis, see Claire Elise Katz, *Levinas, Judaism, and the Feminine: The Silent Footsteps of Rebecca* (Bloomington: Indiana University Press, 2003). For further influence of Levinas on biblical exegesis, see Katz, 172, n. 50. In a recent book Claire Katz examines Levinas's pedagogical importance; see her *Levinas and the Crisis of Humanism* (Bloomington: Indiana University Press, 2012).

[13] Martin Shuster, "Being as Breath, Vapor as Joy: Using Martin Heidegger to Re-read the Book of Ecclesiastes," *JSOT* 33 (2008): 219–44 at 230, n. 48. In a private communication, Shuster clarified that his use of vapor was simply consonant with its frequent listing with the true *peshat* (breath) and that he "wouldn't want to draw a firm distinction between vapor and breath."

[14] Ibid., 241. He is quoting Robert K. Johnston, "Confessions of a Workaholic: A Reappraisal," *CBQ* 38 (1976): 14–28.

Abbreviations

AB	Anchor Bible Commentary
Abot	Pirkei Abot [Ethics of the Fathers]
BT	Babylonian Talmud
CBQ	*Catholic Biblical Quarterly*
CC	Levinas, *Carnets de Captivité*, vol 1
ch./chs.	chapter/chapters
GKC	Gesenius, Wilhelm, E. Kautzsch, and A. E. Cowley, *Gesenius' Hebrew Grammar*, Oxford, Clarendon, 1906
HALOT	*Hebrew and Aramaic Lexicon of the Old Testament*, Koehler and Baumgartener and Stamm. Brill, 1994ff.
JBL	*Journal of Biblical Literature*
JPS	The Jewish Publication Society
JSOT	*Journal for the Study of the Old Testament*
MT	Masoretic Text (the standard Hebrew version)
n./nn.	note/notes
NJPS	*Tanak: The Holy Scriptures: The New JPS Translation According to the Traditional Hebrew Texts*
NRSV	New Revised Standard Version of the Bible
OTL	Old Testament Library
PS	Levinas, *Parole et silence et autres conférences inédites*
Qohelet	Both the Book of Ecclesiastes and its chief narrative voice; literally "Collector"
Radak	Rabbi David Kimhi (1160?–1235?). See *Torat Hayyim*
Rashi	Rabbi Shlomo Yitzhak (1040–1105). See *Torat Hayyim*
RSV	Revised Standard Version of the Bible
Tanak	Hebrew Scriptures (**T**orah, **N**eviim, **K**etubim)

TI	Levinas, *Totalité et Infini*
v./vv.	verse/verses
vs.	versus

Biblical books are abbreviated according to guidelines published in the *SBL Handbook of Style*. All references to the Bible and to classical texts give chapter followed by verse or appropriate subdivision. I cite Hebrew Scripture according to the chapter and verse of the MT and give the English when different. All biblical and other translations are mine unless otherwise noted.

For the transliteration of Hebrew, because in all cases the goal is less to reproduce the exact spelling of MT than to recall the shape of the Hebrew words, vowels are transliterated as they would sound in an English reading. Consonants are transliterated according to the "General Purpose Style" in the *SBL Handbook of Style*.

List of Credits

"Connoisseur of Chaos" and "The Poems of Our Climate" from *The Collected Poems of Wallace Stevens* by Wallace Stevens, copyright © 1954 by Wallace Stevens and copyright renewed 1982 by Holly Stevens. Used by permission of Alfred A. Knopf, an imprint of the Knopf Doubleday Publishing Group, a division of Random House LLC. All rights reserved.

"Of Mere Being" from *The Palm at the End of the Mind: Selected Poems and a Play* by Wallace Stevens, copyright © 1967, 1969, 1971 by Holly Stevens. Used by permission of Alfred A. Knopf, an imprint of the Knopf Doubleday Publishing Group, a division of Random House LLC. All rights reserved.

Introduction

The Path of Moral Philosophy and Beyond

[The Writings of the Hebrew Bible provide] precepts for the conduct of human life.

Josephus[1]

Isn't it greatness to have been the first, perhaps the only, to have taught us how to live on this earth without any conditions other than those of life itself?[2]

Divrei Qohelet: *The Book's Title and Plot*

While Jewish tradition designates Solomon as the author of Qohelet, the book speaks of a surrogate, if you will: Qohelet, the "Collector." At a simple literary level, this pseudonym points to both the form or style of his book and also to its content; and in fact the Collector could serve as a pen name for all such "authors" of proverb collections, from those anonymous ones of the ancient world to Ben Franklin and Bartlett. What has he collected? Let the anonymous presenter explain:

> These are the words/things (*debarim*) of Qohelet.
>
> Qoh 1:1

By the end of the book we learn that the simple collector of fragments has carried the enterprise to more weighty proportions: he also collects the words of others as well as his own, and he, further, gathers students to pore over and discuss them, through this process perhaps becoming a sage in his own right. Thus, a simple word collection such as a telephone

---

[1] Flavius Josephus, *The Life. Against Apion* (Cambridge, MA: Loeb Classical Library, Harvard University Press, 1976), 2: 40.

[2] Geoffrey Hartman, *A Scholar's Tale* (New York: Fordham University Press, 2007), 177. The quotation, as recalled by Henri Peyre, is Eric Auerbach's appraisal of Montaigne's importance.

book has before our very eyes become almost an essay on human experience. Small wonder that Montaigne, the inventor of the essay genre, held Qohelet in such high esteem.[3]

These fragments bespeak a fragmented existence, shards of personal experience and observation: *debarim*, "things" of life, things of speech. Their collection under a single rubric, here called a doublet, reveals a double project that defines the book's plot, the conversion of Qohelet from being a collector of pleasure and power "things" to a collector of words.[4] One of his literary challenges will be to bring the pieces into some kind of unified meaning while remaining true to their existential fragmentation. An important question, if posed historically, is unrecoverable: did Qohelet begin as a mere collector – a hobbyist or raconteur – and only later develop a full-blown national business? Or perhaps it was the concluding wisdom enterprise that led to his dedicated hobby of collecting. The evidence of the book itself points to a cycle, for "the end is in the beginning." By the time we get to the fuller wisdom project at the end of the book, we return to the opening words with a deeper understanding: the fragmentary word/things and action/things of his life are also "words of reproof," Qohelet has a moral message to impart.[5]

These observations are confirmed by a second linguistic doublet,[6] the author's name. Just as there are two kinds of *debarim*, there are two Qohelets. First of all, since Qohelet is not a proper name, one cannot say that "this book was written by Qohelet." This point is even stressed at the end, where it is affirmed, in the closing summary: "Vanity of Vanity said THE Qohelet." Thus, it is not a real name but rather a pen name or pseudonym pointing to an activity or profession. The root word itself has a meaning in biblical Hebrew: to gather together or collect. Thus, Solomon, as recorded in 1 Kings, gathered the congregation together for a public reading of the law. So too, in the last chapter of our book, Qohelet, here also referred to as the Convoker, is seen as gathering together or convoking scholars and students, and this group sets itself the task of collecting and studying proverbs and other fragments of traditional and popular wisdom. This sage, by gathering the research staff

---

³ See Eric S. Christianson, *Ecclesiastes through the Centuries* (Oxford: Blackwell, 2007), 44–46.

⁴ For the concept of doublet, see Appendix 6, "Doublets."

⁵ For *debarim* as words of reproof, see T. A. Perry, *Dialogues with Kohelet: The Book of Ecclesiastes: Translation and Commentary* (University Park: Penn State University Press, 1993), 177.

⁶ Just as the literary figure of hendiadys brings two related words into a single concept, a doublet or bifurcated figure takes a single word in two related but distinct directions. See Appendix 6, "Doublets."

and setting up a curriculum of proverb study and collection, went on to found a school, and these activities are both referred to in his name "Collector."

These two doublets – the pen-name and his "things" – forecast the book's main plot: the personal progression of the pseudo-author from being a collector of power-things to a collector of word-things, as Maurice Blanchot might put it.[7] This is not a mere shift in interest; it records a spiritual transformation. Some might prefer to call it just growing up or getting a life. Additionally, Qohelet's autobiography from the very start is doubled with a moral agenda. If we miss this dual (literary and spiritual) perspective of the Book of Qohelet, we will have missed a great deal.

André Neher, in his great and much neglected essay on Qohelet, focuses on the perennial problem of the book's "contradictions" in a rather innovative way. While still clinging to the usual notion of their troublesome incongruity, he evokes the multiplicity of Qohelet's voices, their complexity as rich as the human existence they both reflect and inspire. Two very different and pervasive moods hold the critic's attention in particular: on the one hand, Qohelet's clear and reasonable directions on how to live one's life; on the other, a meditation that "transcends rational categories and uncovers the mystery of the world's suffering." Let Neher himself set the terms:

> In Qohelet two contradictory ethics confront one another. The first, a reasonable wisdom; the second, a perplexing un-reason. The one, comfortably installed in the golden mean; the other, prowling at the outskirts and provoking an uneasy questioning or cynical irony or disabused pessimism. Prudence and adventure have concluded a pact in Qohelet and walk together.[8]

It is fair to say that critical attention has been coopted by the second of these, by what has been viewed as the work's irony and pessimism. It is also the case that the first, Qohelet's ethical teaching, is typically either misunderstood or neglected altogether, so that even Neher can speak of

---

[7] Blanchot states it in reverse, speaking of a "guarantee which forbids a man of words from becoming a man of power" *L'Écriture du désastre* (Paris: Gallimard, 1980), 21.

[8] André Neher, *Notes sur Qohélét* (Paris: Les Éditions de minuit, 1951), 12. His phrase "prowling at the outskirts" ("rôdant aux extrêmes") corresponds nicely to Qohelet's project of the Outside ("le dehors," see Chapter 7. The contrast between prudence and adventure seems an allusion to Guillaume Apollinaire's "quarrel between Classical Order and Adventure" in his famous poem "La Jolie rousse," in *Oeuvres Poétiques: "Calligrammes"* (Paris: Gallimard, Bibliothèque de la Pléiade, 1956), 313–14.

it as merely "comfortable" or, worse, "viscous and unctuous like a bour-geois catechism."[9]

Hebel: *The Book's Motto and Refrain*

> One's translation and understanding of *hebel* will largely determine one's understanding of the book as a whole. This cannot be emphasized enough![10]

Caveat Lector: Qohelet is a poetic text, at the center of which and throughout is the polysemic word *hebel*, whose *peshat* or literal meaning "breath" is subject to many different interpretations. In my analysis four levels are especially prominent: vanity-*hebel*, transience-*hebel*, disaster-*hebel*, and word-*hebel*. Often these areas are distinct. For instance, "vanity-*hebel*" typically refers to human behavior, whereas transience-*hebel* characterizes the entire cosmos but with special emphasis on the nonhuman realm. In all instances of interpretation, however, the *hebel* designation is attached in order to remind one of the *peshat* or literal meaning that traverses them all: life/wind-breath.

Hebel #1: *Vanity Living*

My goal in Part I is to relocate Qohelet's pessimism within a spiritual (i.e., *real*-life) perspective, mainly by asking whether these two tendencies are in real contradiction or rather, quite the opposite, mutually supportive. For if, to take up Neher's image, ethics and spiritual exploration walk together, they must be walking in the same direction. The first order of business is to provide a full and clear description of Qohelet's ethical impulse toward moderation. Like many moralists, both ancient and modern (Epicurus...), Qohelet's ethical meditation arises from a consideration of human suffering, asking what its causes are and how it can be understood and neutralized, perhaps even transformed.

Now it is a prevalent opinion, held by even the best of critics, that King Qohelet, most notably in the "royal fiction" of 1:12–2:26, holds life to be "completely meaningless and absurd."[11] As a corrective to this view, I am

---

[9] Neher, *Notes*, 15. For research on the possibility of a dialogic reading of Qohelet, see my *Dialogues with Kohelet*.

[10] Mark R. Sneed, *The Politics of Pessimism in Ecclesiastes: A Social-Science Perspective* (Atlanta: Society of Biblical Literature, 2012), 155.

[11] Thomas Krüger, *Qoheleth, a Commentary* (Minneapolis: Fortress Press, 2004), 206.

reminded of Montaigne's critique of the thesis that our lives are ruled by chance:

> It is small wonder that chance has such power over us since we [choose to] live by chance."[12]

Here too, Qohelet argues, much of the *hebel*-vanity of our lives is not a given but rather a human invention and pursuit. Quite distinct from the *hebel* out there in the cosmos (we shall, in Part II, refer to it as transience), which God seems to place there for our confusion and distress but also for the adventurous of heart, there is the *hebel* that humans create, with the things and actions and attitudes that *are* within our moral control to change and regulate.

Qohelet's How-To-Live book is, in the first instance, a manual for achieving such a transformation. His method is an interwoven series of dense meditations on the concept and experience of *hebel*, "breath," often viewed as something unsubstantial and fleeting, thus interpreted as "vanity." Applied to human pursuits, it is frequently parsed by its companion, "chasing the wind," suggesting that our actions are reflexive. Just as the wind turns only upon itself (1:6), the pursuit of emptiness produces an empty person:

> They have gone after vanity *(hebel)* and have become vanity *(yehebalu)*.
>
> Jer 2:5; also 2 Kgs 17:15

Using Qohelet's own terms, the obvious meaning is that they have become vanity *because* they pursued it. When, through analysis and experience, we become aware of the "vanity" of our lives, the smart first move is to shrink the tumor, to withdraw from the bad *hebel* and limit the damage, to "just say no." In Qohelet's view this first level of *hebel* perception can be turned to enormous profit by being smart, modifying unhealthy behaviors and attitudes by following those simple precepts that make up a goodly portion of the book and that place it squarely in the perennial tradition of moral guidance. For, beyond just living, there is the wisdom goal of living well or wisely.[13]

---

[12] Montaigne, *Les Essais*, 337 (II:1).

[13] "Life is a gift of the immortal gods, but living well is the gift of philosophy." Seneca, *Letters*, Letter 90, start; also Plato, Crito 48: "Not life itself but the good life is chiefly to be desired." Krüger (*Qoheleth, A Commentary*, 46) thus views 1:3–4:12 as a "discursive laying of the foundation of ethics," the latter term being defined as a "theory of the human conduct of life." The focus on *bene vivere* is the adverb, not so much what you do but *how* you do it. "It is in the *manner* in which one is present, in which one lives, that there is ethics" Emmanuel Levinas, *De Dieu qui vient à l'idée* (Paris: Vrin, 2004), 144. See Appendix 3, "*Vivere* and *bene vivere*."

We have missed this central concern of the Book of Qohelet by jumping too readily into the theological morass that blames God and things out there for our unhappiness. Qohelet in fact believes just the opposite: that pursuit of vanity is not only unproductive but sinful, offering his own curriculum vitae as an example *not* to follow, and perspectivizing his entire book through a prism both autobiographical and confessional.[14] Once the issue of collection is clarified, the confessional purpose cannot be limited to 1:12–2:26 but rather extends throughout the entire book and gives it its own kind of unity. Such a confessional perspective, both literary and spiritual, opens up neglected possibilities for interpretation.

Hebel #2: *Cosmic Hebel*

At a second and broader level, one that moves from personal *hebel* to universal transience, a brief prolegomenon is needed, what one might call the truth criterion.[15] This means looking intently and seeing not what you or your readership would like to see but what in fact is there.[16] This criterion is put forth in the Hebrew Bible as the absolute basis of jurisprudence and is called *mishpat.* In modern times it forms the bedrock of scientific inquiry and, like *mishpat,* is to be totally independent from the incursions of self-interest, power, and politics. In both courts of law and the laboratory, the truth is pursued. Critical thinking is a spin-off of the scientific method and requires the same level of probity.

Michael V. Fox has argued that Qohelet's new path was to extend this approach to epistemology, which he characterizes as use of the independent rational intellect as the sole instrument of investigation.[17] He loosely terms this approach empirical, meaning that the foundation of

---

[14] Hugo Grotius spied the repentance theme, attaching it to the ascription of Qohelet to King Solomon. See summary in Krüger, *Qoheleth, A Commentary,* 34, and Chapter 1. See also André Barucq, *Ecclésiaste* (Paris: Beauchesne, 1968), 29, who refers to Qohelet's various "confessions in the first person," and one can surely trust the Catholic clergy to detect the liturgical genre.

[15] "The sole function of philosophy is to discover the truth about things divine and things human" Seneca, *Letters,* Letter 90 (II, 395).

[16] The criterion of truth is nicely put by Isaiah (42:3): "to bring forth judgment unto truth (*'emet*). See Chapter 10, "Mortal Remains: Writing Fragments...."

[17] Michael V. Fox, *A Time to Tear Down and a Time to Build Up: A Rereading of Ecclesiastes* (Grand Rapids, MI: Eerdmans, 1999), 76. Also his "The Epistemology of the Book of Proverbs," *JBL* 126 (2007): 669–84. Peter Machinist has further analyzed Qohelet's pursuit of explicit conceptualization and abstraction, notably in his attempt to define the limits of human understanding; see his "Fate, *miqreh,* and Reason: Some Reflection of Qohelet and Biblical Thought," in *Solving Riddles and Untying Knots,* ed. Z. Zevit et al. (Winnona Lake, IN: Eisenbrauns, 1995), 159–75.

knowledge is experience. I view this correct thesis as a major advance in Qohelet studies and would like to give it my own slight push forward. I think that, like scientific and judicial inquiry, Qohelet's method can be extended in many directions. Qohelet's additional innovation is to take his experiential method and apply it to experience itself, and in its most daily manifestations. It is small wonder that the founder of essayistic inquiry – Montaigne – was a devoted admirer of Qohelet, his favorite biblical book, and that his final and crowning essay is entitled "De l'Expérience," meaning both personal experience and the experimental or truth method that brings it to the light of day.

In my reading, Qohelet's analysis of our human condition focuses on two existential areas where the truth criterion must be applied. The first is nicely described by Thomas Krüger:[18]

> Human beings and all that they do are transitory and "fleeting." And all the convictions and wishes that do not do justice to this transitoriness of humankind are untenable and "futile." This in no way means that life is completely "meaningless" and "absurd," as the king holds in 1:12–2:26.

Krüger, in one sentence, turns traditional suppositions on their head, arguing that the absurd is not transience itself but rather the failure to be honest about it. Rami Shapiro is forthright about life's messiness and the need to take it as given:

> This is what I mean by being present to the moment. Nothing magical or extraordinary, just life as it is – often messy and rarely scripted. The more I empty myself of self and of the quest for surety, permanence, and control for permanence that defines the self, the more I am at home in the chaos of my life... And in this there is a grace – an ease of doing – that we cannot imagine as long as we seek to control and manipulate things to meet our ends.[19]

In addition to *hebel*-transience, the truth of human life involves opposites that constitute stable structures – usually binary ones – regulating knowledge and behavior: no day without night, no life without death. Does this mean that night and death are good (or bad)? Thoreau would say that they are better than that: they are true, they are integral to the reality we are given. This is what Qohelet sought to give: "words of truth" (12:10). And what are they? Roland Murphy goes to the point in a single sentence: " 'Truth' [*'emet*] is meant in the profound sense of capturing

---

[18] Krüger, *Qoheleth, A Commentary*, 206.
[19] Rami Shapiro, *The Way of Solomon: Finding Joy and Contentment in the Wisdom of Ecclesiastes* (San Francisco: Harper, 2000), 117.

reality."[20] The implications of this criterion are vast. For one thing, it blows away the usual overconcern with Qohelet's contradictions. As Montaigne says, if my subject is change and transience, I change with it. If reality is contradictory, then my writing must exemplify that reality. If human knowledge is limited, shall I try to seem all-knowing?

Hebel #3: *The Hebel of Dis-aster*

As already stated, since the Book of Qohelet loosely but persistently gathers itself around the concept of *hebel,* this study will have four focal points, one dealing with each of Qohelet's evolving senses of *hebel*: as sinful vanity (Part I); as universal transience (Part II); as the great void that is the source and wellspring of creativity and all new beginnings (Parts III and IV).[21] Part IV attempts to draw these fragments together and reconstruct Qohelet's practical theory of joyous living, both in the here and now "under the sun" and also in the "Outside" or somewhere else, and on the relation between these two forms of behavior and awareness. He consequently offers two solutions: a practical guide to living wisely in this world, and a metaphysical meditation from *beyond* the sun (also a *hebel* perspective!) as a source of renewal and creativity (Part IV).

To clarify and access these dimensions of *hebel,* it is crucial, at the start, to uncover Qohelet's perspective on his own life experiences and failures. Let me therefore try to restate and expand a bit on these various aspects. Part I deals with those human passions and behaviors that cause unhappiness. It proposes mainly a negative morality, focusing on the need for control and excision. Since its focus is personal and experiential – King Qohelet offers himself as the prime example of negative or *hebel* behavior – his autobiographical *and confessional* perspective provides the lens through which the morality is explained and justified. Part II advances to the *hebel* in the social and especially the natural world out there, both beyond individual control. Its main characteristics are unpredictability

---

[20] Roland E. Murphy, *Ecclesiastes,* Word Biblical Commentary 23A (Dallas: Word Books, 1992), 125. This important point – that Qohelet's goal is the truth or description of reality – is the motivating impetus of Fox's important rereading of Qohelet, *A Time to Tear Down,* especially pp. 3–4, on the necessity – not the problem – of Qohelet's contradictions. On the view of Qohelet's contradictions as a deliberate pedagogical device for encouraging strong readings, see Perry, *Dialogues with Kohelet,* pp. x-xii.

[21] In an exegetical tradition traceable back to Origen, medieval commentators viewed Solomon's three books as guides to the three spiritual states: The Book of Proverbs taught humans how to live virtuously, Qohelet taught how to despise the world as transient, and Canticles focused on the love of God (see summary in Beryl Smalley, cited in Krüger, *Qoheleth, A Commentary,* 34). My proposal is to view all three stages as forming the backbone of the Book of Qohelet, unified by the focus on the *evolving* sense of *hebel* and by the "empty" (but how resonant!) words that bring them forth.

and transience, both suspect and typically judged to be negative (e.g., absurdity, vanity, etc.). However, Qohelet offers much positive advice on avoiding negative consequences, and the surprise is that the correctives are modeled and available in the natural universe itself.

Part III adventurously pushes Qohelet's negative method to its philosophical extremes, no longer focused on either a quietism of the passions or their moderation but rather on a withdrawal from the world of things to a no-thing universe or great void, to an almost ontological Outside that opens up risky but joyous possibilities for living and creativity. Put differently, if indeed our Book of Qohelet is, insistently, a meditation on the world "under the sun" or "under the heavens," we attempt to imagine what that could possibly be. Critics respond that, of course, this refers to our own little globe, especially our social world. This is undoubtedly true, but with the perspective of an invitation to rise above things, to consider our lives from a totally different space – different because it is a *non*-place, a *hebel*-place, if you will. Italo Calvino imagined such a journey for his character Astolfo, in search of a cure for a demented Orlando:

> On the white fields of the Moon, Astolfo meets the poet… He thinks: "If he lives in the very middle of the Moon … he will tell us if it is true that It contains the universal rime book of words, if this is the world full of sense, the opposite of the senseless Earth."
>
> "No, the Moon is a desert" – such was the poet's response… "[But] from this arid sphere all poems and all discourse originate. And every voyage through forests, battles, treasures, banquets, bedrooms bring us back here, to the center of an empty horizon."
>
> "Storia di Astolfo sulla luna"

With our progressive vanity-withdrawals and refocusing, we have, with Qohelet and in Calvino's language, gone to the moon and, with Blanchot's and the rabbis' help, well "outside" or beyond. With this, Qohelet invites us to the vanity or void of outside (celestial? prophetic?) perspectives, in order to reconsider and perhaps refocus the origin and value of our primary discourse and desires.

Hebel #*4: Word-Hebel, the Souffle Poétique, Singing in Truth*[22]
Here we return to the traditional "vanity" aura or interpretation of *hebel*, but now with deep irony. If things are vanity, what of the airy words that reproduce them? Are they not, as Montaigne (ironically) remarked, the

---

[22] For Qohelet's use of *hebel* as a structuring *terminus technicus*, see Norbert Lohfink, *Qoheleth: A Continental Commentary* (Minneapolis: Fortress), 2003, xiv. See Appendix 1, "Hebel Repetition as a *Terminus Technicus*."

very notion of "vanity of vanity"? Indeed, are they *all* tiring (1:8), forever turning upon themselves into books without end (12:12)? Or perhaps, rather, a breath of breaths, ones that carry thinking and breathe life into the world. Words that penetrate thick skulls and drive them to betterment (12:11).

When it comes to translating *hebel*, its polysemy is further complicated by the changing life engagements of the speaker's voice. The crucial factor here is the speaker's moral perspectivism, his (and the human being's) constant evaluation of things by the terms "good" and especially "bad." Since the speaker's dominant voice is post-transformational, his "hebel" judgment is likely to be Janus-like, designating both the abandonment of "vanity" things and also his awareness of new life-possibilities resulting from these judgments and experiences. So too the wind that circulates in the universe: judged to be both vanity as a pursuit and the very image of transience, but also as life-sustaining, the very breath of life. I have decided to cleave to the *peshat hebel/breath* in most cases and leave the interpretation to the reader, now aware of these expanded hermeneutic possibilities of *hebel*.[23]

Qohelet's deepening concept of *hebel* thus involves a progression from (1) sins of excess to (2) an awareness of universal transience, both yielding to a removal and bracketing as preconditions for the ongoing (3) creation and re-creation of the world through fresh thinking and wise words and discourse. And, at every stage, Qohelet plants the notion that these "evil" (1:13) *hebels* are given by God for our enjoyment and growth. The essential message of Qohelet, no different from Thoreau's *Walden*, is one of joy and self-renewal.[24] This underlying message becomes most visible when the dominant *hebel* motif is directed away from its popular negative *interpretation* of "vanity" and returned to its basic *peshat* or simple meaning of "life-breath"; whereupon the entire work can now be read as a paean: To Life![25]

[23] For further discussion see Appendix 3, "Quotationals." For an unusually focused discussion of the neglected importance of Qohelet's *hebel*, its polysemy and nonjudgmental status previous to the interpretive accretions that have muddied the waters of understanding, Kathleen A. Farmer's introduction is especially to be recommended (Kathleen A. Farmer, *Who Knows What Is Good? Proverbs and Ecclesiastes* [Grand Rapids, MI: Eerdmans, 1991], especially pp. 143–46).

[24] Sherman Paul, *The Shores of America: Thoreau's Inward Exploration* (Urbana: Illinois University Press, 1958), ch. 7. Quoted in Robert Sayre, ed., *New Essays on "Walden"* (New York: Cambridge University Press, 1992), 91.

[25] See especially Chapter 8 and Appendix 3, "To Lives!"

To summarize, then, this research combines close philology and exegesis, on the one hand, and a modern philosophical perspective inspired to a large degree by broader Levinassian perspectives, on the other. Jewish sages quipped that if there can be no learning without bread, they were also persuaded that there can be no bread without learning. Applied to our task at hand, if there can be no philosophy without philology, the inverse is equally true. Readers familiar with the history of the work's commentary will recognize my departure from interpretations long entrenched and yet hopefully ripe for renewed discussion. Among the major ones, I shall offer the following:

1) The Book of Qohelet is a wisdom manual for living well, according to traditional precepts and with experience as a guide.

2) Popular pessimistic interpretations are of real but limited value in that they occlude the book's prime focus on joyous living.

3) Qohelet is not only autobiographical, as usually thought. As pseudo-authored, it is confessional and transformational.

4) Qohelet is *foundational of a culture that values discourse over power.* I argue that this is the book's plot from start to finish.

5) The book's thesis is its motto (*hebel*), which focuses not on the traditional translation "vanity," which is only an interpretation, but rather its simple meaning "breath," or better yet, wind-breath. Such a reading allows for far different and complex interpretations.

6) Of major interest in Qohelet studies is the issue also at the center of Levinas' concern: how do we talk about God? As against the pervasive view that Qohelet blames God for the world's "vanity," careful reading reveals the opposite, blaming *human* malfeasance and insisting that *God is not to be judged.*

PART ONE

HUMAN *HEBEL* ("VANITY"): SINS OF COLLECTION

The Lord knows the desires of man, that they are *hebel.*

Ps 94:11

When someone declared that life is an evil, he corrected him:

"Not life itself, but living ill."

Diogenes Laertius[1]

Men labor under a mistake.... They are employed, as it says in an old book, laying up treasures which moths and rust will corrupt and thieves break through and steal. It is a fool's life, as they will find when they get to the end of it, if not before.

Thoreau[2]

It would not occur to people, upon reading this Thoreau passage, to blame the moths or rust or even thieves for the folly of their misplaced trust, and certainly not "the world" (or God!) for its being made subject to decay and corruption. And yet, when reading Qohelet, we hypothesize complaints about such things as wasted effort or loss of inheritance, since "this too is a breath!" But isn't the focus in both cases upon human foolishness, on our marketplace values, on a mistaken conception of work ("toil"), on our illusions of complete control over the results of our actions, on our foolish desire for excess and absolute security? Are Thoreau's fools so very different from Qohelet's? For starters, then, let us follow Qohelet's parting advice to "remove anger from your heart and dismiss sadness from your flesh" (11:10), for the world is as glorious as

---

[1] Diogenes Laertius, *Lives of Eminent Philosophers,* "Diogenes," trans. R. D. Hicks. Loeb Classical Library, 2 vols; (Cambridge: Harvard University Press, 1970), II:57.

[2] Henry David Thoreau, *Walden, or Life in the Woods* (New York: New American Library, 1999), 3.

ever, and exalting. But, if only for credibility's sake, let us start with the bad news and the easy pedagogy, the one accessible to one and all.[3]

Qohelet's pedagogical agenda as a wisdom teacher and moral guide is transparent and sustained. At the start, he sets out to "discern what is good for humanity under the heavens during the numbered days of their lives" (2:3). This project has two components: the personal one to enjoy life, which he will go on to pursue.[4] The second is summarized at the book's end, where it is stated that Qohelet "was not only himself a sage but also added to wisdom by teaching the people knowledge" (*da'at*, 12:9). This level of knowledge is targeted at the start of the Book of Proverbs as well (1:4). It refers to experiential wisdom, survival skills appropriate also for the *na'ar* or youth, in order to learn to stay out of trouble and see the consequences of one's actions. In the words of Qohelet, "the advantage of the practical knowledge (*da'at*) of wisdom: it gives life to those who have it" (7:12).

---

[3] "For the world ... the bad news" is a direct quote from Annie Dillard, *For the Time Being* (New York: Alfred A. Knopf, 1999), 8, a valuable spiritual meditation for what follows here.

[4] Choon-Leong Seow relates the concept "good" to the imperative in 2:1 to enjoy life (literally "see the good"); *Ecclesiastes: A New Translation with Introduction and Commentary* AB 18C (New York: Doubleday, 1997), 150. "The numbered days of one's life" is a reminder that our days are limited and death is around the cor(o)ner, but Norbert Lohfink, *Qoheleth: A Continental Commentary* (Minneapolis: Fortress, 2003), 134, commenting on 11:8, in an astonishing meditation bravely connects this notation with the theme of joy: "The sweetness of the world does not automatically follow from success in human affairs. Joy as a further human activity is interposed. People must appropriate happiness by being joyful and at the same time reflecting on death – only then will the light be sweet. The thought of death in no way relativizes joy, but rather gives it its strength and justification."

1

"I *Qohelet* Was King" (1:12): The Collector Theme (1:12–2:26)

Neither his studies nor life had taught him to live properly. His life was passing in a haze of hopeless anxiety.

Aharon Appelfeld[1]

For true language to start, it is necessary that the life that is going to carry that language have undergone the experience of its own nothingness.

Maurice Blanchot[2]

Objectivation is produced in the very work of language, where the subject detaches himself from things possessed, as if he were hovering over his own existence, as if he were detached from it, as if the existence he is existing had not yet completely happened to him. A distance more radical than any distance in the world. It is necessary that the subject find himself "at a distance" from his own being....

Levinas TI 230

Autobiography and the Confessional Perspective

Critics have uncovered two levels of autobiographical writing in Qohelet. On the one hand, there is a royal autobiography focusing on deeds;[3] on

---

[1] Aharon Appelfeld, *The Conversion* (trans. Jeffrey M. Green; New York: Schocken, 1998), 58.

[2] Maurice Blanchot, *La part du feu* (Paris: Gallimard, 1949), 327. Blanchot's "langage *vrai*" as arising from personal transformation and rebirth corresponds nicely with Qohelet's own journey from vanity/emptiness toward the pursuit of "words of *truth*" (12:10).

[3] For a summary of the autobiographical element, see Tremper Longman III, *The Book of Ecclesiastes* (Grand Rapids, MI: Eerdmans, 1998). See also Michael V. Fox, *A Time to Tear Down and a Time to Build Up: A Rereading of Ecclesiastes* (Grand Rapids, MI: Eerdmans, 1999), 153–55.

the other, a reflective inquiry into the meaning of his personal experience.[4] Thus, the book's opening line,

> [These are] the things (*debarim*) of Qohelet…
>
> (1:1)

refers both to his things of speech, his words, and also to the nonverbal things of his experience, with a strong opening focus, as we shall see, on his experience and pursuit of literal *debarim*: things of possession, collectibles.[5] When Qohelet opens his autobiographical discourse, it is in the voice of a king; then, going through most of the entire book, there is the voice of Qohelet the philosopher, one who pursues knowledge and/or wisdom. But even from the very start of his personal narrative, there is also a further possibility:

> "I, Collector [i.e., Qohelet], was king…"
>
> (1:12)

The voice is not yet the philosopher's, nor is it any longer the voice of the king ("I *was* king"). As the narrative progresses, one begins to sense a third voice as well, an existential voice that gives a broader coherence to the other two, once the autobiographer has put aside, or looks beyond, his royal crown and philosopher's gown and has become in some sense an Other or re-formed person. This possibility is neither casual nor academic, since it could extend the conclusion of the "pious" epilogist ("Fear God and keep the commandments" 12:13) to the entire book and make Qohelet sound more spiritual or "religious" from the very start. Alternatively, it could perspectivize a simply human voice from a point "outside the box" – that is, beyond the thickness and illusions and disappointments of daily experience. For, indeed, Qohelet's opening concern focuses on humans' frustrations and sufferings due to the failure of their efforts: What profit *to humans* from all *their* labor? (1:3) A subtext gradually unfolds, as his concern for general humanity is doubled – perhaps

---

4 Fox, ibid., 155.

5 Whether this meaning of nonverbal things can be extended to individual literal things (pools, forests) is unclear. See the discussion in Appendix 6, "Doublets." Equally debatable (but possible) is the abstract concept of "thing" in the Hebrew Bible, the closest example being perhaps *khefetz* (thing desired, see Qoh 3:1). The hapax *tiklah* in Psalm 119:96 offers a further possibility, if the word can be related to *kalta*, "desire" (Ps 84:3), as Amos Hacham thinks (*The Book of Psalms*, 2 vols [Jerusalem: Mossad harav Kook, n. d., Hebrew] 2:408). Another possible synonym – this one a favorite of Qohelet – is *'inyan*, "matter, business," at least in later Hebrew. See also below, p. 89, n. 20.

activated as well – by the sense that he himself has failed his life: it is all *hebel*, empty vanity, a mere breath.[6]

As the opening verse alludes unmistakably to King Solomon – what other king in Jerusalem was also son of David? – we are invited to explain the pseudonym or pen name, since the other two books of the Hebrew Bible ascribed to him are more explicit at the same juncture:

> [This is] the song of songs which is Solomon's.
>
> Cant 1:1

> [These are] the words of Solomon, son of David, King of Israel.
>
> Prov 1:1

One typical explanation – who would be surprised nowadays? – leans to the political and/or ideological.[7] While not denying the possibility that at least some of the book may go back to Solomonic times, scholars speculate that later editors or compilers simply appended the name to give the book greater authority – we might say, in today's market culture, to sell more books. Such a possibility cannot of course be discounted, especially in view of later attempts to do exactly that.[8] Such an explanation skirts even the literary issue, however, by seeking an explanation – an insufficient one, as we shall see – only of the name Solomon, which does not occur in our text. It does not explain the use of the pseudonym. In other words, if the main purpose is one of appropriating an authority figure, then Solomon's name itself should have been used. Skip the *nom de plume* altogether!

To unpack this dense self-introduction, a comparison may be helpful:

> Now the man [*'ish*] Moses was very humble, more so than
> all other humans on the face of the earth.
>
> Num 12:3

---

6 This could be hinted in an additional level of meaning that the rabbis detected in the book's opening "word": What kinds of words? "Words of reproach and admonition," opined the rabbis. But whom is the speaker reproaching? See T. A. Perry, *Dialogues with Kohelet,* 177.

7 For the ideological, see Michael V. Fox, *Qohelet and His Contradictions* (Sheffield: Almond Press, 1989), 96, who refers to "the prestige attached to that archetypal wise man."

8 Noteworthy is the tendency in the Septuagint to homogenize that great Solomonic compilation known as the Book of Proverbs, so that the entire Book comes to be ascribed to him. In the earlier MT text, other sources and authors are clearly acknowledged: Agur (Prov 30:1, also a "collector" according to the etymology of his name; Lemuel King of Masa' (31:1); perhaps also, to a certain extent, Hezekiah (25:1).

This verse says three things concerning the subject Moses:

a) his proper name: Moses
b) his principal social excellence: *'ish,* According to rabbinic tradition, this means an important person. This verse in fact is proof of this notion, since it specifies that he was this kind of *'ish* "above all other humans."
c) What kind of *'ish?* He possessed that quality or character trait through which he is an *'ish:* humility.

This paradigm clarifies Qohelet's own literary presentation:

"I Qohelet was king...."

1:12

Here too three items are put forth:

a) his proper name: Qohelet. Both the presenter (1:1) and Qohelet (1:12) use the term as a proper noun.
b) his principal social attribute: king. Just as the *'ish* Moses is humble above all other humans, so too Qohelet is a supreme something (1:16). We want to say, "of course, he was king!" except that his self-presentation focuses on a particular aspect or characteristic of that kingly quality – one, moreover, that would not qualify at the top of the list of kingly virtues:

"Behold, I have grown great by amassing wisdom, more so than all others before me in Jerusalem."

1:16

Whereas typical readings focus on gathering *wisdom* (see below), his subsequent and lengthy listing (1:16–2:26) suggests a quite different emphasis – on the meaning of the name "Qohelet." For the more general focus is not on *what* he amasses but rather the fact that he does collect.
c) the quality through which he, the king, has "grown great": he is the Qohelet/Collector. The opening proper noun is now doubled by its literal meaning, as Mr. Qohelet will also come to be dubbed THE Qohelet (12:8).[9] There is widespread agreement that the reference is to some form of collecting, and various possibilities have

---

[9] Possible also 7:27; see below, p. 126, n. 6.

been extracted from the text itself. Thus, the collector collects students, wisdom sayings, and the like. Further, it has been suggested – reasonably I think – that the feminine form of the name is not an indication of gender (it is used with masculine verbs) but rather of profession: just as a *soferet* is one who counts, a counter, a *qohelet* is a collector or gatherer.[10] The bottom line, then, is that Qohelet's kingly qualities are best characterized – initially and throughout – by the epithet that he so richly deserves: the Collector King. The king's profession is collecting and amassing, and in this he is without pair: THE Collector. Given the symbiotic relation between a king and a collector (or an *'ish* and a humble person), the point is not that kings are necessarily collectors but rather that the most advanced form of collectors – those having the personality trait of gatherers, hoarders – is best exemplified in kings, perhaps because they have the greatest potential, as persons of power, to achieve their goals. That this initial goal was abandoned – or, better, transmuted – is the subject of the plot of the Book of Qohelet: "I Co[he]llector WAS king."

Sins of Collection: The Theme of King Qohelet

A notable literary feature of the autobiography is its extended vocabulary and grammar of acquisition and possession. The stress from the start is on the greatness and grandeur of his deeds (2:4), but these actions all find their purpose and result in newly acquired possessions (houses, gardens 2:4–6) rather than other kingly activities. Although the dominant verb here is "to make" (*'asah*), the stress is more on the pride of acquisition and possession – one of the meanings of the verb – than on creation or construction.[11] This suggests that even the opening boast may be read as ambivalent: "I greatly increased my possessions" as well as "I did great deeds" (2:4). Notable too is that verb that served as the basis for Cain's name (Gen 4:1), thus

---

[10] For the *Qal* form of the verb, see Appendix 5, "Miscellaneous."

[11] For *'asah* with the meaning of collecting and accumulating, see also 12:12, which refers not to the making of books but rather to stockpiling them (see James L. Kugel, "Qohelet and Money," *CBQ* 51 [1989], 34 n. 9). Kugel also points out the meaning of *ma'asim*, often "deeds, handiwork," as "possessions"; for its frequency in Qohelet see also Appendix 2, "*Hebel* and Friendship with the *Ruakh*." In Gen 12:5, "all the 'souls' they had *acquired*" refers to the servants. Rashi homiletically takes this as referring to the souls that Abraham had converted, thus he "made" or remade their very souls.

I acquired... acquisitions
>   (*qanah*, 2:7)

Or the kingly grandeur of

> I collected (*kns*) silver and gold;
> I got me (*'asiti li*) singers...
>   (2:8)

What are we to make of this grab bag of boasts? In his summation of the
opening autobiography, Qohelet issues his conclusion as a *hebel* judgment, expressing disappointment:

> [God] gives to the man that is good in his sight, wisdom and knowledge
> and joy; but to the sinner (*khote'*) He gives the task of gathering (*'asap*) and
> amassing (*kanas*, 2:8).... This also is a breath and a striving after wind.
>   (Qoh 2:26)

We read the words but miss the reference. This is not only a statement
about sinners in general, since the author has just pointedly and repeatedly ascribed such tasks to himself (2:8)! The point of this self-accusation
should be taken for what it is: Qohelet views himself as a (former) sinner.
Although academic criticism has advanced to the point of considering
the book as autobiographical, it is now time to move closer to the truth,
since this autobiographical conclusion transforms Qohelet's personal
narrative into a confession.[12]

Further considerations come readily to mind when connecting "the
Qohelet" to the penitential or "return" mode. It is well known, for example, that use of a pseudonym or name change can signal a change of life,
spiritually speaking. The case of conversion comes readily to mind (Abram
to Abraham, Sarai to Sarah), but other possibilities must be considered as
well. An important occasion for name change, at least in Jewish practice,
is in cases of serious illness. It is believed that if the moribund Reuven is
renamed Shimeon or Khayim ("life"), then the angel of death becomes
confused and cannot locate the victim. These two cases – undergoing spiritual rebirth and escaping death – are residually present in the third kind
of name change we wish to present. Maimonides states the case clearly:

> The penitent should ... change his name, as if to say:
> "I am another person, I am not the person who did those actions."[13]

---

[12] For the meaning of k*hote'* (sinner) as "one who does evil," see 8:12. This word is
commonly used in Qohelet in this sense: 7:20, 26; 8:12; 9:2; 9:18; 10:4. Notice the title
of one of the best studies of Qohelet, Robert K. Johnston's *"Confessions of a Workaholic':* A
Reappraisal."*CBQ* 38 (1976): 14–28.

[13] Moses Maimonides, "Laws of Repentance," in *Book of Knowledge* (*Mishneh Torah, Book I,*
trans. Moses Hyamson; New York: Bloch, 1937), 2:4.

From this perspective, Solomon becomes Qohelet in order to achieve a more perfect turnaround, and the pseudonym is of a piece with his confession and the detailing of his multiple *sins of collection.*

Yet another confessional issue has to do with the descriptor "Son of David." What has distinguished the Davidic line – spiritually rather than politically speaking – is a quality of righteousness based on the ability to own up to one's wrongs, to repent, to confess and admit to the truth. This note of repentance can be traced to the progenitor himself, to Judah, whose name can be attached etymologically not only to thankfulness but also to acknowledgement. Witness his magnificent admission of guilt before an open court:

> And Judah acknowledged and said: "She [Tamar] is more righteous than I, inasmuch as I did not give her to my son Shelah."
>
> (Gen 38:26)[14]

A related case is of course David himself, who sins abominably both through adultery with Bathsheba and the murder of her husband Uriah. Yet, when confronted with the facts and rather than sweeping them under the carpet, he makes complete confession:

> I have sinned against the Lord!
>
> (2 Sam 12:13)[15]

From this perspective, the king's insistent recital of his *hebel*-pursuits sounds like a *mea culpa.* For is it not likely that the attribution of sin to "gathering" in 2:26 evokes, now in a confessional mode, that Collector King who is ostentatiously portrayed in 1 Kgs 10:26 and 2 Chr 1:14 ("Now Solomon collected [*'asap*])."? Is this not also the Solomon of Canticles, who discovers that *all* his royal wealth and power can conquer neither love's beauty and freedom, nor the simple life that nurtures it?[16] Is it not possible, plausible even, to imagine, in a spiritual text, that the notation "Son of David" is intended, beyond the mere specificity of attribution (compromised by use of the pseudonym rather than the direct name), the distinct glory of ancestors who placed the absolute power of kingship beneath a power more absolute still?

Yet a third issue bound up with our innocent introductory verse is the popular tag "royal fiction." *King* Qohelet, whose watchword and constant

---

[14] See T. A. Perry, *Wisdom in the Hebrew Bible: God's Twilight Zone* (Peabody: Hendrickson, 2014), 13–15.

[15] See ibid., 16.

[16] For this possibility see T. A. Perry, "Love's Philosophy in Canticles: The King and the Pastoral Setting." Edited by J. Harold Ellens. In *Bethsaida in Archeology. A Festschrift in Honor of John T. Greene* (Cambridge Scholars, 2014), 318–29.

refrain is "Vanity of Vanities," is the story of personal failure told by one who had every reason to succeed. The whole project of a detailed documentary of failure is again characteristic of a confession, made by one who indeed thought to "have it all" and ended up with considerably less. Later he declares that "I *was* king," suggesting that he no longer is! From the confessional perspective, however, this comes as no surprise. In fact the opposite would be more surprising because it is precisely his past that he is judging and that he has transformed. H. L. Ginsberg takes the remark as an historian and denies its validity. The point, however, is one of moral distance: "[Qohelet] takes on the persona of a king, Solomon, to be precise. But in what follows he undertakes such criticism of royal power that he couldn't possibly have accepted the dignity. He rather steps back in order to judge it."[17]

2:24–26

The concluding verse of Qohelet's explicit autobiography has allowed us to refocus his main activities as those of a "sinner," perhaps merely as one who has "missed the mark," perhaps because of a vague sense of guilt because things are not going all that well.[18] This disclosure is framed by a wider and equally dense conclusion, one crucial for the interpretation of the entire book[19] and perhaps ripe for a refocus. In particular, Qohelet came to hate his life (2:17) for several reasons. For one thing, the results of his culpable labor (*'amal*) will no longer be in his power after he dies, and his heir may not even be deserving (2:18–19; continued in 5:14–15). Secondly, even in the present a human has no reward for all his (excessive) labor and anxiety to heap up an inheritance or even to increase his pleasures in the here and now (2:20–23):

> 2:24 [Therefore][20] a human has no greater good than eating and drinking and taking pleasure in his work. I saw that this too is from the hand of God.
>
> 2:25 For who eats and enjoys if not I [alone]?
> 2:26 Indeed, to the one who is good in His sight He gives wisdom and knowledge and contentment. But to the sinner He gives the task of harvesting

---

[17] André Barucq, *Ecclésiaste* (Paris: Beauchesne, 1968), 10.

[18] Fox, *A Time to Tear Down*, 191.

[19] See Graham Ogden, *Qoheleth* (Sheffield: JSOT Press, 1987), 47–48.

[20] I insert "therefore" to stress these verses as a conclusion and their continuity with what precedes.

and amassing, to give it over to one who is good in God's sight. This too is a breath and chasing after the wind.[21]

(2:24–26)

Each of these verses has unsuspected treasures. The general point here is the focus on human *'amal* as properly directed to the task of self-survival and maintenance, a message delivered by the exclamation of 2:25:

"who eats and enjoys if not I [alone]?!"

The contextual meaning is the astonished question:

"How much food and drink does one person need?!"

Even providing for one's basic physical needs is contextualized, however, by the preceding verse, which also talks about the labor of earning a living (here: food and drink). This, asserts the writer against all who demean the activity, is the human being's greatest good: *eating and drinking and taking pleasure in the activity* of eating what has been earned by one's own efforts. In other words, to understand Qohelet's point, "eating and drinking" cannot be separated and thought of as an isolated activity. Rather, they form a hendiadys, a single concept of working for one's *necessary* sustenance, which includes the enjoyment of both the work and food as a part of its purpose. Even at the level of simple *peshat*, moreover, Levinas loved to quote the Talmudic exclamation that "eating is a great thing."[22]

The next and concluding verse adds an important qualification – both a limitation and an expansion – to this ongoing discussion. Qohelet's vanity argument raises two problems. The first is the issue of success:

Take a person who works with wisdom and knowledge and success [*kishron*]; yet He will give his rightful portion over to one who has not labored for it.

2:21

Here Qohelet grants the argument: If God wills it so, then that is God's will (2:26). Yet the burden may not only be on God's (arbitrary?) will, for this person has labored not only with/for knowledge and wisdom (see

---

[21] Contrasting this positive use of *hebel* with its negative connotations in 2:21, Ogden establishes the principle of polysemy for *hebel*, indicating clearly that "the traditional rendering 'vanity' is most inappropriate" (*Qoheleth*, 49).

[22] "Grand est le manger." See BT Sanh 103b. For a moving commentary, see Blanchot, *L'Écriture du désastre*, 133.

below) but also for successful possession. The problem is one of purpose and intention.[23]

The second problem is one of the nature of time, summarized in the astonishing appearance in Biblical Hebrew of the concept of the present:

> [Even in the present] what does a person have?
>
> 2:22

Literally "what is [*howeh*] to a human being." In the previous example success was achieved in the present but intended for the future. A later verse returns to this issue with a distinction between two senses of the present:

> Sweet is the sleep of the poor laborer, whether he has eaten much or little...
> But the full belly of the wealthy person is not enough to let him sleep.
>
> 5:11

The wealthy person is always hopeful or fearful of results and thus still committed to the future, whereas the poor laborer (as in 2:24) thinks only of the present in the present. We now can return to the God "problem" presented in 2:21 with a different perspective. In both cases the person had knowledge and wisdom, but with opposite results. Is this only God's doing? Perhaps, although the full text gives a different indication:

> wisdom and knowledge and [the hope of] success (2:21)
> wisdom and knowledge and joy (2:26)

God seems to favor those who are contented with what they have to eat and drink and do in fact eat and drink *in the present*, whether much or little. Perhaps because they are contented with their portion, with what they were apportioned.[24]

We now come to Qohelet's fuller distinction between those who please God and the "sinners" who do not:

> ... to the sinner He gives the task of harvesting [*'asap*] and amassing [*kanas*],
> to give it over to one who is good in God's sight.
>
> 2:26

---

[23] The word occurs only in Qohelet and only two further times, each of which expands the negative intention of the one who labors. "All effort and success [*kishron*] arise from envy of one's neighbor" (4:4). "When wealth multiplies, so too do its spenders. And what success [*kishron*] can owners derive except from what is within their range of vision?" (5:10).

[24] If in such cases gratitude is also present, it comes not as a replacement for sensual pleasures but rather as added value. See my *Dialogues with Kohelet*, 90, 114, 115, 145, 170.

This statement is puzzling and gives reason to those who see the message here as God's arbitrariness. Like *da'at* and *hochmah* (see below), so too *'asap* and *kanas* form a hendiadys. Taken as a single hybrid concept, they indicate gathering together, collecting, and then bringing in and storing, grain for example.[25] And there is nothing wrong with such activities, certainly not the ingathering of life's necessities such as food, even knowledge and people (for the military, for learning). It is only when these activities pass from collecting to amassing, from gathering to heaping for its own sake that problems arise. The first concerns the issue of bypassing what is needed for the task at hand and hoarding excess for its own sake. The second is more attitudinal, founded on the belief that mere possession of goods is a goal in itself. Thus, money may be required, but "He who loves money will never be satisfied with money" (5:9); when it becomes a *goal* of possession, one will never have enough. Jankélévitch sketches the existential lifestyle of such practices and the restrictions it imposes on one's human purpose:

> Opulence in itself would condemn us to the management of our patrimony, to accumulation, to treasure-hunting [*la thésaurisation*], to managership, and consequently to the worship of possessions [*le culte de l'avoir*].[26]

What happens, then, when these normal needs of survival are exceeded? What if, in a different kind of economy, money or horses or swimming pools instead of needed food itself are stored, or when the gathering instinct becomes excessive and habitual? In view of these distinctions and nuances, the better translation would be, given the context of eating and drinking:

> … to the sinner He gives the task of harvesting [*'asap*] and amassing, hoarding [*kanas*], to give it over to one who is good in God's sight.
>
> 2:26

Qohelet uses *YaSaP*, a near homonym of *'asap*, to stress the connection between grandeur and love of excess:[27]

> "Look, I have grown great by amassing
> (*hoSaPti*, 1:16)"

---

[25] Exod 23:16; Deut 16:13, where *'asap* includes collection and also processing and storing.

[26] Vladimir Jankélévitch and Béatrice Berlowitz, *Quelque part dans l'inachevé* (Paris: Gallimard, 1978), 47.

[27] Conversely, *'sap* can be used for *yasap*; see Exod 5:7. There similarity can facilitate their interchange and hence a play on words, as in Qohelet; see also Joseph's name *yosep*, explained as derived from *'asap* (Gen 30:23–24).

"I grew great and amassed"
        (*hoSaPti*, 2:9)

The essential contrast to this human activity is soon to follow:

I know that all which God has made, that is what will be into eternity: To it there is no adding (*'ein le-hoSiP*)....

3:14

Even the acquisition of the highest values is subject to close scrutiny and limitation, since "in *too much* wisdom is much anger, and whoever increases (*moSiP*) knowledge increases pain" (1:18). Moreover, the entire series is introduced by a verbal form of *GaDoL*, "large," calqued on an expression always used positively when referring to God's admirable work but which, when applied to humans, can only signify, by contrast, a grandiose manner of behavior:

"I acted in grand style."

2:4[28]

With this adjusted perspective in mind, we can now hear other overtones in the book's opening project of *'amal*, labor:

What profit to a human from all the *'amal* that he *'amal*'s under the sun?

While *'amal* may surely refer to activity (especially excessive) and as surely to money, its frequent goal and sometimes result, may it not also echo a word with which it is frequently paired in the Hebrew Bible: *'amal wa-'awen*, sinfulness?[29]

Another false start is the so-called enallage or change of pronouns. Why, it is wondered, does an autobiography begin in the third person: "Vanity of vanities *said* Qohelet"? The standard hypothesis is of course plausible, that the prologue is part of a frame narrative spoken by someone else. But might not Qohelet's distancing from his sinful self also be seen as but a variant of the change of names and the taking of a pseudonym?

The repentance argument of this narrative is further strengthened by yet other aspects of the experiential "I" as they occur especially in

---

[28] This is Robert Gordis's translation, *Koheleth – The Man and His World* (New York: Schocken, 1968), 150. See also 1:16 and 2:9, cited in this chapter. Indeed, from Joel 2:20–21 one gathers that only God can act in such a manner, and that when humans do so it is reprehensible. See James L. Crenshaw's perceptive comment, *Joel: A New Translation with Introduction and Commentary* (AB 24C; Garden City, NY: Doubleday, 1995), 152.

[29] See p. 42, n. 15. For *'amal* as wealth, the result of labor, see Ps 105:44 (NRSV).

wisdom writing. Such a wisdom use may be evoked by extraordinary declarations of hypostasized wisdom such as

"I am Wisdom."
> Prov 8:12

It is a strong reading to claim that this refers all wisdom to the subject – unless you think like Emerson and Thoreau – but it does give a strong imprint to Qohelet's highly personal and experiential search of wisdom in such texts as the declaration of his wisdom experiment:

Behold, *I* have grown great and collected wisdom.
> 1:16

This does not claim that "I am Wisdom," but the enterprise is arguably in the same ballpark. His wisdom conclusions are based on neither tradition nor authority but rather on a personal experiment, on reflecting on his own life experience. And his desire to tell about it extends beyond both scientific curiosity and pedagogic interest, although it of course includes these. Its ultimate claim is that wisdom is an earnest journey *through* experience rather than its avoidance.

It is thus curious that some pedagogical and religious interests have drawn the opposite conclusion. The *a posteriori* argument has been advanced that the sage Qohelet is doubled with the figure of the king not in order to further personal research but precisely to avoid it, as if to say: "If *I*, Solomon, couldn't succeed with all my power and wisdom, why should *you* even try?" In other words, even admitting that I conducted an experiment with experience, others should learn from my failure. It is thus not infrequently argued that what has been called the book's conclusion ("Fear God and keep the commandments, for this is the whole of man") dispenses one from ever again reading the book, for Solomon has declared the whole to be vanity: the world, the wisdom enterprise, and the books that try to grasp it.

If this were the case, however, then his later advice toward experience would make no sense: cast your bread upon the waters, enjoy your youth! The game or role is of course serious, even risky (and God is watching), but it is certainly no pullout into inexperience or pseudo-experience, what could be called alterism or living through another.[30] It seems

---

[30] For a wonderfully positive and even necessary aspect to the risks involved, see John D. Caputo, *The Weakness of God* (Bloomington: Indiana University Press, 2006), 82. See also Perry, *Wisdom in the Hebrew Bible*, 173.

more likely that the pedagogical point works in the opposite way: rather than swallow Qohelet's "conclusion" undigested, one is advised to imitate his method, as the high incidence of verbs in the first-person singular would suggest, driving home the example of a methodological self-consciousness and even self-examination. Further, the personal search based on experience rests on what Seneca termed the very foundation of wisdom itself: self-confidence, friendship with one's self:

> There is only one good, the cause and foundation of a happy life: trust in oneself.
>
> Seneca[31]

Qohelet's confessional mode, stated at the outset and setting its perspective on the entire work from start to finish, helps solve what has been a perennial problem in Qohelet's criticism: its contradictions. In an earlier study I ventured to show how the book can be ordered as an ongoing dialogue between an optimist and a pessimist (Qohelet himself).[32] In view of the above, it is now possible to reformulate this extensive conflict as an interior dialogue within Qohelet/The second sense is discussed self and his present re-formed self. Both voices are still present, because the confession involves a complete narration of past mistakes, from the perspective of one who acknowledges them as false starts and judges them, still incorporating them into his present awareness. Qohelet lists each one of his mistakes in order to rid himself of them but also to acknowledge their pedagogical value. This also suggests an alternative to viewing the pseudonym for ideological purposes, for here the royal autobiography makes an a fortiori argument that is precisely the obverse of the one usually assumed (the king failed, so how could *you* possibly succeed?): If I could learn from my failures and change direction, with all my fabulous wealth and "wisdom," then so can others. Rather than being viewed as a preacher, the author Qohelet seems rather a self-teacher or autodidact, an out-reacher. The point could be encapsulated in a Qohelet-like aphorism on the value of experience:

> The fool is one who gets burned twice.
> The worse fool is one who never gets burned.[33]

---

[31] Seneca, *Ad Lucilium Epistulae Morales*, 3 vols. (trans. Richard M. Gummere; Loeb Classical Library, Cambridge, MA: Loeb Classical Library, Harvard University Press. 1971), *Letters,* Letter 31 (I:222). For friendship with one's self see Seneca, *Letters,* Letter 6 (I:28).

[32] Perry, *Dialogues with Kohelet.*

[33] See below, Appendix 8, "Qohelet from the Geniza."

Wisdom: A Collectible or a What?

We begin by drawing a crucial and perennial distinction on the status of *debarim.* On the one hand, there are things of basic human need and enjoyment, such as the usual triad of food, clothing, and shelter; and, on the other, the function of things – often but not always the same ones – as collectibles, objects of pointless and usually excessive acquisition. I have suggested that Qohelet's long litany of vanity objects is, more than a simple literary exercise in autobiography, a bitter critique of the pursuit of grandeur, one most typical of kings and moneyed or power people but, to varying and lesser degrees, to others as well: "What profit to *humans?*" The mea culpa litany regarding collectibles has a prologue, however, and it is one that seems to undo Qohelet's very enterprise of wisdom self-analysis and self-correction:

> I gave my mind over to study and to probe [in, through]
> wisdom concerning all that happens under the sun.

1:13

> I said to myself: "Behold, I have grown great by collecting wisdom,
> more than all that ruled before me in Jerusalem,
> and my mind has seen *very much wisdom and knowledge."*

1:16

> And I gave my mind over to *know wisdom and knowledge,*
> and [also] *to know* madness and folly.
> I now know that this too is a chasing after the wind.

1:17

> For in *much* wisdom is much anger,
> and to *increase knowledge* is to increase pain.

1:18

The first problem, which has bothered critics and remains undecided, concerns the function of wisdom in 1:13. Does it indicate wisdom as the instrument through which experience is to be ingested and analyzed? Or is wisdom the grammatical direct object, leading to the notion that the goal is to probe wisdom as one probes any other object of knowledge? Quite possibly it means both, leaving the real question to be exactly what kind of wisdom Qohelet has in mind. This is an urgent question in that it must decide on the status of wisdom itself, namely whether it is also to be included among the collectibles and thus to be avoided as well.

In v. 1:16 wisdom is clearly the direct object; it is the accumulation of wisdom that is a source of greatness and superiority. When the same expression recurs in 2:9, the direct object is unstated, leaving room for some other types of collectibles, the more visible sources and manifestations of kingly greatness just stated in 2:4–8.

> I grew great by accumulating, more than anyone before me in Jerusalem;
> and [*'ap*] my wisdom did not abandon me.
>
> 2:9

In this typical reading Qohelet is rejecting the possibility of a contradiction between his pursuits of wisdom, on the one hand, and power and pleasures on the other: "My wisdom survived!" In fact, he goes one better:

> I grew great by accumulating, more than anyone before me in Jerusalem;
> and [*'ap*] my wisdom even assisted me.[34]

Although wisdom clearly functions as an instrument here, its compatibility with riches – the ones listed in the preceding four verses – is retained as well. Such was indeed the dual attraction of Solomon's glory to his foreign visitors:

> And King Solomon was greater than all the kings of the earth for riches and
> for wisdom.
>
> 1 Kgs 10:23; also 5:14

Such a view of wisdom as itself a collectible is hardly surprising; it is already fully presented in the opening series:

> I said to myself: "Behold, I have grown greater by collecting wisdom, more
> than all that ruled before me in Jerusalem, and my mind has seen *very much
> wisdom and knowledge.*"
>
> 1:16

I think that Qohelet's main point is captured in the particular kind or level of wisdom expressed by the hendiadys (two words forming a single concept) *hochmah wa-da'at*:[35]

> wisdom and knowledge (v. 16)
> to know wisdom and knowledge (v. 17)
> wisdom … knowledge (v. 18)

---

[34] This reading of *'amdah li* reflects the Targum's understanding; see my *Dialogues with Kohelet*, 78.

[35] See Fox, *A Time to Tear Down*, 173, and more clearly in *Qohelet and His Contradictions*, 177.

And again crucially, as a summary in his conclusion to the entire confessional autobiography:

For to the man who pleases Him, He gives wisdom and knowledge....

2:26

The focus of Qohelet's criticism should be kept clearly in mind: he means that kind of *wisdom based on knowledge* (there are other sources, such as wisdom based on inspiration, or intuition, or *a priori* data, or tradition). We thus must ask: what is a wisdom based on knowledge? What are its advantages and its limitations and even dangers?

Although the possibility is rarely perceived, the autobiography reaches back not only to the past when Qohelet was king, but also to a distant past when he was still young. He does not have the addressee typical of wisdom pedagogy, however ("my son," i.e., my disciple), nor is his advice of the traditional moralizing sort. Rather,

Youngster, enjoy yourself while you are still young....

11:9 to 12:1

Differences notwithstanding, the rapprochement with the very first category listed in the programmatic opening of the Book of Proverbs is highly significant:

[The proverbs of Solomon ... were collected] to know (*la-da'at*) wisdom.

Prov 1:2[36]

Although Proverbs' program goes on to list other levels of wisdom, the opening call to *know wisdom* is directed at youngsters of whatever age, those who need knowledge of a particular kind, one that is especially appropriate to the clueless and empty-headed:

To give cunning to the callow, and to the young, knowledge of shrewdness.

Prov 1:4

If then knowledge-wisdom, wisdom of knowledge, in the first instance is a survivor skill (rather than a higher intellectual or moral one), one need not attempt to explain away or apologize for the presence of "madness and folly" in Qohelet 1:17, since these too, both in the outer world and in each individual, are part of the risks of

---

[36] The added words are Bruce K. Waltke's excellent suggestion, in order to bind the preamble to the title, thus clarifying the elliptical thought of the two opening verses (*The Book of Proverbs: Chapters 1–15* [NICOT. Grand Rapids, MI: Eerdmans, 2004], 174).

survival.[37] As in Proverbs 1:2, Qohelet's analysis of knowledge is *la-da'at hochmah* (1:17), to know a wisdom based on *da'at*, knowledge and experience, worldly-wise knowledge, if you will, a cumulative and necessarily early pursuit.

The result, assessed almost immediately, is mixed:

> In much wisdom much anger
> and one who accumulates knowledge accumulates pain
>
> 1:18

I would like to suggest that the key words here are not wisdom and knowledge (again: wisdom based on knowledge) but rather the unusual repetition:

> MUCH wisdom MUCH anger
> ACCUMULATING knowledge ACCUMULATING pain

From the very start and ongoing, all knowledge or *da'at* is achieved by accumulation, by the pursuit of things that one adds on, collectibles. Even those who have an expansive and inclusive view of *da'at* cannot escape this aspect.[38]

We have already seen the dangers of collecting things, but these are not limited to castles and singing ladies. Whatever else the Book of Qohelet may be, it is surely a diatribe against the view that the worth of life is one's *avoir* or possessions, that collecting and hoarding things are protections against loss, marks of valor and sources of true happiness, fantastical desires for totalizing control of the world. However, his analysis is extended to all levels of collection, of *savoir* as well as *avoir*, one based on the exhaustive pursuit of knowledge "from start to finish" (3:10–11).[39]

Can we be more precise about the dangers of collecting *too much* knowledge-wisdom? Isn't more always better, and can there ever be *too* much?! One answer comes from the possible school environment of the wisdom movement. If learning is good, indeed good in its own right, then why not spend one's entire life in school? The opening curriculum of Proverbs provides an answer, by also projecting further steps beyond

---

[37] Fox, *Qohelet and His Contradictions*, 177, imagines "a scribe seeking to provide a more acceptable target for the *hebel*-judgment."

[38] For an interesting possible parallel of the pursuit of excessive knowledge, see Goethe's *Faust* I:601: "Zwar weiss ich viel, doch möcht' ich alles wissen." (trans. by Walter Kaufmann [New York: Anchor], 1990).

[39] Can there not here be an allusion to the tree of the knowledge of good and evil, (*da'at tov wa-ra'*), especially if "good and bad" is a binary expressing everything, the All. See Nahum M. Sarna, *Genesis: The Traditional Hebrew Text with the JPS Translation* (Philadelphia: JPS, 1991), 19.

the mere acquisition of knowledge: application in the "real" world, and *binah*, inference from learned experience to deeper forms of understanding. Qohelet contributes to this discussion in a slightly different way, suggesting that the mind is not a mere storehouse for collectibles, nor is knowledge merely to be ingested and regurgitated. Rather, knowledge has a transformational purpose, as Montaigne was to propound in his influential essay on education (*Essais* 1:14).

What then does Qohelet propose? If memory is faulty at best (1:11), being mainly a storehouse for those involved in *thésaurisation*, in having an agenda of collections, then one must consider alternative goals and methods and forms of attention – and the goals are in the methods – of living wisely. I like Jankélévitch's promotion of subtlety and intuition, the art of letting one's self be solicited by surprise. The question revolves, perhaps, on the formation of personal identity:

> What I am I do not yet know; what I know I am no longer that .... And yet in this perpetual and paradoxical back-and-forth from one to the other... we succeed in gathering odds and ends, crumbs of knowledge (*savoir*), luminous flickers which make up our most precious knowledge because it is not a "*savoir*": this tangency of intuition with the intangible has its own intangible consequences. It is an introduction that introduces you to nothing, an encounter without tomorrow or visible consequences. And the only message it leaves us is not at all an enrichment but rather something that cannot be formulated, an imponderable touch. And this gentle touch, without visible stigmatas, will, after the fact, have transformed our life.[40]

"I Qohelet *Was King" (1:12): Aging and Vulnerability*

Let us pursue Jankélévitch a bit further:

> It is here that we touch upon the mystery of human destiny. It is quite possible that in this labor of casting aside, humans recognize and fraternally greet their own destiny. Now this destiny is both a decline and a search for another wisdom and often even another language, both together. At the very moment when, through the ongoing accumulation of experiences and knowledge and memories, the aged person should be reaching the peaks of wisdom, he denudes himself... To impoverish one's self while growing rich, to advance in decline: such is human life.[41]

Qohelet's book is bracketed by a self-presentation at the start ("I Qohelet...." 1:12) and the image of withdrawal and decline and

---

[40] Jankélévitch and Berlowitz, *Quelque part dans l'inachevé*, 50–51.
[41] Ibid., 196.

demise in the closing elegy on dying (12:1–8), already foreshadowed at
the very beginning: "I Qohelet *was* king." I would like to reflect on the
implications of this arrangement. My focus until now has been on the
concept of repentance, a bit in the sense that many of our theologies
have made popular and here connected especially with human acquis-
itiveness. But there is also a let us say natural sense of a changed life
perspective, one arising from vulnerabilities such as aging and from the
earnest experience of what is commonly known as life's downsides: not
sin or even workaholism but less glamorous ones such as disappointments and boredom and, of course, mortality.

Much has been said about Qohelet's autobiographical perspective,
and it is both true and also besides the main point. To be sure, to speak
of one's self as another ("Je est un autre," Rimbaud said famously) is
to apply the same standards of otherness to one's self as to others,
since the autobiographical "I" is now seen from the outside, with all
the limited but real chances at objectivity and heightened knowledge
about one's personal experience that now seem possible – of course,
such objectivity may be compromised by self-promotion. Levinas, however, aware that autobiography's usual purpose is to strengthen the
self, points to deeper levels and in a different direction: away from
personal experiential knowledge of the self, indeed toward the self's
dissolution:

> The attempt was not to present my relation with an other person as an
> attribute of my substantiality, as an attribute of my hardness as a per-
> son, but rather, on the contrary, as the fact of my destitution, of my
> being deposed (in the sense in which one speaks of a sovereign being
> deposed).
>
> Levinas[42]

This perspective is precious in what it says about self-portrayal as a stepping back from one's ego hardness. It offers not a social or political
change – does one ever cease being a pope (whoops!) or a parent or a
king? – but rather a transformation of perspective. Could we not for a
moment step beyond the hardness of our under-the-sun ideologies and
take our wisdom texts as joyous opportunities for transformation?

Qohelet has turned from the world and now has another perspective, one epitomized by his closing elegy on aging and dying. Levinas
(in another context) calls this the discovery of vulnerability, and also of

---

[42] Emmanuel Levinas, *De Dieu qui vient a l'idée* (Paris: Vrin, 2004), 133.

deterioration, to be sure, but a discovery to be faced with one's eyes open and with patience:

> Vulnerability is the power to say adieu to this world. We say adieu to it by aging. Time wears on, endures, as a function of this adieu and also the a-Dieu [to God].[43]

> What is human is not simply what *inhabits* the world but what also *grows old* in the world, what withdraws from it in a way other than by opposition – which withdraws from it through the passivity of aging (a withdrawal which, perhaps, confers upon death itself its meaning, in lieu of having it thought from the starting point of a negation which is a judgment) ....[44]

Perhaps, then, those sages were right who thought Qohelet the product of a writer at the end of life.[45] Qohelet did of course bring negative judgment against the world, or rather against his acquisitive relation to that world. However, aging and even death are here projected as powers of the spirit, as opportunities for human growth, as passivity that is no longer seen as negation, as the mere dialectical opposite of activity, but rather as infinite patience, one that puts us in contact with the infinite future.

I think we tend to simplify the more existential aspects of the book in favor of externals: that Qohelet was rich and wrote only for the rich, that he studied the world and threw up his hands at what he found. However, the kingly fiction, the insistent I-narrative, point rather to a personal and transformational quest, undertaken not because he was an authority figure but more like Appelfeld's fictional character who comes to the awareness that "Neither his studies nor life had taught him to live properly. His life was passing in a haze of hopeless anxiety."[46]

Finally and from the point of view of Jewish liturgy, Qohelet is a confessional text and could be read on the Day of Atonement. Why Jonah is read instead is because Jonah and Yom Kippur really focus on God, whereas Qohelet narrates a personal quest that takes life on its own terms and without the help of clergy. It is therefore read instead at the "time of our joy," on the Festival of Succot, asserting that humans can, through their own efforts at living earnestly, have the possibility of changing their lives. For Yom Kippur only wipes the slate clean; Succot models realistic modes

---

[43] Ibid., 134.
[44] Ibid., 141.
[45] Midrash *Shir ha-Shirim Rabba* 1:1, section 10.
[46] Appelfeld, *The Conversion*, 58.

of contentment and joy: living in simple succah-huts rather than castles, in houses we and the environment can afford, crying out for compassion for those who feel no comforter from anywhere (4:1), casting aside our kingly addiction to pleasure and power in favor of the fellowship and hospitality of learning and eating.

2

Fool's Toil (1:2–3)

Ye toil, O men, for paltry things and incessantly begin strife and war for gain; but nature's wealth extends to a moderate bound, whereas vain judgments have a limitless range.

Diogenes Laertius[1]

Between the first verse presenting the author as "Qohelet" and the opening cosmological poem (1:4–7), the following lines occur:

"hebel of hebels," said Qohelet.

"hebel of hebels:

All is hebel.[2]

What profit[3] for humans from all the toil that they toil under the sun?"

1:2–3

Although some readers prefer to translate *hebel* in its more literal sense as "breath" rather than the more traditional "vanity," the negative impact is the same: Qohelet's watchword or slogan or motto is a declaration of insubstantiality. But regarding what?

---

[1] Diogenes Laertius, *Lives of Eminent Philosophers*, "Epicurus" (trans. R. D. Hicks. Loeb Classical Library, 2 vols. Cambridge, MA: Harvard University Press, 1970), II:541.

[2] "Let us realize that nothing is important and that if, from the outside, things seem different, at bottom they are all equally vain." Seneca, *De tranquillitate animi* X. In *Moral Essays*, trans. John W. Basore (Cambridge MA: Harvard University Press, 1989), ch. 10.

[3] Alternatively, "what remains?" Or, as will be proposed here, "what extra?" The first sense becomes prominent in the discussion of *hebel* as transience (see Part II) The second sense is discussed in Chapter 3, where the point is not the constant complaint that "there is nothing extra," but rather the more probing question "Why do we desire more than we really need?"

37

Before looking at the answers proposed by the text, let us notice the quite unusual repetition of "hebel of hebels." Surely once would have been enough, as the concluding summation in fact puts it:

"hebel of hebels. All is hebel."

12:8

(Note that along the way we have lost one of the "hebel of hebels"!) But if the opening repetition adds nothing to the sense, it certainly does have a performative meaning, exemplifying the excessive *hebel* by its own pointless exuberance.[4] Because this verbal extravagance is in fact brought under control by the end – forming an *inclusio* or parenthesis that must make deliberate recall of 1:2 to be effective[5] – one wonders whether Qohelet's confessional mood of regret has not been made to spill over into the very statement of motto.

Alternatively, if indeed Qohelet is talking about something out there, then he is verbally mimicking everything he sees: "ALL is *hebel*! All is *hebel*! The world speaks its own excess!" Or perhaps even, as I once suggested:[6]

> *hebel* of *hebels*.
> Qohelet has *spoken* a *hebel* of *hebels*.

Surely we have here, as Montaigne was quick to realize in his essay on the same subject (*Essais*, III:9), the point that words exemplify *hebel* through their sheer insubstantiality, so that words about *hebel* can appropriately be termed a *hebel* of *hebels*.

The view that *hebel* is increased in the world through excessive speech was of concern to Qohelet:

The fool multiplies words.

10:14

Through a constant ambivalence of *debarim* ("things") referring both to human speech and behaviors:

So many wearisome things:
No person can express them all

1:8

---

4 The present discussion draws on the negative valence of the *hebel* repetition. For its performative use in a more upbeat mode, see Appendix 2, "Breathe in breathe out."

5 For some implications of this extravagant *inclusio*, see Chapter 10, "The Great *Inclusio*."

6 T. A. Perry, *Dialogues with Kohelet: The Book of Ecclesiastes: Translation and Commentary* (University Park: Penn State Press, 1993), 53–55.

And, in direct (and partial) response to our passage:

> There are so many things that increase *hebel*:
> what profit are they to humans?
>
> 6:11

We shall see that both kinds of excess – wordiness and greed for things – are related, in Qohelet's thinking, to intemperance. The repetition may also hint at the depth of Qohelet's existential crisis, his sense that his life has gone nowhere.[7] We assume, along with Pascal (you write the beginning last), that the opening declaration "*hebel* of *hebels*, *hebel* of *hebels*" is already a conclusion, in which case the opening exactly coincides with the ending "all is *hebel*" and the repetition is indeed tautologous, a mere rhetorical gesture.

With the introduction of the *All* concept ("All is *hebel*"), we are in deeper water still. Some would like it to refer to absolutely everything in the universe. The rabbis, for instance, counted seven occurrences of the word:

hebel = 1
hebels = 2, the minimum plural
hebel = 1
hebels = 2

Thus, all of the works of the six days of creation, plus even the seventh day, are *hebel*. What this might suggest about the Creator is severe indeed, but it allows an escape. By interpreting "*under* the sun" as "*in exchange for* the sun" (a common meaning of *takhat* in Biblical Hebrew)[8] and through symbolic extension of "sun" as "the Law" (as per Prov 6:23), they have Qohelet conclude that in comparison with Torah all is without value.[9] The Qohelet text does not bear out such a reading, however, for Qohelet goes on to examine things that do matter; and if there are then degrees of *hebel*, then all is not *hebel*, at least not entirely.[10]

---

[7] See the Appelfeld epigraph quoted at the start of Chapter 1.

[8] Although this notion may seem imaginative to some moderns, it was unanimously accepted in traditional Jewish exegesis (Michael V. Fox, *Ecclesiastes: The JPS Biblical Commentary* [Philadelphia: JPS, 2004], 4). This was perhaps prompted by a common secondary meaning of *takhat*, "beneath, instead of," as in the expression "an eye for an eye," meaning "in exchange for an eye."

[9] Alternatively, one can read the text as follows: "*under* the sun all is vanity, but *above* it, in the realm of spirit." This midrashic suggestion is explored in Parts III and IV.

[10] Two further possibilities can be proposed. On the one hand, the "all" may be mere rhetorical exaggeration, such as "*All* I see in this world is getting and spending!" Another possibility is that in our text "all" quite frequently has the meaning of "both"

As for the proximate referent of *hebel* at the start, the text in its opening moment attaches its meaning to that of toil, for what the text most directly means by "all" is immediately specified in the very next verse: "*All* the toil that one toils." Attempts have been made to dislodge this clear reading by artificially separating the two verses, thus stopping the direct quotation at the end of "All is *hebel*," although there is no textual reason for so doing. Indeed, once this slight change is allowed, then a more serious one ensues, a disruption of the sequential reading of the two verses (1:2–3). It seems more natural, however, to retain the integrity of the sequence, so that, even if v. 2 is plausibly understood as a special kind of saying – a motto perhaps – the continuation is still presented as a statement of what "Qohelet said," rather than, say, something by someone else who may not quite agree with the presented speaker. And, in fact, the function of v. 3 is precisely to interpret, by limitation, the preceding one. The meaning that arises from a sequential reading, then, is that it is the vanity *of humans ('adam) and the labor that they labor* that is to be characterized as a universal *hebel*. Subsequent support for this reading comes from Qohelet's summation of this entire section, where the two concepts and verses are again joined:

> I considered *all* the works that I did and the *toil that I toiled*, and, behold, all was *hebel* and a striving after the wind, for *no profit* remains under the sun.
>
> 2:11; also 2:22

For those who (correctly) read vv. 2–3 together but insist that human labor is but part and parcel of universal *hebel*, rather than its entirety, "all" is understood as "any," and Qohelet is seen as arguing that no effort has any value. When we later must admit that "something does accrue from the various activities that occupy human beings during their waking hours,"[11] then they must rely on the notion of death's finality – a dubious strategy, since it displaces the debate to the other world. Rather, we would do better to return to Fox's notion that extra effort does not *adequately* compensate our efforts.[12] To Fox's very pertinent question we

---

(7:15, 18; 2:14; 3:19). Thus, "Vanity of Vanities, *hebel* of *hebels*, both are *hebel*." While the exact reference is yet to be presented, we are warned at the start that two kinds or levels of *hebel* are to be discussed: human and cosmic. In terms of the omnipresence of binaries and doublets in Qohelet's thought, this interesting possibility must be considered. See Chapter 8.

[11] James L. Crenshaw, *Joel: A New Translation with Introduction and Commentary* (AB 24C; Garden City, NY: Doubleday, 1995), 60. See also R. N. Whybray, *Ecclesiastes.* New Century Bible Commentary (Grand Rapids, MI: Eerdmans, 1989), 83–84.

[12] Michael V. Fox, *Qohelet and his Contradictions* (Sheffield: Almond, 1989), 68. The sense was expressed by Seneca (II, 345): "An advantage is that which contains more of

give a different answer, however, since Qohelet's complaint may be not against the system – the world, God – but against ourselves, not against what we shall call naturally conditioned action and activity but against excessive enterprise, pursuit of the superfluous (what Seneca termed "*supervacua,*" super vanities) and its requisite toil as opposed to normal work – thus Qohelet can question the value of action only inasmuch as it mushrooms into '*amal.*[13] For, the system being what it is, Qohelet asks whether our response is adequate or even wise. And if not, then maybe we have misread the system's very purpose or nature. In other words, if my expenditures are not compensated, then maybe I am making the wrong kind of expenditures; maybe I should cut back on anxiety-producing labors and reduce worry about things over which I have doubtful control at best.

One common understanding of the key term '*amal* is "toil," but in its entirely negative aspect of that fruitless drudgery that seems character-istic of our human condition. Thus, the word's common connotation of misery strongly colors our understanding, and it does so by seeming to imply passivity: this is the way the world is made, no fault of ours. However, a more aggressive sense is implied in the following:

> All a man's toil ('*amal*) is [only] for his own sustenance,
> Yet his appetite is never sated.

6:7

There is a remarkable parallel in Proverbs, which even uses the same verb:

> The hunger of a worker ('*amel*) works for him [alone],
> For his mouth urges him on.

Prov 16:26

In another context, Qohelet ascribes such ceaseless striving to jealousy:

> I considered all '*amal* and all achievement, that they arise from envy of one's neighbor: this too is *hebel* and chasing after the wind.

4:4

---

usefulness than of annoyance." André Neher puts a perhaps more pertinent stress on a *durable* advantage, on what is PERMANENTLY left over or survives (*Notes sur Qohélét* [Paris: Les Éditions de Minuit, 1951]), 36.

[13] See, for example, 3:9. Heschel puts it nicely: "There is happiness in the love of labor. there is misery in the love of gain" (Abraham Joshua Heschel, *The Sabbath* [New York: Noonday, 1951], 3). For *supervacua* see Seneca, *Ad Lucilium Epistulae Morales,* 3 vols. (trans. Richard M. Gummere; Loeb Classical Library, Cambridge, MA: Harvard University Press. 1971), *Letters,* Letter 31 (I:18).

Or, as Diogenes Laertius put it,

> "Ye toil, O men, for paltry things and incessantly begin strife and war for gain."
>
> Diogenes Laertius[14]

"War for gain" crosses the line, so to speak, recalling a more active sense of *'amal*, a perspective that stresses, rather than the passive sense of misery, quite another sense of the term in Hebrew Scripture and especially appropriate to Qohelet's confessional context:

> Behold he travails with iniquity (*'awen*) and has conceived mischief (*'amal*)
> and brings forth falsehood....
> His mischief (*'amal*) shall come down upon his own head,
> and his deceitful dealing (*khamaso*)....
>
> Ps 7:15, 17[15]

With this, Qohelet's inquiry is suddenly and dramatically refocused. Instead of looking at what humans suffer from outside, the concern is now what we ourselves do to cause suffering, both our own and that of others. We now read with different eyes the "programmatic question" that sets up the debate of the entire book:

> What profit from all the toil at which *he* toils under the sun?
>
> Qoh 1:3

The focus is now on human responsibility, on the sins that lead to and require a turning about.

---

[14] Diogenes Laertius, "Epicurus," II:541.

[15] For the coincidence of *'awen* and *'amal* see Hos 10:13, Ps 90:10, Job 4:8, Prov 22:8 and Num 23:21. These often occur sequentially: *'awen* and *'amal* (Hab 1:3, 13; Ps 7:15; 55:11); *'amal* and *'awen* (Isa 59:4; Job 15:35; Ps 10:7). Fox (*Qohelet and his Contradictions*, 54; *A Time to Tear Down*, 99) lists further parallels but neglects their importance, opting for *'amal* the more general sense of "evil" or trouble," or "lie, deceit" (ibid., 29), thus deflecting the possibility of human responsibility for such. Similarly, *hebel* is acknowledged to mean *'awen* or "sin." The medieval poet saw the ambivalence more clearly: "Against his will man is born to toil [*'amal*] / And all his thoughts and desires are sinful and evil [*'awen we-'amal'* Moses Ibn Ezra, "I Long for You at Night," strophe IX, quoted in Adena Tanenbaum, *The Contemplative Soul: Hebrew Poetry and Philosophical Theory in Medieval Spain* (Leiden: Brill, 2002), 115. Also Hab 1:13. Ha-Meiri equates the word with Qohelet's dominant theme in his commentary on Ps 90:10: *"and most of them [our days] are 'amal and 'awen.* That is to say, *hebel* and emptiness [*rik*]" (Menahem Ha-Meiri, *Commentary on the Book of Psalms*, ed. Menahem Mendel Zahav [Jerusalem: Otsar ha-Poskim, 1971, Hebrew], 179). *'amal* also occurs by itself in Ps 7:15, 17; 94:20; 140:10; Prov 24:2; Hab 1:13, where it is equivalent to *ra'*, evil. Also, rather than its frequent meaning of "violence," *khamas* here refers back to "falsehood" in v. 15 and in this instance also means deceit (also Ps 35:11).

It is quite astonishing that critics have tended to disregard this *hebel*, all the more so because this theme is intoned at the very start. *'Amal*, as everyone points out, often refers to the troubles of existence, as it does in other instances in our book. However, this sense could have been conveyed by "all his troubles under the sun." Here, the word has a more active sense: "the troubles which humans themselves cause." There are, of course, lesser pursuits, where the things pursued are "things of naught" but not intrinsically evil. Here the person has followed Qohelet's requirement to dissociate labor from its results, which are not in our control, and to perform it for its own sake. Here too, however, the important distinction remains between simple "doing" and the excessive "overdoing" connoted by *'amal*, the opposition between "work" and "overwork," what is today known as workaholism.[16]

A sequential reading of 1:2–3 thus yields important insight on the valuation, or rather devaluation, of toil, as opposed to simple work or even labor: it is to be regarded as *hebel*, now seen as having two levels: negative, as sinful, and neutral, as having no more substance or value than a *hebel*. It is this latter valuation of toil that Seneca characterizes quite precisely:

> This [trust in oneself and the happy life to which it leads] cannot be attained unless one has *learned to despise toil* and to reckon it among the things which are neither good nor bad.[17]

If toil is (almost) nothing, indifferent and thus neither positive nor negative, it has no value whatever and therefore is not worth worrying about, surely not worth getting all worked [i.e., toiled] up about! We must remember this basic notion each time we encounter Qohelet's pet refrain: *gam zeh hebel* – this too is a mere *hebel* and therefore not worth getting upset about.

---

[16] See Robert K. Johnston, "'Confessions of a Workaholic': A Reappraisal," *CBQ* 38 (1976): 14–28. Following Ginsberg, Michael V. Fox (*A Time to Tear Down and a Time to Build Up: A Rereading of Ecclesiastes* [Grand Rapids, MI: Eerdmans, 1999], 99) sees an occasional further meaning to *'amal*: profit, especially property, what one acquires. This meaning or echo would then reinforce the collector's signature activity.

[17] Seneca, *Ad Lucilium Epistulae Morales, Letters*, Letter 31 (I:223).

3

Excess and Its Passions (1:8–11)

It is the quality of a great soul to scorn great things and to prefer that which is ordinary rather than that which is too great. For the one condition is useful and life-giving; but the other does harm just because it is excessive.

Seneca[1]

The Vocabulary of Excess

Qohelet's confession has yielded the secret of his unhappiness and the focus of his *hebel* condemnations: his pursuit of excess, his Qohelet or collector's (CEO's) mentality, now put aside ("I *was* king…, I collect*ed*, I acquire*d*") as a pursuit but very much on his mind (otherwise why write a book about it?) both as a lesson to others and perhaps too as a warning to himself.

Qohelet's careful analogy between macrocosm and microcosm, between the world of nature and that of humans, is elaborated, as we shall see in Part II, by a series of metaphors that apply to both levels, thus stressing their interdependence.[2] It is seldom noticed, however, that the analogy is also reflected in a carefully crafted parallelistic verse sequence. The book's opening prelude to the actual "words of Qohelet" in 1:12 ("I, Qohelet…") can be described as follows:

1:1 The presenter's introduction

1:2–3 The motto ("*hebel* of *hebels*") and theme: human toil and its (partially negative) benefits. The entire remaining space between these opening

---

[1] Seneca, *Ad Lucilium Epistulae Morales*, 3 vols. (trans. Richard M. Gummere; Loeb Classical Library, Cambridge, MA: Harvard University Press, 1971), *Letters*, Letter 39 (I:261).

[2] See Chapter 9 for further development of this central notion. For the cosmology, see Chapter 5.

verses and Qohelet's confession narrative is occupied by two parallel and equal sections of four verses each:

1:4–7 presents the cosmology (macrocosm)

1:8–11 responds with a human behavior (microcosm) set in explicit contrast.

The transition from macrocosm to microcosm is made by noting, in successive verses, the insatiability of the sea and that of humans: the sea is never filled (*male'* 1:7) and the human ear is never (ful)filled or satisfied (*timmale'* 1:8). The development of the second series, beginning where the previous one leaves off, thus presents an inversion of the first, both structurally and ideologically, because it ends where the first began, which is the topic of the generations and either their recurrence (1:4) or their disappearance (1:11).

The cosmology sets forth the conditions of the natural world "under the sun" and, by analogy, those parameters within which human life *should* be conducted. In contrast to the glory of natural cyclical regularity that the cosmology presents, however, the sorry state of human affairs immediately follows. As opposed to the directed and limited desires of the natural elements, the world and pursuit of *'ish*, of humans, is sadly one of excess:

> SO MANY things/words in ceaseless activity![3]
>
> Even a great person (*'ish*)[4] cannot express them all:
>
> The eye is never satisfied with seeing
>
> Nor the ear filled with hearing.
>
> Qoh 1:8

[3] The RSV understanding of *yege'im* ("in ceaseless activity") as "full of weariness" has moved interpretation in unproductive directions, and Whybray's careful remarks on 1:4–11 should provide a corrective: "Nothing in this passage suggests that there is anything futile about the behavior of the elements. On the contrary, Qoheleth sees their intense activity as both predictable and positive, contributing to the stability of the earth" R. N. Whybray, *Ecclesiastes*. New Century Bible Commentary (Grand Rapids, MI: Eerdmans, 1989), 39–40. The sense of "wearisome" occurs only here and seems to be based on a haplography, reading *meyag'im* from the contiguous *debariM*.

[4] The tradition in Jewish exegesis of distinguishing between human beings in general (*'adam*, 1:3) and an *'ish*, a great person such as a king or collector – in which case the narrator's irony is turned against himself here – goes back at least to Rashi (on Num 12:3) but can be grounded in such a text as Ps 49:3: "Both *bnei 'adam* (humans) and sons of *'ish*, the rich and poor together." In Ps 49:3 the distinction seems to hold as well, although some regard *'ish* as merely a poetic substitute. See T. A. Perry, *Dialogues with Kohelet: The Book of Ecclesiastes: Translation and Commentary* (University Park: Penn State University Press, 1993), 62.

In other words, although it is true that human speech and eye and ear are "incapable of taking it all in,"[5] Qohelet seems to argue that humans *should not try to do so!* These words are thus neither a complaint on the universe's monotonous futility nor even primarily a lingering admiration of nature's wonders.[6] Rather, they take note of the vanity of our boundless striving for what we imagine to be fulfillment. Indeed, our endless pursuit of newness, our ceaseless curiosity and desire for absolute knowledge, our pretense to have invented the world anew is based on a blissful ignorance not only of nature but of history as well:

> Someone claims: "Look, this is new!" It has already happened for eons. [He is simply unaware, since] Just as there is no memory of former things/people [people make no effort to remember. In the same way, tit-for-tat,] there will be no remembrance by/of those who come after.

Qoh 1:10–11

When we come to the summation of our pericope, the focus is pointedly on human action:

> I saw all the deeds that are done under the sun, And, behold, all is a breath (*hebel*) and a pursuit of wind.

1:14

At this point Qohelet characterizes the situation in the world by giving a radical twist to what must have been two traditional proverbs:

> A crookedness that cannot be straightened

1:15

This can now be understood as referring not only to the natural universe, as is usually the case, but also to the curve and cyclicality of all natural human movements of desire, which humans wrongly try to "straighten." Again,

> an absence/emptiness that cannot be counted

1:15

This can now be viewed as a fruitless desire to count what cannot be counted (because it is too numerous or), resulting in a loss of time and effort. Thus:

> "that which you cannot count (because you will never get to the end of it) is an absence."

---

[5] Ibid.

[6] For the concept of regularity as a source not of boredom but of security and joy, see Chapter 5.

This figure merely repeats, as a conceptual refrain, the previous three in 1:8. In other words, the two proverbs characterize the foolish presumptions upon which fools base their pursuits: "straightness" and number. Had they learned from nature's movements, they would know, for example, that the shortest and wisest distance between two points is often not a straight line, and that the pursuit of quantity for itself is an illusion, since more is less: absences do not respond to number.[7]

The general point, then, is that, contrary to popular thinking, more is not more but less. We may now supply an emphatic translation of the opening rhetorical question:

> What profit for humans from *so much* toil that they toil under the sun!?
>
> Qoh 1:3

Indeed, as we shall now see, it is the human tendency to excess – to reaching or going beyond reasonable (natural) needs – that comes in for what is perhaps Qohelet's main critical focus of the entire work. Isn't this argument graphically enacted by the book's refrain, intoned at the very start by its redundant emptiness that cannot be counted: "*hebel of hebels, hebel of hebels*, all is *hebel*." What better illustration of the focus of Seneca's attack against excess: *super-vacua*, a "super" emptiness![8]

The Passions

Let us recall Qohelet's typical complaints on human insatiability:

> Even though a person's toil is [only] for his sustenance, his appetite is never satisfied.
>
> Qoh 6:7

> If a person begets a hundred children and lives many years: for all the years that he lives, if his appetite does not find satisfaction with the good, then I say that the stillborn – even if it does not have a burial – is better off than he.
>
> Qoh 6:3[9]

In our endless studies of such key concepts as *'amal* ("toil"), we have become stalled on the act and its result while neglecting the cause. Thus,

---

7 For further comment on this verse see Appendix 5, Miscellaneous, "Slanting the Truth."
8 See above, n. 102; also Seneca I:4.
9 The stillborn would be *better* off than he is because the stillborn is simply nonexistent or neutral on the scale of happiness, whereas the perpetual *lack* of satisfaction denotes a negative. One still-to-be-born does not have the addiction to excess that would hamper enjoyment and moral progress. As the thought continues, "all a human's toil is [only] for his own sustenance, and his appetite is never filled!" (v. 7).

the term means both toil and its possible result, wealth, to be sure.[10] But we must not neglect suggestions such as the following, which returns to Qohelet's opening question (1:3) with a hendiadys that adds an important focus:

> What does a man have from all his *toil and his heart's desires* that he toils under the sun.

Qoh 2:22

Behind the abundant toil, we have not sufficiently noticed the *ra'yon libo*, the heart's unnatural passions and desires that produce the "overdoing" and the workaholism in the first place.[11]

For the collector the world is indeed too much with us: too much seeing, hearing, talk (1:8):

> let your words be few: just as a dream come with too much busyness, so too a fool's voice with too many words.

Qoh 5:1–2

The principle of balance applies even where one would least expect it:

> Don't be too righteous and don't play too much the wise man: why should you be destroyed?

Qoh 7:16

A critique of the *passions of the soul* has formed a constant focus of interest among religious and moral teachers from the earliest times. What has not been sufficiently noticed is how pervasive Qohelet's contribution is. We might begin an analysis of his thought here by focusing on the usual dangers. Take, for example, his well-known observation:

> He who loves money will never be satisfied with money.

Qoh 5:9

We might think that this is a standard diatribe against materialism, focusing on the *goal* of desire. And, to be sure, such is the case of all things of breath and wind, as we have seen. We are quite taken aback, however, when we discover that, beyond these usual pitfalls, Qohelet includes wisdom itself:

> For in *too much* wisdom is much anger, And greed for experience is greed for pain.

Qoh 1:18

---

[10] Michael V. Fox, *Qohelet and His Contradictions* (Sheffield: Almond, 1989), 57, refers to the toil/earnings or wealth ambiguity.

[11] Ibid., 54. For workaholism see above, n. 105.

Wisdom and the experience needed to acquire it are also morally dangerous and painful!? What is going on here?

Qohelet takes an interesting approach[12]:

> Humans cannot rule over the wind [*ruakh*], to inhibit the wind – just as there is no rule over the day of death or escape in a war – and passion [*resha'*] will not save its possessor.

Qoh 8:8

Since the word *resha'* is usually understood as "wicked," Radak goes on to explain, in his commentary to Ps 1:

> The wicked (*resha'yim*) are those who are passionate (*kharedim*) in acquiring money and their heart's desires in this world and make no distinction between good and evil, and embezzle and steal and kill because of their heart's passion.

Although money is listed as a typical goal, Radak thinks that the real evil is desire itself:

> For the meaning of wickedness (*resha'*) is passion (*kheredah*).

He then cites, in addition to 8:8, Qohelet 7:17: *'al tirsha' harbeh*, "Don't be *too* wicked."[13] Might one then conclude that Qohelet gives license to be somewhat wicked? Rather: don't be too passionate. For "too much" leads not only to emotional disturbance[14] but also to depravity.

One of the most interesting and revealing refrains in Qohelet is *re'ut ruakh*, which, according to the common understanding, refers to things outside, thus "a chasing after the wind."[15] It would thus parallel such metaphors as Hos 12:2: a chasing after the east wind. Grammatically, however, one may construe this not as an objective genitive but rather as a subjective one: the spirit's desire or pursuit, thus conceptually parallel with the "heart's desires" in 2:22. And it is now becoming accepted to translate alternately as "an affliction of the spirit," so that the focus is now on a problem internal to the subject rather than on a defect of

---

[12] I translate according to Radak (Rabbi David Kimhi, 1160?–1235?). Radak is cited in *Torat Hayyim: Chumash* [The Five Books of Moses], with Classical Commentaries, ed. Mordechai Breuer et al., 7 vols. (Jerusalem: Mossad Harav Kook, 1986–1993).

[13] He further cites the following: "When He gives quietness, who can cause disturbance (*yarshia'*)?" (Job 34:29); "And wherever he turned he caused disturbance (*yarshia'*)" (1 Sam 14:47).

[14] Fox, *Qohelet and His Contradictions*, 235, citing Qoh 1:18.

[15] In Chapter 9, I analyze the verbal ambivalences at the base of Qohelet's cosmology and further explore the case of *ruakh* and its alternation between (cosmic) "wind" and (human) "breath/spirit."

the universe.[16] It seems possible to accept both simultaneously, however, and to see the phrase as stressing the situation of the unquiet spirit that desires or pursues the wind. Consider the following:

> I think that all toil and achievement arise from envy of one's neighbor, and this too is therefore breath and a *chasing after the wind*. The fool folds his arms and eats his own flesh. Better one handful with repose than two fistfuls with toil and *chasing after the wind*.
>
> Qoh 4:4–6

Who can say for sure whether "chasing after the wind" in such a passage may not *also* be understood as an "affliction of the spirit," especially where the stress is so much on the passions (envy) and self-mutilation (eating his own flesh)?

It would even seem, on the basis of this pervasive ambivalence, that Qoh 8:8 could *also* be rendered as follows: "Humans do not rule over the *ruakh*, to inhibit the *ruakh*."[17] We must not abandon the first reading (humans cannot rule over the *wind*), which places limitations on humans' desire for power and control. But we must be willing to see here a moral problem as well – a human refusal to take charge over those internal areas, the *spirit* – that *is* within our control.

Quietism Then?

The degree of our liberation is measured by the number of activities from which we manage to emancipate ourselves, as well as by our ability to convert all objects into non-objects... We shall not regain control over our lives or enjoy life without first nullifying it.

Cioran[18]

In quietness [of spirit] and in turning back you will be saved.

Isa 30:15

With the relentless *hebel* litany Qohelet has proposed a world of no-thing, to be brought about both by a withdrawal from things of naught

---

[16] For the concept of a universe neither good nor bad but neuter, see Chapter 7. For an interesting medieval case, see T. A. Perry, *The Moral Proverbs of Santob de Carrión* (Princeton, NJ: Princeton University Press, 1987), 113, 120.

[17] So too Qohelet Rabba, Rashi, Ibn Ezra, Targum Jonathan.

[18] E. M. Cioran, *La Tentation d'exister* (Paris: Gallimard, 1956), 15. Cioran goes on (p. 16), and in Qohelet's and Seneca's own language, to relate this project to freedom from the emotions: "Every sensation is a link – pleasure as much as pain, joy as much as sadness. Only that person is liberated who, purified of all dealings with beings and objects, focuses on his own emptiness (*vacuité*)."

(including naughty things) and by a quieting of their accompanying passions. To make a meditative shift to such a mood, I propose a scene from the film version of Edith Wharton's *Age of Innocence*. The countess is seated gazing out over the water in a landscape of luminous tranquility. Her lover has lied to his wife and nervously pursued the countess to this appointed spot. As he arrives on the scene his precipitous passions are somehow stalled, bemused, overwhelmed by the flood of serenity and peacefulness that seems to have conquered the countess as well, indeed to flow from her very being. He walks away without accosting his true beloved and later learns that, while she had been aware of his presence, she too chose to remain within the scene and not turn to greet him. Lest one think she turns away from passion out of moral scruple, the final scene recreates the same conditions, and without any possible inconvenience of adultery, as his wife is now deceased. Again, the lovers turn away from their only true emotional fulfillment in life, and we ask why.

Despite our Western cult of passion – the most violent form of which may no longer be romantic love or even scientific curiosity but moral rectitude and religious triumphalism – there has always been a minority opinion. What prevents us from making positive use of *hebel* perceptions may be a *re'ut ruakh*, a breathless chasing the wind that has turned sour on its own extravagances. Qohelet's particular brand of indifference has struck some critics as upper-crust, as a numb and snooty aloofness from all worldly things, a pattern for which might be Voltaire's Senhor Pococurante. We wonder, though, whether in Qohelet we are not dealing with a particular form of mental asceticism, with a philosophical detachment, apathy, passivity, abandon, a mistrust of that passionate intensity that we occidentals have come to view as the very hallmark of the spiritual life or, indeed, of any life worth living whatever.

To access these resonances of Qohelet's *hebel* refrain, we may, propaedeutically, have to divert our spiritual gaze from the very fullness of God's creation and, along with the Dalai Lama and others, recover an awareness of the emptiness that precedes and permeates creation and that seems to be its very support.[19] We may also have to turn from our tense notions of frustration and woe, to withdraw from our forever expansive hatreds and dogmatisms and especially attachments (Qoh 7:8–10). In short, and like the lovers in Edith Wharton or *La Princesse de Clèves*, we may have to relearn to value the tranquility of the void (that is, *hebel* in a positive

---

[19] I like the Rabbinic midrash that regards *hebel* as the breath of school children that constitutes the support of the entire creation (BT Sabb 119b).

sense) more than the turbulence of the passions, the peacefulness of inner calm more than all the fancied grandeur of other times and worlds and dominions. When viewed in its more extreme forms, as proposed by the repetitive conclusion that "this *too* is *hebel*," such a withdrawal from all vanities and passions of excess evokes a sense of things that has much of what we would call quietism.[20]

The quietistic theory should seem especially congenial to those critics who subscribe to Cartesian dualism, as reflected, in Qohelet criticism, by Camus's definition of *hebel* as the absurd. According to this view, our universe is composed of two completely different substances: thinking substance (consciousness) and extended substance (matter). The absurdity would be in neither taken separately but rather in the total disjunction between the two and their coexistence in the same universe. Thus, in the texts that we shall soon discuss, dealing with the nature of the cosmos into which humans are placed (Chapter 5) and especially the time arrangements that define and constrain human existence (Chapter 6), one might paraphrase Rousseau: humans are born free, and everywhere they are in chains to a world totally predetermined by fate or nature or God (*Deus seu natura*). Qohelet's opening question thus returns with renewed (and exaggerated) vigor: if indeed individual appetites and preoccupations (*khepets*) are governed by established cosmic patterns, what is to be derived from human effort? In other words, isn't quietism – rather than the Jobean rage ascribed to Qohelet by some critics – the wiser approach to life? For if everything has its preordained moment, of what possible use are my efforts, anticipations, anxieties, even prayers? Is it not true that even our wisdom is tainted – indeed, driven – by our being so uptight (here termed *ka' as*, anger (1:18, 7:9)?

Such a view may originate from two different but not contradictory perspectives. Viewed religiously: shouldn't perfect acceptance and conformity with God's will, as expressed in the order of things, be the true focus and locus of our spiritual liberation? If so, then pursuit and its passions must, in Cioran's words, be replaced by withdrawal, by a conversion leading from a repetitive "no-thing" to a total emptiness or

---

[20] James Limburg points out some quietistic aspects of Luther's reading of Qohelet; see his *Encountering Ecclesiastes: A Book for Our Time* (Grand Rapids, MI: Eerdmans, 2006), 19. So too does Lohfink, who evokes an affinity between Qohelet and "those currents of popular philosophy that rejected wealth, withdrew from public life, and for happiness in that hesychia (quiet) that is assured by modest restraint in lifestyle" Norbert Lohfink, *Qoheleth: A Continental Commentary* (Minneapolis: Fortress, 2003), 70. Except that Lohfink sees this quietistic aspect in 4:5–6 only, whereas it seems to me much more pervasive.

"nothing." Or, formulated philosophically, we concluded Chapter 2 with the observation that the notion of toil (*'amal*) in Qohelet has, like breath itself, neither positive nor negative value, that overdoing and mental affliction is simply not worth the pain. We must remember this basic notion each time we encounter the constant refrain: "*gam zeh hebel*," "this too is a [mere] breath," which would be one of Qohelet's pet techniques for inducing quietism. It is clear, of course, that breath applies not only to our pursuits (Part I), but also to the world "out there": *everything* is air. The purpose of this constant assertion is usually misunderstood, however, which is to reduce worry about it.[21] Why worry about nothing? For, again, vanity or void means nothing and nothing does not have value, either *or* negative. That's the point: if it were positive I would worry about having it; if it were negative I would worry about avoiding it. Since it is neither, why worry?!

Pushed to their extremes, such quietistic readings – while capturing real moments of Qohelet's pessimism – are to be rejected because things do have relative value, if only in this world "under the sun," as we shall see in Part II. Also and more seriously yet, the quietistic theory supports a false view of Qohelet's philosophy as individualistic and solipsistic. Indeed, the existentialist approach has led some to the point where individual *Angst* and destiny become disregard for the suffering of others. We shall later see, however, that Qohelet's focus is steadily on humans (*ha-'adam*), the individual through whom we all survive as a generation (*dor*), not separate from the universe but rather an integrated part of it.

Rather than a radical quietistic withdrawal from the world of things and their passions, therefore, in Qohelet's view the control to be exercised over our lives is to be a measured one, to be set not against an unfriendly universe but rather in harmony with it, since it alone offers the potential for growth and surprise.

---

[21] "Make life as a whole agreeable to yourself by banishing all worry about it" Seneca, *Letters*, Letter 4.

4

A Practical Guide for Living Wisely

Natural desires are limited, but those which spring from false opinion have no stopping point, for there are no limits to the false. When you are traveling on a road, there must be an end; but when astray, your wanderings are limit-less. Therefore, withdraw from vain things (*vanis*); and when you would know whether what you seek is based on a natural or a blind desire, consider whether it can stop at any definite point. If you find, after having travelled far, that there is a more distant goal always in view, you may be sure that this condition is contrary to nature.

Seneca[1]

The more we amplify our need and our possession, the more we involve ourselves in the blows of fortune and adversity. The range of our desires should be circumscribed and restrained to a narrow limit of the nearest and most contiguous good things; and moreover *their course should be directed not in a straight line that ends up elsewhere, but in a circle whose two extremities by a short sweep meet and terminate in ourselves.* Actions that are performed without this reflexive movement, I mean a searching and genuine reflexive movement – the actions, for example, of the avaricious, the ambitious, and so many others who run in a straight line, whose course carries them ever forward – are erroneous and diseased actions.

Michel de Montaigne[2]

---

[1] Seneca, *Ad Lucilium Epistulae Morales,* 3 vols. (trans. Richard M. Gummere; Loeb Classical Library, Cambridge, MA: Harvard University Press, 1971), I:109. See also his *De tranquillitate animi* X. In *Moral Essays,* trans. John W. Basore (Cambridge MA: Harvard University Press, 1989), ch. 10.

[2] Michel de Montaigne, *The Complete Essays of Montaigne* (trans. Donald Frame; Palo Alto, CA: Stanford University Press, 1976), 773, italics added. This idea may be illustrated by 1:15: "a crookedness that cannot be straightened." A positive reading would imply that such a natural crookedness *should not be* straightened. See below, Appendix 5, "Slanting the Truth."

Setting Natural Limits: Cycles

With the analogy of reciprocity between nature and human nature firmly in mind, let us briefly review the cosmology's moral lessons and implications, as presented in 1:4–7.

1:4 People are born and die, generations come and go, forever striving to accommodate change and advance; the earth and also its people do remain.

1:5 The sun rises and sets, "panting with desire" to reach its place of renewal, from which it generates yet another cycle.

1:6 The wind (*ruakh*, also "spirit") blows in a circular and ongoing fashion, always returning upon itself.

1:7 Despite their efforts to fill the sea, which is never (ful)filled or "satisfied" (as per 1:8), the river waters themselves return to their point of departure.

Of the many things that can be said of this cosmology, the following three points seem essential:

1) the fact of universal movement [*halak*], anthropomorphically represented as desire. Only two elements, the earth and the sea, seem at rest, but these too achieve their continuity and renewal, serving as repositories of the transitory generations and rivers.

2) each movement has a definite and limited goal, called its place.

3) each self-contained process is repeated indefinitely. To say "eternally" would be a stretch of imagination, although there is no indication that the process itself would ever cease or change. What does merit this designation is the cosmic earth and its people, which will remain, "standing" to serve *le-'olam*, infinitely.

It is perhaps the cyclical regularity[3] of all things that has most interested critics, but often in a negative sense of monotony and futility. And, in fact, such awareness can itself be regarded as a key feature of wisdom itself:

---

[3] The point is made in the very first word *dor*, "generation," which seems to mean "circle" or even "ball" (Isa 22:18; 29:3). For more on cyclicality, see Chapter 8. For his part, Michael V. Fox (*A Time to Tear Down and a Time to Build Up: A Rereading of Ecclesiastes* [Grand Rapids, MI: Eerdmans, 1999], 332) sees in circularity only "futility and thus absurdity," a view very much contested here. For, in the words of Fox's own hero, Camus declares that "we must imagine Sisyphus to be happy" (*Le Mythe de Sisyphe* [Paris: Gallimard, 1942], 168). Closer perhaps to Qohelet's literary project is Camus's further observation (p. 167): "One does not discover the absurd without being tempted to write a manual on how to be happy." I argue here that Qohelet is precisely such a manual.

> What is vice? It is what you have often seen. Indeed, when anything happens, have this thought in readiness: It is what you have often seen... There is nothing new. Everything is banal and ephemeral.[4]

In the context of renewal and desire, however, the sun's desire for renewal – both in the natural world under the sun and in the human world – focuses on the limited goals and visible ends that make this possible, as the passages from Seneca and Montaigne clarify. What thus may seem to us as a dreadful annoyance – that there is nothing new, and so forth – is in fact viewed by Qohelet as a guarantee against a more serious inconvenience. For it is *un*-natural, linear desires that seek the new, imagining places where there is no memory of past things; and it is the discipline or restriction of desires to their cyclical and natural boundaries that saves us from the vanity of the false infinite.[5] From this perspective, the defining motto "all is *hebel*" is neither ontological nor epistemological. It is a moral teacher's caution against the vanity that we multiply (6:11) through our blind and extravagantly *un*-natural desires and pursuits. Yet another trip to the shopping mall or the stock broker? Ho hum!

The dynamism of this process is, paradoxically, put forth in the notion of place, normally thought to be a position of stasis. However, the formulations are significant:

> [the sun] yearns to return to its place: there is where it rises [again].
>
> 1:5

Notice that the sun does not go to *a* place but rather *its* place, the one peculiar to its journey and desire. The sun's place is not simply the physical location of its rising but its rising itself. For, as Thoreau observed, "the actual place is indifferent to the dead man who comes to life."[6] Similarly, the waters:

> To the place where the rivers go, there they return, to go forth again.

What one's "place" really is, then, is not *where* you happen to be but rather *what* you yearn to do and *be*, less the space where you are headed than the desire to be (to return to) where you take your origin and renewal. This

---

4 Marcus Aurelius, *Thoughts* (2 vols. Cambridge, MA: Loeb Classical Library, Harvard University Press, 1970), Book 7, par. 1.

5 On natural boundaries see, for example, Ps104:9": "You have set a boundary which they [the waters] might not pass over, that they might not return to cover the earth [once again]."

6 Henry David Thoreau, *Walden, or Life in the Woods* (New York: New American Library, 1999), 107.

may be why God has been called *ha-Maqom*, The Place, a place of destinations because of origins, a "remembered future," as Harold Fisch put it.[7] The projected human virtue here is cyclical contentment, and its basis is patience and eternal trust in the renewal that the future can bring.

Organ and Self-Control: Eyes, Hands, Feet

A full code of behavior would include negative as well as positive directives. Thus,

> *Turn from evil* and do good.
> Ps 34:15; 37:27

Such a dual focus would apply not only to ethics but also to the pursuit of happiness:

1. Happy is the one
   who *neither* walks in the counsel of the wicked
   nor stands on the way of sinners
   nor sits in the seat of scoffers.
2. But in the Teaching of the Lord is his delight....

> Psalm 1:1–2

The Jewish religious code of commandments of course contains both, but with a preponderance of negatives over positives: 365 versus 248. This is in keeping with Psalm 1:1–2, where negative prescriptions are named first and outnumber the positives in a ratio of three to one. Such a negative morality is quite characteristic of Qohelet.[8] Here are a few of the behavioral focal points:

What Is within the Range of Vision
The Hebrew Bible warns against what might be called punning on the Hebrew *tur*, "to wander," a kind of a visual *tour*-ism:

> And you should not wander after your own heart and after your own eyes, which you go a'whoring after.
> Num 15:39

---

7 See T. A. Perry, *Jonah's Arguments with God: The Honeymoon Is Over!* (Peabody, MA: Hendrickson, 2014), 119. For *maqom* see also p. 229, n. 107.

8 For some of the characteristics of negative morality, see T. A. Perry, "Just Say No: Montaigne's Negative Ethics," in *Approaches to Teaching Montaigne's Essays*, ed. Patrick Henry (New York: MLA, 1993), 78–83.

Rashi, by reversing the terms, not only stresses the close connection between heart and eyes but also a possible causality not to be overlooked:

> *The eye sees* and the heart desires and the body commits the sin.

This focus was not lost on Qohelet:

> *The eye* is never satisfied with seeing
>
> 1:8

> There is no end to so much toil, yet *his eye* is never satisfied with his wealth.[9]
>
> 4:8

Although, as Crenshaw observes, "no motive is given for the person's endless desire," since merely to see is a strong provocation to want; the cure is also implied: control over the eyes.[10]

Such control does not suggest blindness, however, but rather the necessity of remaining within natural limits, of attending to what is available *without* excessive pursuit, of sticking to real needs rather than imagined ones.

> When wealth multiplies, so do its spenders,
>
> And what benefit can owners derive
>
> Except what is within *view of their eyes?*
>
> 5:10[11]

While retaining its simple or physical meaning, the view of one's eyes easily morphs into a metaphor for the range of one's appetites and desires. Thus,

> Better what the eyes can see than the wandering of the appetite.
>
> 6:9

---

[9] For the paradox to be effective, then it must be admitted that, normally, toil does produce wealth.

[10] James L. Crenshaw, *Ecclesiastes: A Commentary* (OTL, Philadelphia: Westminster, 1987), 110. The warning in 15:39, while noting the close connection between seeing and appetite, reverses the causation: "Do not follow after your heart and eyes in your lustful urge."

[11] Whether pursuit should be limited to really basic needs or should enjoyment also play a part by motivating pursuit is an important issue, one suggested perhaps by the close relation between the biblical verb *ra'ah*, "to see," and the same word followed by the preposition *b-*, "to enjoy." See Emmanuel Levinas CC, 119: "This property is legitimate insofar as it is a condition of individual enjoyment that nobody should try to bother. One's only property is the 'at home' (*le chez soi*)." For the importance of enjoyment, Levinas's further meditation should also be carefully pondered (CC, 245–46).

The moral: control your eyes, satisfy your needs with things within your range of vision. Or, to use a parallel focus, when Henry Thoreau was asked, at a smorgasbord, what he would like to be served, he replied: "whatever is within reach."[12]

The Near at Hand

Given the collector's addiction to acquisitions and his subsequent withdrawal, it becomes crucial to define what he now considers the legitimate limits of property and possessions. Levinas's phrase captures the action at its most basic level: "La possession – de la main qui prend."[13] Its easy metaphorical extension focusses on the concept of *Zuhandenheit*, of being within reach, at hand.[14]

Gordis's translation of this latter verse illustrates the natural affinity of the two figures:

> Better a joy at hand than excessive desires.

6:9[15]

Even when the sense is metaphorical, the image stresses the close at hand or readily available, whatever is within one's natural reach:[16]

> Better one *handful* with repose than two fistfuls with effort and *chasing after* the wind.

Qoh 4:6

This verse also suggests one of Qohelet's favorite images for remedying human excess, the focus on what may be termed the near at hand. This is meant quite literally, but the metaphorical extension is an easy one:

> Do with strength whatever your hand finds to do.

9:10

---

[12] The thought is a stoic commonplace. See, for example, Epictetus, *Enchiridion* #15.

[13] CC, 125, Levinas never lets the metaphor entirely depart from its *peshat* or literal reference: "The organ of power is the hand" CC, 247.

[14] " *Zuhandenheit* de l'activité tient à la *Zuhandenheit* de prendre et de posséder" (CC, 127).

[15] Robert Gordis, *Koheleth – The Man and His World* (New York: Schocken, 1968), 170, renders *halak nefesh* as "longing for distant pleasures," while adding, in the notes (pp. 261–62), the meaning "wandering of the appetite."

[16] Traditional moral teaching abounds with the notion that whatever we really need is close at hand: "Parabile est quod natura desiderat, et adpositum... Ad manum est quod sat est" Seneca, *Letters* I:4, 18. Cf. also Montaigne: "We must direct and fix our desires on things that are easiest and nearest" *Essais*, 820 (III:3).

> It is good to hold on to this, and also not to rest your hand from that.
>
> 7:18

> In the morning sow your seed, and in the evening do not rest your hand…
>
> 11:6

One cannot resist the rabbinic-type limitation: do *what is within reach,* but to what is beyond give no regard!

Underlying the valuation of the proximate and available and familiar is the emotional contrary pull of the unavailable, the "grass is always greener" syndrome (envy), the touristic attraction to the new (undercut by 1:10). Of special interest in this regard is Qohelet's warning:

> Do not say: "How can it be that the former days were better than these [present ones]?" For such questions do not arise from wisdom.
>
> 7:10

Nor do such questions arise from harmless nostalgia and fantasy. They are part and parcel of the myth-making that removes humans from clear thinking and concrete living and *real* self-interest.

Feet

Rather than making theoretical distinctions, Qohelet focuses his analysis on very local and practical prescriptions, on the order of the plea to a youngster invited to join a gang of criminals: "Keep your *foot* from their paths" (Prov 1:24). Such figures of restriction and restraint account for much of Qohelet's advice, his first line of defense against unwise living.

"Traveling on a road" is one of our most popular metaphors for expressing a *"way* of life," for exploring the meanings of living as "taking a particular path." Whether Dante's generalized *"cammin* di nostra vita" or Robert Frost's *"miles to go* before I sleep," it typically incorporates broader existential vistas with physical images, never entirely leaving the realm of concrete experience. An outstanding example of the first is the introduction of our prayerbook, the Book of Psalms, which sets the tone of the entire collection:

> Happy the person who… does not stand on the *way* [*derek*] of sinners.…
> For the Lord knows the *way* of the righteous; but the *way* of the wicked will perish.
>
> Ps 1:1, 6

Like *derek*, "way" can highlight the metaphorical, as here: "a way or manner of life," while still planting the concrete notion of physically walking:

> And these words which I command you this day shall be upon your heart. And you shall teach them to your children, and you shall speak them when you sit in your house and *when you walk on the way* and when you lie down and when you rise up.
>
> Deut 6:7; also 11:19

I think that it is this latitude, this ability to range broadly while never entirely leaving the *peshat* or literal level that is especially appealing to moralists and poets alike. Seneca's choice of the image of "traveling on a road" achieves this dual purpose, here to concretize the process of human desire. Qohelet would have loved it.

Concepts of Time: The Present, Dailiness

> My philosophy is in action, in natural and present practice, little in fantasy.
>
> Montaigne[17]

Montaigne advises a withdrawal from frivolous and imagined pleasures by restricting his activity to things available now, proximate both in space and in the present time. His great admirer Pascal took up the theme, observing that humans, always distracted, live in the past or the future, never in the present. With good reason, perhaps, since, as one wag complained, "the present moment is already far from me," a remark that Qohelet would have accepted, albeit in a more positive vein. Montaigne's focus on action or practice seems innovative, since contemplation and certain forms of meditation are more congenial to such an exclusive focus. Sensing the problem and aware of the vanity of both past and future, Qohelet settles on what has been called the Epicurean solution: eat and drink and be joyful, since this alone is in the present. Otherwise, in a stunning neologism, he asks: what (else) is *present to humans* – that is, what else do we really possess?[18] Since the past is past and the future not yet, and since at any rate nothing of any worth is within our power to guarantee, then what remains, what is the *yitron*? In Qohelet the focus of *carpe diem* is on the very traditional notion of seizing

---

[17] Montaigne, *Essais*, 842 (III:5).

[18] *Mah howeh la-'adam* (2:22); see Neher, *Notes sur Qohélét* (Paris: Les Éditions de Minuit, 1951), 93. I think that "eating and drinking" may also be a figure for the legitimate boundaries of those danger zones that drive the collector's impulse: imagined utility and pleasures.

what Emerson called the "potluck" of the *dies* or day.[19] Just as Thoreau thought that living a life of "true integrity" involved nothing less and nothing more than a "day by day" focus ("Economy"),[20] Qohelet, in response to the limited natural range of our vision of the future, advises what we may call dailiness, a focus on what occurs or can occur within the range of twenty-four hours.

Dailiness is one of the richest topics of traditional moral literature, as can be seen in this brief sampling:

> My travel plan is everywhere divisible; it is not founded on great hopes; each day's journey forms an end. And the journey of my life is conducted in the same way.
>
> Montaigne[21]

> I act as if each and every day were a complete life.
>
> Seneca[22]

The reason is Qohelet's: we have only the present in which to live:

> There is no person whose life does not look forward to the morrow. "What harm is there in this?" you ask. Infinite harm; for such persons do not live, but are preparing to live. They postpone everything.
>
> Seneca[23]

The restriction of one's needs and desires is common in Hebrew Scripture, and not always in a positive sense. Thus Pharaoh's taskmasters command the Israelites to postpone nothing, but rather to "fulfill your work, *each daily thing in its own day* (Exod 5:13, 19). This same formula is used as a test of faith in the distribution of manna in the desert: "the people shall go out and gather each day [only] that day's portion" (Exod 16:4; also Deut 8:2–3). In a more positive sense, the same formula is used to regulate the festival sacrifices (Lev 23:37; 2 Kgs 25:30; Neh 11:23). The formula did allow some flexibility, acknowledging that different days can bring different needs, as in Solomon's prayer at the inauguration of the Temple (1 Kgs 8:59). And if the individual day signals the quick renewal of necessities, it also specifies that such requirements

---

[19] Ralph Waldo Emerson, "Experience," in *The Portable Emerson*, ed. Carl Bode (New York: Penguin Books, 1981), 276.

[20] Thoreau, *Walden, or Life in the Woods*, 3.

[21] Montaigne, Essais, 978 (III:9).

[22] "Id ago ut mihi instar totius vitae dies sit." Seneca, *Letters*, Letter 61 (I:424).

[23] Seneca, ibid., Letter 45 (I:299).

must be met on a daily basis, with no interruption (Neh 11:23; 12:47). In this respect it parallels the phrase *yom yom*, "day by day," indicating persistence, regularity and continuity (Prov 8:30, 34).[24]

In Qohelet dailiness is closely linked with skepticism, with our inability to know the future. Human ignorance and "things at hand" come together in Qohelet's focus on present time. Just as the pursuit of time past is *hebel* (because it is irretrievable), even more so is future time:

> Who can tell humans what will be after them?
>
> 6:12; also 3:22; 7:14; 10:14b

Ignorance of what will be after death extends to the more proximate future as well:

> No man knows what will be.
>
> 10:14a

> For man does not know what will be, for who can tell him how things will be.
>
> 8:7

This is consistent with other wisdom texts, such as

> Do not boast of tomorrow, for you do not know what a day may beget.
>
> Prov 27:1

If that is the case for every single day, then an a posteriori meaning may be suggested: "for you do not know what even today may bring." That is to say, there is risk even in the present. That is perhaps why Blanchot discusses dailiness (*le quotidien*) as beyond the dialectic and close to the neuter.[25] In direct reference to our text and tying together the various strands of human ignorance and dailiness and especially acceptance, Montaigne offers a summarizing observation:

> Ecclesiastes says: "Accept all things in good part, just as they seem, just as they taste, day by day. The rest is beyond thy knowledge."[26]

---

[24] Cioran cynically provides a parody of this ideal. Referring to a beggar, he remarks that "to live day by day is to live nose to nose with eternity" *La Tentation d'exister* (Paris: Gallimard, 1956), 13.

[25] See the commentary in William McKane, *Proverbs: A New Approach* (London: OTL, 1970), 607. Also Bruce K. Waltke, *The Book of Proverbs: Chapters 15–31* (Grand Rapids, MI: Eerdmans, 2005), 373. For Blanchot, see his "La parole quotidienne," in *L'Entretien infini* (Paris: Gallimard, 1969), 355–66. See Chapter 7.

[26] Montaigne, Essais, 506 (II:12).

The concept of timeliness expands the limits of the daily in the direction of yet other time events, ones that have no dependence on human interests and yet, like the sun (1:5), have their own pantings and agendas. The whole point can be brought to mind by a report on the annual tomato crop in the State of Maine, which we will come to momentarily.[27]

Attitudes, Expectations, the Joy of Contentment

> I compare notes with one of my friends who expects everything of the universe and is disappointed when anything is less than the best, and I found that I begin at the other extreme, expecting nothing, and am always full of thanks for moderate goods.
>
> Emerson[28]

There is an area distinct both from the organs' passions and behaviors but crucial to safeguarding human happiness. This is the area of attitudes and expectations. Not directly related to physical needs and pursuits, this is the domain of character and of one's broader conceptions concerning the world and God.[29]

In Qohelet studies the negative view has been thoroughly put forth, the sense that Qohelet sees this world as the den of inequity (God's) or iniquity, take your pick.[30] Religious thought, at least from Job on, has had to deal with the situations of "when bad things happen to good people," and if God is not to blame, then, as Camus would have it, the fault lies with the existence of humans in an inhuman – or, better, nonhuman – environment, apparently a practical consequence of Descartes's radical distinction between thinking and extended substance. Thus, we have the unfortunate situation of *l'homme absurde*, the victim of *hebel*: alienation from the world, a distancing of the "I" from the event with which it seems to be bound.[31]

Qohelet's evidence is well taken: inequity is a fact of life, people do bad things, justice is uneven at best, and things often seem, well, out of sync in a radical way. But to see such everyday events as absurd one would have to

---

[27] See below, Chapter 6, "An Indifferent Universe."

[28] Emerson, "Experience," 276.

[29] See the good discussion in Eunny P. Lee, *The Vitality of Enjoyment in Qohelet's Theological Rhetoric* (Berlin/New York: Walter de Gruyter, 2005), 53ff.

[30] Michael V. Fox has been an eloquent spokesperson of the negative view in *Qohelet and His Contradictions* (Sheffield: Almond, 1989), and with increasing reservations, in his wonderful *A Time to Tear Down*. See especially his discussion of *hebel*, 30–42.

[31] Ibid., 31.

postulate an angelic existence and edenic world. What is then absurd, as Fox himself admits, is the presence of such expectations in such a world.[32] But, one would then like to ask, what sensible person would entertain such expectations in such a world?! In other words, while some would have Qohelet complain that the world is not perfect, Qohelet seems in fact to impugn, rather, the absurdity of human expectation.

A second response might be that this same complaint – a distancing of the "I" from the event – could be used to describe not the disease but rather, in Qohelet's mind, the cure. Here Fox arrives at his conclusion of the absurdity of human existence by relying on the same evidence – a sense of alienation – that religions have used to justify their own opposite conclusions. Most notable here is the Jewish sense of wandering and exile as intrinsic to the spiritual condition of humanity at large, taking Abraham's words as emblematic of the entire situation: "I am but a resident alien among you" (Gen 23:3). The related question we shall discuss later on is whether the mind's detachment is to be termed an alienation leading to complaint or rather, as Thoreau would have it, a doubling that allows both truer insight and appreciation.[33] Or, closer to Qohelet, there are perspectives from "beyond" the sun that quite simply cannot be evaluated and judged from our condition "under the sun."

I have argued elsewhere that Qohelet's defining attitude toward life is joy.[34] My point is summarized by the usual reaction of a colleague's mother, when presented with something new or when suffering some material loss: "We have enough." These words – I would call them a wisdom saying – were often voiced by the older folks in Maine where I grew up, but they are rarely heard today. The apparent gap between joy and sufficiency is easily bridged in the famous rabbinic Mishnah:

> Who is rich? One who is contented with what one has.
>
> Abot 4:1

The Hebrew is more precise: "One who is joyful [*sameakh*] with his portion [*kheleq*]." This is not primarily a material matter but rather one of attitude and character, adjusting one's expectation to reality, as the Sephardic proverb puts it:

> Si no es lo que quiero, quiera yo lo que es.
> If it is not what I wish, may I wish what it is.

---

[32] Ibid.

[33] See p. 99 and the Thoreau text quoted there.

[34] T. A. Perry, *Dialogues with Kohelet: The Book of Ecclesiastes: Translation and Commentary* (University Park: Penn State University Press, 1993), 29–32.

In Qohelet this topic is always delicately theologized: it is the portion *that God has given* and for which gratitude is appropriate.[35]

We come then to the end of Qohelet's moral directives, all structured on the concept and experience of *hebel.* The value of these distinctions is manifold. For one thing, Qohelet's *hebel* tag can no longer be invoked as a blanket condemnation of all of creation. His negative view of *hebel* is of course real enough, but it applies mainly to what we can call *hebel* #1, the wrong behaviors and attitudes that humans actually bring into the world, mainly through their pursuit of excess and sense of entitlement. At the next level (*hebel* #2) is the world out there, whose most general characteristic is transience. These things in flux are the mere circumstances of our lives, the rules of the game that we do not invent but to which we are subject, or perhaps invited to play. Axiologically, they are regarded as always located on a sliding scale of good and bad, yes and no, depending on factors of time and occasion and not intrinsic merit: indifferent rather than either good or bad, and, from God's point of view, *yapeh,* beautiful or perfect in their time (3:11). Wishing to avoid or change them would be, in the words of Robert Frost, like wishing to play tennis with the net down.

Our normal world is seen as usually manageable, if lived with moderation and in accord with natural rhythms. In fact, it is a source of contentment. What does one do, however, when other kinds of trouble come upon us: I can't sleep at night, lose my job, get cancer? Qohelet would reply that there are three steps. The first one is that the sufferer should first inspect his/her own deeds (1:13), should ask: Am I in some way responsible? Am I eating right, do I have a grip on my emotions or "passions," am I upset because I have treated someone poorly? Or, closer to Qohelet's own situation: am I addicted to wealth and power and unreasonable expectations? For when the king, now turned philosopher from his anguished *hebel* judgments, allows his heart to investigate and explore all things that happen, could this research program not, in its deeper motivations and as I have argued above, be a first step to recovery and a wiser life?

If this first step – the possibility that one's own actions are the cause of one's unhappiness – proves unproductive and it is correctly decided that the matters are truly beyond one's control – truly "out there" – what does one do then? The answer is strikingly simple, since we already have

---

[35] This is stressed no fewer than seven times: 2:24–26; 3:12–13; 3:22; 5:17–29 (E18–20); 8:15; 9:7–10; 11:8–10.

the therapy in the analysis and conclusion: the thing is truly beyond my control![36] If undeserved physical suffering is involved, we have the Book of Job to help sort matters out. If we just don't like this or that or, indeed, our life itself, then this is the point at which important work on one's self, one's awareness and attitudes, can truly begin. Qohelet proposes that here our domestic ideals of happiness begin to yield to stronger imperatives, the chief of which is the truth criterion, the full awareness and acknowledgment of the true (i.e., transient) conditions of our lives.

The most tentative and interesting of the three is *hebel* #3, which comes more clearly into view, at least in Qohelet's personal narrative, once all the frustrations arising from the other *hebel*s have been lived through and seen and accepted for what they are, and then canceled, as it were. What remains is a no-thing, hardly a simple nothing, however, but one laden with possibility. Perhaps, for example, the very possibility of metaphysics:

> ... the not-knowing where philosophical knowledge begins coincides not with just plain nothingness but rather with the absence of objects.
>
> Levinas[37]

---

[36] This is Epictetus's basis for stoicism; see his powerful distinction between what is and is not within our control, at the start of his *Enchiridion*.

[37] "A moins que le non-savoir où commence le savoir philosophique coïncide non avec le néant tout court, mais seulement avec le néant d'objets." TI, 9.

PART TWO

UNIVERSAL *HEBEL* ("WIND"): TRANSIENCE, TIME, AND INDIFFERENCE

What is free from the risk of change? Neither earth, nor sky, nor the whole fabric of our universe, though it be controlled by the hand of God.... All things move in accord with their appointed times (*certis temporibus*); they are destined to be born, to grow, and to be destroyed....

Whatever is will cease to be, and yet it will not perish, but will be resolved into its elements. To our minds, this process means perishing, for we behold only that which is nearest; our sluggish mind, under allegiance to the body, does not penetrate to bournes beyond. Were it not so, the mind would endure with greater courage its own ending and that of its possessions, if only it could hope that life and death, like the whole universe about us, go by turns, that whatever has been put together is broken up again, that whatever has been broken up is put together again, and that the eternal craftsmanship of God, who controls all things, is working at this task.

Seneca[1]

It is only through the corrected reading of *hebel* as "transience" rather than "vanity" that we may understand the structure of the book of Ecclesiastes, and thereby learn its message. For Ecclesiastes does not offer a single, static teaching from beginning to end, but a thematic progression, one that follows Kohelet's own discovery of meaning.

Ethan Dor-Shav[2]

Our focus thus far has been on the "Qohelet" or collector's theme, the human desire to gather and hoard things of collection or collectables, and this would include even knowledge and wisdom based thereon. The

---

[1] Seneca, *Ad Lucilium Epistulae Morales*, 3 vols. (trans. Richard M. Gummere; Loeb Classical Library, Cambridge, MA: Harvard University Press, 1971), *Letters*, Letter 71 (II:81).

[2] Ethan Dor-Shav, "Ecclesiastes, Fleeting and Timeless," *Azure* 18 (2004): 67–87 at 76. This interpretive essay is required reading on this subject.

king's review of his past activities listed all of these, with predominance on objects, *things* that occupy space and that have a place. We now move to an analysis of things in their place or *maqom*, which, as we shall see, has a dynamic quality that moves beyond stasis and its characteristic dimensionality and toward its conjunction with time. Jankélévitch's observation can point the way:

> Becoming (*le devenir*) is a series of continuing occasions: these appearing/ disappearing things reappear at any time without there being any scalable progress, without there being any further closeness to a goal fixed in advance. In space the goal does not change place, whereas in time it changes as it goes and drags me along after it. The infinite number of occasions reconstitutes at the extreme a continuity in the discontinuous, a flux through successive fluxions.[3]

The question then becomes the status of time's dynamism: does it have limits? Is the future infinite and indefinitely open; or, at least, does the notion of the "unachieved" project a usable context for the adventurous?

Closely connected with the universe's transience, axiologically speaking, is its independence from human concern, its status as a gold-feathered bird (see below) and the challenge this poses to both morality and poetic representation.

---

[3] Vladimir Jankélévitch, Béatrice Berlowitz, *Quelque part dans l'inachevé* (Paris: Gallimard, 1978), 89.

5

Cosmic Patterns of Return and Renewal

Just as the heavenly bodies yearn ardently toward their origins and seek to ascend and attain the substance out of which they were separated, so everything that is brought into being out of the four elements seeks only to join its origin… Thus as they revolve, ascend, and incline, the fiery, airy, and earthy forms seek only to attain that source from which they were formed, in accordance with the desire and longing that God imprinted in them.

Ibn Ghiyath (1038–89)[1]

The Opening Cosmology (1:4–7)

That verse which has been taken as "a brief statement of Qohelet's whole undertaking"[2] moves us nicely from confessional and private concerns to more cosmic perspectives:

> I set my heart to investigate and explore through wisdom all the things that happen under the heavens: it is an unhappy business that God has given to humans to busy themselves with.

Qoh 1:13

The focus has broadened considerably beyond human malfeasance, beyond what comes from within me, and now extends to the universe out there and even to God's dispositions with that universe.[3] And, in fact like

---

[1] Ibn Ghiyath (1038–89) is commenting on Qoh 1:5–7; trans. by and quoted in Raymond P. Scheindlin, *The Gazelle* (Philadelphia: Jewish Publication Society, 1991), 50. Lohfink comments beautifully on Qohelet's vision of the elements' duration in time: "The solid earth is the eternal stage upon which the equally eternal other elements of the world gloriously repeat their performance without using themselves up" *Qoheleth: A Continental Commentary* (Minneapolis: Fortress, 2003), 1.

[2] R. N. Whybray, *Ecclesiastes*. New Century Bible Commentary (Grand Rapids, MI: Eerdmans, 1989), 49.

[3] Bonaventura, in his persistently Trinitarian mode (e.g., his *Itinerarium mentis in Deum*), structures his intellectual model on three levels, proceeding from lower to higher:

the Bible itself, the Book of Qohelet leads off with a cosmology, a description of the structure and functioning of the physical world of nature. In both cases the cosmos is first presented as its own self-contained, independent, and glorious entity; then it is related to the humans and other creatures that will inhabit it. In the Genesis account humans are seen in a positive role, as its custodians (or, in some self-serving readings, its exploiters). What is the case in Qohelet?

> 1:3 What profit for humans from so much labor that they labor [at] under the sun?
>
> 1:4 One generation goes [forth] and another generation comes in
>
> [i.e., dies];
>
> And the earth *remains* forever.[4]
>
> 1:5 And the sun rises and the sun sets,
>
> And it pants to return to its place where it rises again.
>
> – It goes southward and *returns* northward –.[5]
>
> 1:6 The wind goes forth around and around,
>
> And it *returns* upon its turnings.
>
> 1:7 All the rivers flow into the sea,
>
> And the sea is not filled.
>
> To the place where the rivers go,
>
> [From] there they *return to go forth again.*[6]

Qoh 1:3–7

There is a critical tendency – similar to the sequence of vv. 2–3 – to separate 1:3 from 1:4 because, it is claimed, at 1:4 a new pericope is formed.[7] But how does one know this? One would rather think the opposite, first of all because the thematic phrase "under the sun" is followed almost immediately by a description of … the sun! Secondly, because the cosmology projects an analogy, suggesting a fundamental parallelistic structure

---

　　a) what is outside of us or *extra nos*; b) what is within us or *intra nos*; c) what is above us or *supra nos*. In Qohelet's analogue, the confessional perspective places the "within us" first.

4　The usual translation sees an opposition here, consistent with the thesis, which we reject, of a conflictual relationship between the individual and the cosmos: "*But* the earth remains forever."

5　Since it is unclear whether this refers to the path of the sun or the wind, I render this as a self-contained statement, which hopefully clarifies the point that "it" refers to both and thus can be read "above and below," as I shall argue further on.

6　Reading *mi-sham* as a haplography, with the preposition *min* carried over from the previous ending letter of *holekim*.

7　Whybray, *Ecclesiastes*, 39; also James L. Crenshaw, *Ecclesiastes: A Commentary* (OTL, Philadelphia: Westminster, 1987), 62.

of reality between the world of human beings and that of nature, arguing that humans are part of nature and must learn something crucial to their well-being from that circumstance. It is especially this analogy that we shall explore here, in the world "under the sun," which is inhabited both by humans and by nature, as suggested precisely by the juxtaposition in v. 3 of *'adam* (humans) and the *shemesh* (sun).

A remarkable stylistic feature of the cosmology is that it constantly plays on both registers, that its metaphors sustain ambivalence. Thus,

> A *generation* comes forth and a generation dies,
> And *the earth* remains forever.

There is ambiguity from the start, since "generation" (*dor*) suggests both nature and people (see below). Further, the plain meaning of *'erets* is "earth," making it a cosmological reference. Yet scholars have quite correctly, in view of the verse's topic of generations, suggested another meaning: "the *people* of the earth,"[8] thus insisting on a human reference as well. Both schools of thought miss the point, however, in their demand for either/or, since the terms mean *both*, thereby reinforcing the main argument, which is the didactic analogy of the entire passage.[9] This then allows the verb "standing" its rich ambiguity: not only "standing in, enduring," but also "standing to serve," appropriate in the first instance only to humans.[10]

The argument for *stable structures of transience* in the human as well as the natural realm is suggested by a stylistic peculiarity little noticed: the repetition of *dor*.[11] The text could more naturally have said "a generation comes and goes." That would be the case if the stress were on its passing: the same generation that is born passes away. The repetition, however, refers to a *different* generation; the focus is on replacement and

---

[8] See Gen 6:11, 41:57; Ps 33:8.

[9] Although Occam's razor requires an either/or choice, literature is more flexible than logic. I fear we critics have learned our trade with some help from the universe of Orwell's *Animal Farm*. For, on the one hand, we are quite fond of reducing the pool of available words, by excising those that do not fit our readings or theories. And, on the other and having failed at that, we then insist – by applying Occam's rule to literature – that such words can have only one meaning, neglecting Qohelet's own advice: "Perhaps BOTH will succeed" (11:6). As if to mock such reductionism, the figure of *antanaclasis* uses a single word in close proximity to mean different things. So too with doublets. For Qohelet's use see Appendix 6, "Doublets," "*Antanaclasis*."

[10] For some theological resonances of "standing" as service, see T. A. Perry, *Dialogues with Kohelet: The Book of Ecclesiastes: Translation and Commentary* (University Park: Penn State University Press, 1993), 180.

[11] For the exception see Crenshaw, *Ecclesiastes: A Commentary*, 62–63. I argue that this repetition constitutes a mild form of *antanaclasis*; see Chapter 8, p. 107, n. 6.

succession, so that the earth's endurance and productivity stand and are grounded, as it were, in the generations themselves. Thus,

> a [new] generation comes forth as the [previous] generation passes on.

The doubling of *dor* also evokes the rich meaning of continuity of the phrase *dor wa-dor*, generation to generation, most notably in its frequent association with the concept of *'olam*, "eternity" or "great length of time, forever."[12] This remarkable parallelism requires ascribing identical valence to both members. Now if le-*'olam* ("forever") is positive, then so is the time projected by *dor / dor*. This involves, among other things, revising our usual translation of the *waw* connective as oppositional:

> One generation goes forth and another generation comes [in], *but* the earth remains forever.

For there is scant basis, either in our text or in Hebrew Scripture, for an opposition between the succession of generations and the duration of *'olam*, since both project permanence in time. Thus,

> A [new] generation goes forth as another generation comes [in], *and* [in this way] the earth [alt: the people of the earth] remains forever, continues on.

From this perspective the crux of 3:11 becomes a bit more understandable:[13]

> God has made everything beautiful in its / His time.[14] He has also put eternity [*'olam*] into their hearts; except that it is not given to humans to know, from beginning to end, what God has made.

The verse starts by explaining that God has arranged things according to their fixed, limited times; and the verse ends by the observation that God does not allow humans to understand things from start to finish. The verse then considers the expanse of time from the smallest to the longest possible unit. Between the two, Qohelet asserts that God still instills in the human heart the *'olam*, the sense of permanence. Of what kind? First of all, the one that can be observed in the orderly succession of natural

---

[12] Exod 3:15; Deut 32:7; Isa 58:12, 60:15; Joel 4:20; Prov 27:24.

[13] Some critics have tried to solve the difficulty by claiming metathesis, reading *'amal* (toil) instead of *'olam* (forever). This certainly reverts to Qohelet's favorite theme, but it introduces a concept that is the antithesis of Qohelet's thought, namely that God introduces "toil" into the human heart! Michael V. Fox (*Qohelet and his Contradictions* [Sheffield: Almond Press, 1989], 194) tries to tease this meaning out of Qohelet 8:17, but the effort fails for the simple reason that Qohelet nowhere ascribes mankind's folly arising from toil, *over*work, to God.

[14] For the probably intended ambivalence of its/His, see p. 147, n. 17.

events such as *dor wa-dor*, the projection of an ongoing and extended time precisely opposed to the false sense of endurance and security provided by human toil or *'amal.*

The earth and its people are followed by the sun. This is surely a cosmological reference, except that in Qohelet the sun not only shines but also "pants with desire" like a living creature. Then the *ruakh* appears, referring primarily to the wind here (also 11:4) but with a strong secondary reference throughout Qohelet to the human spirit, the one that pursues inquiry (1:17), that gets angry (7:9, 10:4), that returns to God at death (12:7), that is common to all living and therefore a synonym of *hebel*-breath (3:19, 21) and is often linked to "vanity" (e.g., 5:15), that symbolizes the unknowable mystery of human reproduction (11:5) and, in its basic meaning, refers to the breath of life or the life spirit (8:8).[15]

The final element is the waters – that is, the rivers and the sea. The latter is declared to be never filled, *male'*, and if other resonances are not immediately sensed, one has only to wait until the next verse, to hear about *human* lack of fulfillment: "The ear is never filled, satisfied [*male'*] with things to hear." Between the two references to lack of satisfaction, there is a summary of sorts:

> All things/words [*debarim*] are in ceaseless activity.
>
> 1:8

Again, critics are unsure as to the meaning of the *debarim*, but, again, only the retention of *both* possibilities allows sufficient stress on the ambivalence and interrelation of (natural) things and (human) words.[16] I also proposed above that the remainder of the verse repeats the human/cosmic binary:

> The eye is not filled with seeing [things], nor the ear filled with hearing [words].
>
> 1:9

Finally, as if to beat the thing into the ground, the summarizing verse:

> What was is what will be [in the universe]; what was done is what will continue to be done [by humans]…
>
> 1:9

---

[15] Commenting on this verse, Lohfink (p. 106) cites Ps 146:4, "when breath (*ruakh*) leaves us, we die."

[16] For further discussion see Appendix 6, "Doublets."

Far from mere poetic repetition, the text attempts, in very deliberate ways and from start to finish, to stress the ambivalence resident in the analogy and dependence between things cosmic and things human.

Some of these ambivalences and analogies have of course been noticed, but their use or meaning continues to evade. Some claim, for example, that Qohelet was interested only in humans, and they thus view the cosmology merely as elegant analogies.[17] However, it seems to be also the case that the analogies are not simple literary devices, that Qohelet saw no discontinuity between the two, that humans exist and labor "under the sun" just as, according to the stoics, human nature is part of universal nature.[18] The question on human effort (1:3) is thus directly addressed by the cosmology, which uses psychological terms and metaphors to describe the elements, as well as elemental facts of the natural world, to portray (ideal) human behavior. In Chapters 3 and 4 we pursued these recommendations of Qohelet at a more practical level.

What then, to summarize, is the momentous sequence of vv. 1:3–4? The former introduces the true focus of the book: "what profit to *humans?*" The very next verse situates and perspectivizes the lead topic: humans ("generations") come and go, "and the *earth* remains forever." The important point of reading is to notice and accept the polysemy of '*erets*, meaning both the "earth" and the "people of the earth." In this book humans are presented in their earthly existence and as part of, continuous with, the earth, humans and nature are one, unified by the metaphor.[19] And there is more. As the sequence develops as a presentation of the four elemental levels of nature (earth/sun/air/water), the human's persistence in existence is based in his very physical being as dependent on all four. For how long could biological life continue without the sun – a year maybe? Without water, not even a week. Without air to breathe? Of the four it would seem that *ruakh,* the air of each breath, is both momentous and the most momentous, since at death "the *ruakh* returns to God who gave it" (12:7).[20] Translators may of course prefer "air, wind" in some cases and "spirit" in others (also Gen 1:2), but the metaphor

---

[17] For example, Whybray, *Ecclesiastes,* 39. Alison Lo ("Death in Qohelet," *Journal of the Ancient Near Eastern Society* 31 [2009]: 85–98 at 86) gives a succinct summary of both positions (p. 86), but always returns to the either/or position rather than the both/and.

[18] Even Fox, despite his pessimistic interpretation, admits the analogy: "The poem shows ... the persistent movements of natural phenomena, of which mankind, taken as a whole, is one...." (*Qohelet and his Contradictions,* 171).

[19] See Chapter 9.

[20] See ibid. for the synonymy of *ruakh* and *hebel,* life-breath.

speaks rather of their commonality and, beyond that, of the unity and integration and dependence of humans and nature: wind-breath.

Wechseldauer: *The Stable Structures of Transience*

The waterfall I now behold with growing

Delight as it roars down the ravine.

From fall to fall a thousand streams are flowing,

A thousand more are plunging, effervescent,

And high up in the air the spray is glowing.

Out of the thunder rises, iridescent,

Enduring through all change [*Wechseldauer*] the motley bow,

Now painted clearly, and not evanescent,

Spreading a fragrant, cooling spray below.

The rainbow mirrors human life and strife;

Consider it and you will better know:

In many-hued reflection [*Am farbigen Abglanz*] we have life.

Goethe's *Faust*, Part II, vv. 4715–27.[21]

Nothing endures but change.

Heraclitus, as per Plato's *Cratylus*

In the biblical account, life's permanent existence after the flood is sealed with a covenant, the sign of which seems tentative, if not risky in the extreme: a bow made of rain, a rainbow *brith* (Gen 9:12–17). Although rain occurs as a natural and (somewhat) predictable phenomenon, the rainbow does not, depending for its appearance on the coincidence of water with the sun, its opposite. As such it is a strange reminder of the eternal permanence of the *brith*. God explains:

> … water shall never again become a flood to destroy all flesh. When the bow is in the clouds, I will see it and remember the everlasting covenant…
>
> Gen 9:15–16

Strange but also glorious, being the very image that for Ezekiel pictured the appearance of God's glory:

> As the appearance of the bow that is in the cloud in the day of rain.
>
> Ezek 1:28

---

[21] Translated by Walter Kaufmann (New York: Anchor, 1990), 428.

Whether connected with the Genesis account or not, Goethe selected the rainbow as the very symbol of our earthly existence and coined a neologism to express the paradox: *Wechseldauer*, literally permanence in change, posits a world of permanent transience [sic], of a beauty whose stability is founded on evanescence. Goethe took an esthetics of transience and carried it forward – using a cosmic symbol, as does Qohelet – into the ethical realm.[22] Just as the rainbow in Genesis will serve as a sign (an *'ot*), Faust's rainbow and Qohelet's four elements will reflect or perhaps project the path of human endeavor. The concept is an important one in wisdom texts, the wonder occasioned by transient things that pass and leave no trace:

> Three things are too wonderful for me,
>
> Four that I cannot fathom:
>
> The path of the eagle on the heavens,
>
> The path of a snake upon the rock,
>
> The path of a ship upon the high seas,
>
> And the path of a man upon a woman.
>
> Prov 30:18–20

To be carefully noted is the parallel with the four elements in Qohelet's cosmology: air, earth, water, and the fiery element of sexuality.[23] These here exemplify the domain of the "wonderful," which in wisdom writing acts as a (possible) sign (*'ot*) of divinity. Additionally, the focus here is on the path, repeated anaphorically four times, and suggesting the primary qualities of *hebel* itself: without substance and producing no *yitron*, no trace or residue and no advantage.

Returning to Qohelet's cosmology, commentaries typically stress the transience and instability of all four elements, seen to either rise and fall or to turn around and around to no purpose, monotonous in their binary movements.[24] The truth of the matter, however, is that the motion

---

[22] For an esthetics and ethics of transience in the Hebrew Bible see T. A. Perry, *Jonah's Arguments with God: The Honeymoon Is Over!* (Peabody, MA: Hendrickson, 2014), 160, 150.

[23] For commentary see T. A. Perry, *Wisdom in the Hebrew Bible: God's Twilight Zone* (Peabody, MA: Hendrickson, 2014), 157–70. For Qohelet's use of the four elements see also my "A Poetics of Absence: The Structure and Meaning of Chaos in Genesis 1:2," *JSOT* 58 (1993), 9–11.

[24] One may question the paradoxical instability of the earth element, since it shows no movement whatever. The point, however, is twofold. On the one hand, Qohelet's primary focus is on the rise and fall of the (people of the) earth, here called the "generations" precisely in order to stress their movement. And, on the other, even at the level of the earth-as-primary element, its parallel motion is shown in the dust's combination with

of each of the four elements that make up the nature analogy has not two but three moments: not rise and fall, but rather rise / fall / rise again. The stable element is its *maqom*, its place, which is both its terminal point of rest and especially the transit point of its immediate new departure:

earth (human race)	birth	death	rebirth (permanence)
sun	east	west	east
wind	north	south	north
water	reservoirs	sea	reservoirs

Thus, despite change, there is, as in Goethe's explanation, a *Wechseldauer*, an eventual and ineluctable return to one's place. The focus, moreover, is dynamic, everything is in perpetual movement. That is to say, the usual density and stability of one's "place" here denotes not fixity but rather a fluid, transitional space, a paradoxical point in time – paradoxical and unreal because, as Bergson has shown, any *instantanée* of Zeno's arrow is only an intellectual construct. Or one might prefer to think of this minuscule point of instant as a Janus figure of the eternal renewal of the cycle of creation, the desire for genesis being also the genesis of desire.

We can refer to these as *stable structures of transience* because of the equilibrium that is built into transience and guarantees its permanence. Thus, humans chase the wind, an almost nothingness, but typically fail to learn from it its universal law of cyclicality, its inevitable and necessary return upon itself as a condition of its very existence. So too, the sun sets as surely as it rises, but it rises again and again; individuals die, but the human race "stands," endures. This point becomes even more convincing when, disregarding the complaints about vanity and lack of newness, we notice the cosmological poem's majesty, the absence of any semblance of pessimism. Right from the very start, the orderly succession of generations projects permanence, stability, regularity, an enduring presence and source of strength attributed also to God:

A prayer of Moses, a man of God:

"Lord, you have been our dwelling place *from generation to generation* [*dor*]. Before the mountains were born and before you formed the earth and the world, and *from eternity to eternity* [*'olam*] you are God."

Ps 90:1–2

and separation from the spirit at birth and death (12:7). Ben Sira (29:10) in fact stresses their continuity: "All people are of clay, for from earth humankind was formed" (trans. Alexander A. Di Lella; AB 39: 394).

6

The Catalog of Human Times (3:1–8)

Unless there exists, in the mind of whoever dreamed up humans (all the way to himself), an exact count of *the pure rhythmical motifs of being*, which are its recognizable signs.

Mallarmé[1]

Our life is composed, *like the harmony of the world*, of contrary things, also of diverse tones, sweet and harsh, sharp and flat, soft and loud. If a musician liked only one kind, what would he have to say? He must know how to use them together and blend them. And so must we do with good and evil, which are consubstantial with our life. Our being cannot subsist without such a mixture.

Montaigne[2]

The nonhuman environment is present not merely as a framing device but as a presence that begins to suggest that human history is implicated in natural history.

Lawrence Buell[3]

A Merismic Universe

After the interludes on the negative value of human excess (1:8–11) and its illustration in Qohelet's autobiography and confession (1:12–2:26), the text resumes the evaluation of the "All is *hebel*" thesis with the "Catalog of the Times" in Qohelet 3:1–8. Now we are presented with a second characteristic of the All. In addition to its *hebel*, we now learn that the All

---

[1] Quoted in Maurice Blanchot, *L'Écriture du désastre* (Paris: Gallimard, 1980), 14. The phrase "all the way to himself" attempts to render *jusqu'à soi*, omitted in the Smock translation (*The Writings of Disaster* [trans. Ann Smock; Lincoln: University of Nebraska Press, 1995], 5), italics added.

[2] Michel de Montaigne, *Les Essais*, 1089–90 (III:13).

[3] Lawrence Buell, *The Environmental Imagination: Thoreau, Nature Writing, and the Formation of American Culture* (Cambridge, MA: Harvard University Press, 1995), 7.

has time, a *zeman*. The momentous proportions of this step in the argument actually mark a transition of perspective from the world of things to the world of time. For now, continuing with Heschel's words, Qohelet has discovered that "things, when magnified, are [only] forgeries of happiness."[4] The focus now begins a shift, from space and its "things" that we possess, to the inner spaces of events and time where humans really live: eternity (3:11) in the making.

Thomas Krüger has carefully spelled out the close parallel between this catalog and the cosmological poem that starts the book (1:3–9).[5] Noting the "lack of evaluation of the described state of affairs" in both poems, Krüger suggests "a sort of meditative pause" common to both, perhaps a stepping back from a *hebel*-judgment that could be taken as a condemnation, so as not to preclude a broader perspective. This axiological suspension of judgment conditions the critical stance put forth here, that the universe (both natural and human) is neither positive nor negative but neutral and thus available to human evaluation according to appropriate "times," typically in the form of "good" and "bad."

Krüger's view of the Catalog as a "continuation and expansion" of the Cosmology requires a brief review of the latter, now focusing no longer on its dynamic regeneration through return but rather as a static and binary system (the one that has so impressed the pessimism proponents), one that charters the course of the four elements, their linear motion and direction from start to finish:

earth (human race)	birth	death
sun	east	west
wind	north	south
water	rivers	sea

The focus here is on each single element at its two extremes of activity or process or "going forth" (*halak*). Thus, the sun or fiery element is pictured through its oppositions of rising and setting; the generations, at their birth and death; the wind and river waters as their exhaustion and disappearance.

Now, there is a pervasive but poorly studied rhetorical figure called merismus or merism, meaning "the use of opposites to express a completeness or totality."[6] It is clearly the case that merism is the figure through which

---

4 Abraham Joshua Heschel, *The Sabbath* (New York: Farrar, Straus and Giroux, 2005), 6.

5 Thomas Krüger, *Qoheleth, a Commentary* (Minneapolis: Fortress Press, 2004), 75.

6 So noted by Crenshaw (*Ecclesiastes: A Commentary* [OTL, Philadelphia: Westminster, 1987], 93) in the case of the Catalog, without naming the rhetorical term. I am unaware

the Hebrew Bible is launched, and not once but repeatedly. The first has been often noticed, designating the universal totality about to be created:

> At the beginning of God's creating of *heaven* and *earth*....
>
> Genesis 1:1

A second merism follows immediately, this one more insistently (six times):

> And it was *evening* and it was *morning*, one day.
>
> Gen 1:5; also 8, 13, 19, 23, 31

Again, just as the entire creation is referred to as the union of two spatial opposites (heaven and earth), two opposing points designate the entire temporal unit of creation, "day." An identical structure is projected as well for the survivors of the flood and onward:

> For all the [remaining] days of the earth,
>
> Seedtime and harvest,
>
> cold and heat,
>
> summer and winter,
>
> day and night
>
> will not cease.
>
> Gen 8:22

It seems that what Lyn M. Bechtel has referred to as "God's oppositional forces" – operative in the human realm – has a solid basis in the universe's ongoing dynamics of unity through oppositional contrast.[7]

I posit that in the Catalog of the Times, no less than in the Cosmology, Qohelet is engaging in intra-biblical exegesis, in this case a commentary and/or application of the Bible's foundational theology: the creation of the world as structured by merisms. I suggest that Qohelet's two passages attempt to approach an understanding of what kind of a "totality" is being created by such a figure. How pervasive is it in the created world being described? And how is it to be interpreted? His argument is that the merismic structure of reality applies to the human as well as the cosmic realm, to daily life in all its possible variations. Before discussing the

of any previous attempt to describe Qohelet's Cosmology as a sustained series of merisms, although focus on its binary opposites is pervasive. For several examples, see Anton Schoors, *The Preacher Sought to Find Pleasant Words* (Leuven: Peeters, 1992), 218.

7 Lyn M. Bechtel, "Rethinking the Interpretation of Genesis 2.4B-3.24," in *A Feminist Companion to Genesis*, ed. Athalya Brenner (Sheffield: Sheffield Academic Press, 1993), 1–18, at 8.

concept of totality, we must briefly outline its constitutive dynamic in the human realm, the dialectic.

Humans "Under the Sun": The Dialectic

Krüger's argument for a close parallel between the Cosmology and the Catalog would allow an expanded translation of the hinge verse of 3:1, one that could highlight the double focus:

> Just as there is an appointed season (*zeman*) for the cosmic "All" in the opening cosmology [i.e., the one composed of the four Aristotelian elements and including humans]; so too in the human realm there is a time for "all" human endeavors and desires/projects (*khepets*) under the heavens.[8]

> 3:1

The switch from the opening and more frequent "under the sun" (1:3) to "under the heavens" (3:1; see also1:13, 2:3) may seem only a stylistic variant (compare 1:13 and 1:14). However, "under the sun" is the more comprehensive in that it includes the human realm, whereas "under the heavens" refers specifically to human activity:

> On behalf of wisdom I allowed my heart to investigate and explore all the things that happen *under the heavens*: It is a badly arranged affair that God has given *to humans* to be exercised with.

> 1:13; also 2:3[9]

It thus is a better introduction to the Catalog of the Times – emblematically captured by the ancient merismic figure of heavens (*shamayim*) as composed of the opposites fire and water (*'esh/mayim*) – and its dialectic of oppositional forces of *human* projects and desires (*khepets*).

Here is the celebrated text of the Catalog:

> 3:1 For the universal All there is a season, and a time for every human purpose [*khepets*].
> 3:2 A time to beget and a time [for your begotten] to die;[10]
>   a time to plant and a time to uproot the planted.
> 3:3 A time to kill and a time to heal;
>   a time to break open and a time to build.

---

[8] Specifically those of the individual in 3:2, and those of the collective in 3:8.

[9] See T. A. Perry, *Dialogues with Kohelet: The Book of Ecclesiastes: Translation and Commentary* (University Park: Penn State University Press, 1993), 57. Lohfink makes a precious observation (p. 47) that here in 1:13 the discourse about God is being introduced.

[10] For the evidence of "birthing" over "being born," see the excellent discussion in Choon-Leong Seow, *Ecclesiastes* AB 18c (Garden City, NY: Doubleday, 1997), 160. See also Appendix 3, "Giving Birth vs. Being Born."

3:4 A time to weep and a time to laugh;
     a time to mourn and a time to dance.
3:5 A time to cast stones and a time to gather stones;
     a time to embrace and a time to refrain from embracing.
3:6 A time to seek and a time to destroy;
     a time to retain and a time to cast away.
3:7 A time to rend and a time to sew;
     a time to keep silence and a time to speak.
3:8 A time to love and a time to hate;
     a time for war and a time for peace.

3:1–8

In his interpretation of the Catalog, Krüger focuses on the degree to which activities are either predetermined or available to human freedom. He summarizes as follows:

> The common denominator of the phenomena named in vv. 2–8 seems to consist above all in the fact that favorable or unfavorable temporal circumstances both allow and limit the success of human actions.[11]

To be sure, there is value in what can be called a soft reading of the Catalog of the Times, focusing quite correctly on appropriateness (to the time and the circumstances). Thus, there are times when lovemaking is suitable and times when restraint is the rule, and so forth. Qohelet's term for these typical (life cycle, business cycle, etc.) activities is *khepets*, desire, whether of what we want to have or want not to have.

The limitation of this approach is that, in so doing, Krüger has put aside the parallel with the cosmology, except as a broad compositional device. What both have in common, at a deeper structural level, is neither the "time" nor the particular desire or *khepets*, however, but the perspective of a totality composed of opposites:

> In the day of prosperity be joyful; and in the day of adversity, consider: God has placed the one opposite [*le-'umat*] the other, so that the human being might not find out anything of His motives.

7:14

Likewise, Ben Sira's formulation leans toward theodicy and dialectic. God created things in pairs:

---

[11] Krüger, *Qoheleth, a Commentary*, 77.

> See now all the works of the Most High: they all come in pairs, the one
> opposite [*le-'umat*] the other
>
> Ben Sira 33:15; also 42:24–25[12]

In both texts merismus is used to support both God and wisdom, both
the mystery of evil in the world – put there by God, as per Isa 45:7 – and
the necessity of a holistic approach, what we have been calling the creation or perception of totalities. In both cases we are urged to increase
the level of awareness of totalities in our daily lives. Take, for example,
the merism life/death as the expression or model for the entire human
life, used as an attempt to comfort a sick person:

> You do not die from being sick, you die from being alive.[13]

Death and life are part of life!? Yes, just as day and night, in Genesis, are
part of the totality concept "day." Just as a full "day" of twenty-four hours
includes the opposites day and night, light and darkness, so too a full
"life" includes life/birth and death; a full fortune, joy and sadness. The
concept "day," as composed of both day and night, is a basic paradigm
also because it stands as a progenitor of human events, since

> You do not know what a day may give birth to.
>
> Prov 27:1

Carefully note that in all such cases the limitations are imposed not only
by transience but by human ignorance as well.

It is noteworthy that both the theodicy and the wisdom focus on
totalities carry the admission that a negative factor is absorbed or balanced out by a positive one. However, it is important also to note that
these values are not regarded as absolutely negative or positive but
rather relative to many circumstances. For the text does not say that
things are *tob* or good in their time, rather they are *yapeh*, beautiful or
appropriate. In such a cosmos all values are relative to one another. For
example, how does one evaluate the activity/passivity nexus, crucial to
ethical thinking? Or any such values that exist in simple oppositional
correlation? We note that *both* terms, depending on their times, may be

---

[12] In its wider context of 33:7–15, Ben Sira also imbricates the human with the cosmological. For its possible connection with stoicism, see Sharon Lea Mattila, "Ben Sira
and the Stoics: A Reexamination of the Evidence," *JBL* 119 (2000): 480–84. The connection with the dialectic is noted by Georg Sauer, *Jesus Sirach/Ben Sira* (Göttingen,
Germany: Vandenhoeck & Ruprecht, 2000), 234. See also Qohelet 5:15, which confirms
the notion of a merism, of a totality consisting of opposites.

[13] Montaigne, *Les Essais*, 1091 (III:13).

called "good."[14] Thus, to take an extreme case, war is sometimes good, and death is too!

The shifting and relative nature of dialectical evaluation, of plus and minus values, is crucial to understanding the movement of transience and change embedded in the very nature of things/concepts (*debarim*) as they occur in our merismic world and human practice. Here there appears to me a perfect consonance between the dialectic and the Qohelet text. Take, for example, oppositions derived through negation such as speech/silence ("speech is silver and silence golden"). Are there then only these two options? Well, there are the gradations in between: for instance, a whisper. Clearly, when you do not speak you are silent, and vice-versa; but also clear is the "silence that speaks words," as the saying goes. This kind of dialectical analysis is useful for the everyday, and one must master its modalities and appropriate times in order to be considered wise or to succeed and avoid failure.[15]

Negatives

Whether negatives have intrinsic and absolute negative value, as they would in a dualistic system, is constantly challenged. A favorite technique in this regard is what Blanchot calls reversals of language (*renversements de langage*), such as "long is short and short is long":

> Always in a state of return on the roads of time, we shall neither be early nor late: late is early, near [is] far.[16]

Take the example of the dialectical pair wealth/poverty. As commonly understood, wealth is having possessions and money enough to purchase whatever one wants, and poverty is the opposite. Yet, overwhelmed by the vacuity – sometimes invasive – of material acquisitions, many come to Thoreau's subversive or re-versive definition of wealth as the amount of things one can afford to be without! Such revisions of thinking respond, I think, to a rejection of vanity perspectives, a refusal to let degraded language do the job of human thinking and valuation. For if our key

---

[14] Putting the best possible spin on things, in accord with Gen 1, where creation is declared to be "good" and even "very good." For his part, Blanchot complains that we have forgotten death as a beneficial factor of experience. See Chapter 7, "The Outside."

[15] For a silent sound that passes beyond or "outside" the dialectic into another mode altogether, see 1 Kgs 19:15 and the analysis in Chapter 10, "Im-Mortal Remains." For a sound that cannot be heard, see Ps 19:4.

[16] Blanchot, *L'Écriture du désastre*, 96.

concepts are indeed to be wealth/poverty, then they need to be adjusted to healthier contexts. Here are some favorite rabbinic ones:

> There is no poverty except ignorance.
> Who is rich? One who is contented with what s/he has.

The only point on which all agree is that poverty is a lack of something, but it is here that the discussion should not end but rather begin. Is our human happiness only about money, or should it be about knowledge, contentment? One thinks of Mallarmé's poetic intent to upgrade the language of the tribe. Qohelet's focus is that our attitudes and values are also up for an upgrade.

The issue of wealth has been of particular interest to critics of Qohelet. One common view, of possible sociological interest, is that Qohelet is addressing mainly wealthy people. However, if the king has concluded that material possessions are a distraction, then whom better to address than those who are making the same mistake? What then is his bottom-line teaching on money? That it is a neutral value (= breath), neither positive nor negative and thus not worth the trouble *as a pursuit.* Like pleasure, however, if it comes to one without pursuit, then it is to be accepted with gratitude.

The Catalog's grand summary evokes the perspective of a theological meditation:

> God has made everything beautiful in its time. He has also put eternity into their hearts; except that it is not given to humans to know, from beginning to end, what God has made.

3:11

The remarkable similarity of this text with a later one invites comparison:

> When you are having a good day, enjoy! And on a bad day, consider: God has placed the one opposite the other, so that the human being might not find out anything of His motives.

7:14

In both texts God is in control, not only of the events themselves but of our ignorance of their ultimate and complete meaning. Indeed, in the latter text this seems to be God's very purpose. Exception is made of the good days, when one is simply to enjoy, in the present and without any thought of what evil days may follow. Opposites are evoked only when things are *not* going well: "Consider!" Nevertheless, the juxtaposition of good and bad fortune stresses less their perceived opposition than their totality as part of a single dialectical unity. This is in fact the paradigm wherein many values perceived as negatives become integrated into a whole. The theological basis is not only that God created evil along with good, but also that such a mixture is specifically intended for human concern:

> an "evil" business that God has given humans to be exercised with.[17]
>
> 1:13

The puzzle is compounded by the context:

> I gave my heart to seek and search out by wisdom all the things that are done under the heavens....
>
> 1:13

So far so good (or bad...). Humans, then, are to accept the bad things that happen because they are reversible and can thus – at the proper time – be good or beautiful. Should then one prefer to be subjected to anger and disapproval than to experience enjoyment? Of course not! Yet these can actually be useful, since

> an angry *(ro'a)* face can improve the heart.
>
> 7:3

Or, as Emerson would put it, it improves the character. The pun is important, since it makes the crucial point that evil *(ra')* can actually contribute more to human maturity and growth than apparent goods. Seen from this perspective, God's gifts include things we would rather, at least initially, do without. Once it is agreed, however, that the goals of life are the improvement of character, the acknowledgement of God's beneficence, and the acceptance of the real nature of human existence, then other attitudes come into play: suspension of judgment and patience.

We now have two explanations for negatives, those "bad" things that happen to us. In addition to challenging our trust in God, they are seen as necessary growth factors. It is from these two motivations, I think, that people seek wisdom, have children, although (or perhaps because)

> In much wisdom is much grief, and one who increases knowledge increases sorrow.
>
> 1:18

---

[17] For the quotational use of "evil" here, see Chapter 12, "Qohelet's Very First Words." See also Appendix 3, "Quotationals."

An anonymous medieval commentary to this verse sets the issue clearly:

> Although Solomon says… "He that increases knowledge increases pain,"
> nevertheless what he calls sorrow I interpret to be the labor of heart and
> mind. Thus we should not consider such pain as bad, for he did not call it
> *bad* pain. Nor should this be a reason for withdrawing from knowledge and
> science, for knowledge leads the intelligent person to physical and spiritual
> enjoyment.[18]

It seems that the exegete, in stressing the desirability of increasing the
pain of labor, is offering a precious gloss on Qohelet's opening question
on the value of *'amal* or *over*work: to be avoided in the pursuit of things
of vanity but very much to be practiced in the desire for intellectual and
spiritual improvement.

An Indifferent Universe and Its Song of Mere Being

A gold-feathered bird

Sings in the palm, without human meaning,

Without human feeling, a foreign song.

Wallace Stevens[19]

The following reflections focus on how we humans should live and think
our relation to the outside world. It proposes that, axiologically speaking, the world out there is to be regarded as indifferent, neither "good"
nor "bad" in itself.

Qohelet's famous Catalog of the Times is introduced by an ambivalence whose importance has escaped notice:

> There is a time [*'et*] for each and every thing [*khepets*] under the heavens.

Qohelet 3:1

What we have here is another bifurcated figure, a doublet similar to
those that opened the entire book. On the one hand, a *khepets* is a *desire*;
on the other, it is a matter or event or any *thing desired*.[20] Which is the
right one? Both, of course. The word functions as a doublet, a word that
goes in two different but related directions.

---

[18] See T. A. Perry, *The Moral Proverbs of Santob de Carrión: Jewish Wisdom in Christian Spain*
(Princeton, NJ: Princeton University Press, 1987), 172.

[19] Wallace Stevens, "Of Mere Being," in *The Palm at the End of the Mind: Selected Poems and a
Play* (New York: Alfred A. Knopf, 1971), 398.

[20] In terms of our proposed reading, it is crucial to recall that all typical human action and
striving alluded to in the Catalog is referred to as *khepetz*, rendered variously as "matter"

To illustrate one level and as promised above, I finally offer my report on the tomato crop in Maine. It was a bad year! With all the rain and the blight, some farmers produced barely 10 percent of their expected harvest. To make matters worse, I anxiously asked our farmer, "When will we have tomatoes this year?" His downeasterly reply could have been expected: "When they are ripe." Or, in King Lear's words, "ripeness is all," at least for tomatoes.

For *khepets* has a cosmic as well as human reference. Too often overlooked is that the seasonal requirement ("everything in its season") also applies to things, since each thing has its own *khepets* or desire, so to speak. That is to say, human desires occur in a universe that has its own cycles and timetables. Any number of literary examples could be cited:

> The eyes of all wait upon You [Lord,] and You give them their food in [its] due time.
>
> Ps 145:15

Distinct from the following verse, which addresses the people's time of need, the text asserts "in ITS, THE FOOD'S, own time or season."[21] Or perhaps Bergson's famous observation that, before drinking the tea, "il faut laisser au sucre le temps de fondre"– you should give the sugar its time to melt. The point of these and similar examples, of course, is that the things of the world, like Wallace Steven's gold-feathered bird,

---

(Crenshaw, Whybray, Krüger, Fox, Seow, NRSV), "event" (Gordis, Ogden), "experience" (NJPS, Fox), "business" (Barton), "doing" (H. L. Ginsberg), "interest" (Lohfink), "affair" (Murphy), "[un temps] pour tout faire" (Jerusalem Bible). My proposed reading is "desire," thus corresponding to the cosmic sun's "panting with desire" (1:5), as well as the aged or dying person's dwindling engagement with life's pleasures. Michael V. Fox, *A Time to Tear Down and a Time to Build Up: a Rereading of Ecclesiastes* (Grand Rapids, MI: Eerdmans, 1999), 207, notes the possible meaning "desire, pleasure" and cites 5:3, 12:1, 10, but he bypasses its central importance. It indicates a project or interest (Lohfink) that one would not pursue without the desire or perceived need to do so. It is not clear, however, whether Qohelet uses the term to refer to individual things or objects. See also n. 48 and Appendix 6, "Doublets."

21 Especially as outlined or typified in the Catalog of Times (3:1–8), the dominant concept is *'et*, and here the time is determined not only by the agent but also by the thing being acted upon. For a close parallel see Sirach 39:16: "Les oeuvres de Dieu sont toutes bonnes, / à tout besoin il pourvoit en son temps (trans. Mopsik). As in Qoh 3:11, Sirach allows the notion "in His own time," but also projects the possibility of Ps 145:15 and Qoh 3:1–8: each thing in *its* own time. Charles Mopsik comments on Sir 39:16: "C'est moins sur la notion de providence divine que porte l'insistence du texte que sur le parallélisme de synonymie entre le bien et l'utile (ou la bonté et l'utilité)." *La Sagesse de ben Sira* (Paris: Verdier, 2003), 226.

have their own natures and schedules, independent of human need and intervention.

Of possible interest to environmentalists, this point is immediately compromised in the Qohelet text, however, by the immediate sequel, which attaches the time of each thing [*khepets*] to a *human* interest or preoccupation:

> a time to be silent and a time to speak,
> a time for war and a time for peace.

To be perfectly clear, the Catalog's opening *khepets* can be initially taken as referring to all things in themselves, except that they are then illustrated as things of human reference and desire. We are thus made aware of a fatal connection between the human and non- or extra-human worlds, a connection as universal and pervasive as, say, Descartes's distinction between extended and thinking substance (and without even a pineal gland to bridge the chasm).

Here the point is theologically heightened in that the permission for this state of things is none other than God's. However, people will be given food not in their good time and not even in God's good time but rather in the *food's own good time*, when it is ripe or cooked or otherwise ready to be eaten. When we attempt to use or enjoy things outside of their proper or natural time, then, as Montaigne observed, it is like serving mustard with desert, "vain and out of season."[22]

Thus, external conditions cannot be viewed as the mere matter that my decision will affect, for each natural thing or *khepets* has its own appropriate time as well, and it is only when my human decision coincides with the natural one that a wise situation occurs. Behind the primary meaning of *khepets* as "intention, desire" (Krüger) lurks another, that of "thing, matter," and it is never a matter of deciding between a primary or secondary meaning in any given context, since both are always present and one cannot function without the other. For what we have here is yet another ambivalence wherein the human (desire or intention) and the cosmic (thing) function in tandem. Thus, whereas many of the examples in the Catalog focus on the aspect of human agency (most are verbs), their success always depends on an interaction with an object, unstated but always implied (even when the verbs are transitive, they appear without their direct object, which must be supplied at the "appropriate" time). For example, a human decision to speak or be silent is always conditioned by

---

[22] Montaigne, *Les Essais*, 991 (III:9).

the environment and things beyond my control; and whether I destroy or build depends on specific objects and conditions.

Although Qohelet pursued street knowledge of "good" and "evil" (*da'at*) beyond its limited mundane purposes, its overall result has fulfilled its wisdom purposes, for it is through these oppositional forces, as Lyn M. Bechtel puts it, "that the man and woman [Adam and Eve] must become aware of when they begin to mature by eating of the Tree of Mature Knowledge, and begin to experience life as God created it from the beginning. Eating of the Tree of Mature Knowledge means learning to discern and accept both poles of the essential binary forces of life."[23]

What then do my Maine tomatoes and Stevens's golden bird have in common, other than their total indifference to me? Two things matter a great deal to both Qohelet and myself: I can eat the tomato and enjoy the music but perhaps not at the same time unless I am having a really lucky day. For, aside from the dialectical opposites of human pursuit, indeed beyond their totalitarian possibilities and their pretense of conceptual control, is there not a neutralization of such tensions implicit in the very notion of time: not one of catalogs but of that freedom suggested by Qohelet's wonderful poetry: the poetry of time, time as the essence of poetry. Take it from a poet who enjoys a stroll:

> il y a
> de merveilleux livres de poésie
> à un moment ou un autre nous en venons à parler
> de poésie
> c'est-à-dire du temps.
>
> Roubaud

> There are /
> some marvelous books of poetry /
> at one moment or another we come around to speaking about poetry /
> that is to say about time.[24]

---

[23] Bechtel, "Rethinking the Interpretation of Genesis 2.4B–3.24," 1–18 at 15.
[24] Jacques Roubaud, *Cent cinquantes poemes (1991–98)* Paris: Gallimard, 1966.

PART THREE

THE *HEBEL* OF "DIS-ASTER": TOTALITIES, TRANSCENDENCE, AND CROSSOVER CONCEPTS

Qohelet's plea and declaration, to his critics:
"Why are you thinking only that? Why can't you help me?"
Maurice Blanchot[1]

The time is near when only what has remained unexplainable will be able to command our attention.

René Char[2]

The world "under the sun" has yielded its own wisdom for survival and success, consisting of a mode of living with moderation, in accord with the rhythms and cyclicalities of nature. One aspect of this model we have characterized as a kind of quietism, consisting of a quieting or even quitting of the passions.

Recalling Neher's perception of a dichotomy in Qohelet's thinking, however, a more radical "quietism" is also at work, this one dealing no longer with human values (legal, psychological, ethical) intrinsic to the worldly system, but offering rather a perspective of distance and removal to a more radical void: a neuter zone, a wind in God perhaps or, perhaps, only – or rather, also – a wind. At any rate, a very different breath or *hebel*.[3]

---

[1] Maurice Blanchot, *Le Dernier homme* (Paris: Gallimard, 1957), 7.

[2] "Le temps est proche où ce qui sut demeurer inexplicable pourra seul nous requérir." René Char, "Conversation avec une grappe, en hommage à Maurice Blanchot," *Critique*, June 1966, 483.

[3] For André Neher, see the Introduction.

7

Totalities and the Outside (*Dehors*)

a law of inherent opposites,
Of essential unity, is as pleasant as port…
After all the pretty contrast of life and death
Proves that these opposite things partake of one,
At least that was the theory, when bishops' books
Resolved the world. We cannot go back to that.
The squirming facts exceed the squamous mind,
If one may say so.

Wallace Stevens[1]

Foucault had a particularly keen insight into how our lives were endangered, not by existential meaninglessness, but rather by totalized meaningfulness, whether that be articulated in the forms of religious dogmatism, totalitarian theories, or vaunted secular enlightenment.

James Bernauer[2]

Totalities and Their Limitations

As we saw in Part II, there is an urgency, within our world "under the sun," to adapt to natural means and goals, to the "world at hand," and this exigency is self-justified by its local results: contentment, moral rectitude, efficiency, and success. Perhaps even power, understood not only as dominion over things and people but rather over one's own urges and passions. What could be better? Wisdom does have its advantages after

---

[1] Wallace Stevens, "Connoisseur of Chaos," in *The Collected Poems of Wallace Stevens* (New York: Alfred A. Knopf, 1954, 1982), 215.

[2] "Secular self-sacrifice: on Michel Foucault's courses at the Collège de France." In *Foucault's Legacy*, ed. C. G. Prado (New York and London: Continuum, 2009), 157.

all, despite some quibbles:[3] It is, *après tout,* a *worldly* wisdom, claiming at the very least a reduction of pain! What then of the *hebel* litany? Is it to be viewed only as a necessary obstruction, a foil to be overcome on the path to a better way-of- life? For we must also ask what this worldly or totality wisdom perspective *ex*cludes. For example, how do Job's unexplainable and unjustified sufferings fit into a possibly wider picture (Job 38–41)?[4] Or, to take a second and related example: in the Book of Qohelet, usually thought to focus only on the individual, how is the status of the Other narrated and conceptualized?

Returning to Qohelet's confessional perspective, we recall that his autobiographical narrative records a most dramatic transformation: the demission from high office of a king, son of David in Jerusalem no less, to the socially passive roles of school teacher, possibly union organizer, and especially bricoleur and collector of proverbs (12:9–10). The surprise is that the autobiographical literary form, often thought to enhance and glorify the self, can have the opposite effect, just as Appelfeld's hero can draw either proper or unsuccessful conclusions from his personal experience.[5] In the Book of Qohelet the self-reliance required for self-examination leads to an "outside" perspective and eventual destruction-that-is-a-renewal of the self (or recovery of a self-that-is-not-a-self), all epitomized in the transference from Solomon to the pen name.[6] We now wish to explore other implications of this transformation, using Blanchot's categories as rallying points for further reflection and new departures.

As an appropriate subtitle of the Book of Qohelet, as well as an apt modern restatement or translation of some of its key concepts, I nominate Blanchot's book *Writing of Disaster.* By placing our meditations under the Sign of Disaster, we evoke the ancient rabbinic midrash that attempts to explicate Qohelet's recurrent and dominant phrase, intoned at the very start:

All is *hebel* (without permanent value) under the sun.

---

[3] See the caveats expressed in such texts as 3:11 7:23–24; 8:17.

[4] The Book of Job, through the dialogue with God finally granted, suggests that there is an outside perspective, but also that it is beyond our comprehension, or at least our normal interests. But is there no justification from "outside the box"?

[5] See the Appelfeld epigraph quoted at the start of Chapter 1.

[6] For the notion that the 'I' narrative signals active self-examination, the confrontation with one's own soul, see Adena Tanenbaum, *The Contemplative Soul: Hebrew Poetry and Philosophical Theory in Medieval Spain* (Leiden: Brill, 2002), 89–90.

The midrash views the phrase as restrictive:

> "*Under* the sun, yes. But *outside* or above the sun, all is *not hebel.*

So too Blanchot: Everything in this world under the sun or *aster* is literally a dis-*aster.* But beyond a this-worldly perspective and with the disengagement occasioned by a *dis*-aster, other points of view and existences and spaces become possible. Blanchot equated this mode of existence with thinking itself:

> We posit that this disaster is the act of thinking.[7]

Levinas explains:

> We must understand 'disaster' as dis-aster: not to be in the world under the stars (asters).[8]

Disaster is thus, like *hebel* itself, a Janus-concept: it both describes the partial failure and demise of the totality of our cosmos under the sun and, through the dislocation of dis-aster, projects a point beyond the cyclical enclosure where real thinking – not the aster-bound dialectical craftiness of control and power or the "pretty contrasts of life and death" – can be imagined and perhaps even attempted. We shall now explore what such an event or awareness or, indeed, powerful new way of thinking could entail, and how Qohelet attempts to portray these possibilities. Before that, however, we must ask, even in its best mode: what are totality's limitations?

Totalities, as we have seen, are made up of meaningful reconciliations or reductions of opposites into unities, as in the cosmological alternation of evening and morning (= one day) or, in the human realm, birth and death (= one life). In its most general and typical application, its keyword is "all," as in "ALL is breath." Moreover, its focus is relentlessly introverted and deceptively exclusive, as if nothing else mattered or even existed. Consider, from this point of view, the entire opening section to the Book of Qohelet:

> the **All** is hebel (v, 2)
> **all** human labor (v. 3)
> **all** the four elements (vv. 4–7)
> **all** things / words (v. 8)

---

[7] "Nous pressentons que le désastre est la pensée." Maurice Blanchot, *L'Écriture du désastre,* 7, quoted in Emmanuel Levinas, *Dieu, la mort et le temps* (Paris: Grasset, 1993), 165.

[8] "Il faut comprendre le désastre comme dés-astre: ne pas être dans le monde sous les astres." Levinas, ibid.

all that was and will be: **no-thing** new (vv. 9–10)
all is forgotten (v. 11)

Despite the local and personal orientation of human events and desires (*khepets*) to particular times, Blanchot uncovers their totalizing exigency:

> Desire remains in touch with the distant star [*astre*], entreating of heaven, submitting its case to the entire universe.[9]

In a single stroke Blanchot shows the (psychological) unity of the Cosmology and the Catalo: the human need to magnify the "I" – notably both its desires and powers (knowledge, wisdom, etc.) – to cosmic proportions, resulting in a reduction of reality to a (false) unity or totality.[10] This totality, nevertheless, produces results in that area of its greatest concern, power:

> The dialectic proposes to us the achievement of all things possible, if only one knows (by cooperating with it through power and mastery in the world) to allow time to take all its time.[11]

Blanchot here captures both the eager anticipation of wide possibility and the risk or frustration of waiting upon time to take its own sweet time. The irony with respect to the world of dialectic – this world of ours, history – is palpable.

Just as humanistically oriented totalities (generated by the dialectic) have a darker underside, so too does the *all*-inclusive cosmological totality that mirrors and sustains its wisdom:

> Is the cosmic … the temptation to melt into the fiction of the universe, and thereby become indifferent to the tormenting vicissitudes of the near at hand (the neighboring)? Would the cosmic be a little heaven in which to survive, or with which to die universally, in stoic serenity? A "whole" which shelters us, even as we dissolve therein, and which would be natural repose – as if there were a nature outside of concepts and names?[12]

We are locked in by received concepts. Is there no escape?

---

[9] Blanchot, *L'Écriture du désastre*, 81.

[10] Blanchot is said to have poked fun at metaphysicians – in this case Heidegger himself – by noting their tendency to reduce *all* of reality to their own definitions thereof, thereby "thinking only in those spaces in which they hold sway." See Jacques Rolland's introduction to Levinas, *Éthique comme philosophie première* (Paris: Payot et Rivages, 1998), 19.

[11] Ibid., 48.

[12] Blanchot, *L'Écriture du désastre*, 75. For a slightly different translation see *The Writing of the Disaster*, trans. Ann Smock (Lincoln: University of Nebraska Press), 75.

The Outside (Dehors) *and the Neuter or Neutral*

The non-knowing where philosophical knowing begins coincides not with just blank nothingness but rather with no-thingness [*le néant d'objets*]. Without substituting eschatology for philosophy, without philosophically "demonstrating" the eschatological "truths," one can, beginning with one's experience of the totality, rise to a situation where the totality is broken....

Levinas[13]

With thinking we may be beside ourselves in a sane sense. By a conscious effort of the mind we can stand aloof from actions and their consequences; and all things, good and bad, go by us like a torrent. We are not wholly involved in Nature... I only know myself as a human entity... and am sensible of a certain doubleness by which I can stand as remote from myself as from another... a spectator, sharing no experience, but taking note of it, and that is no more I than it is you.

Thoreau, "Solitude,"[14]

Our analysis of the key concept *hebel* has produced two distinct valuations. At the first level it is negative, refers to things and behavior that I need to control or, better, do without, expunging them through a litany of *hebel* imprecations.[15] At a more cosmic level the focus is on universal transience, and since nothing remains, there is no lasting or permanent value, no *yitron*. In both of these (distinct but related) areas of meaning, *hebel* projects no clearly positive implications – *until*, that is, a kind of wisdom reflection takes over and seeks accommodation.

A first level would be a dialectical concept seen to be inherent both in human fortunes and in the cosmic dimension as well. According to this mode of perception, things have a flip side, they come in opposite pairs and thus form a unity. Thus, if day will soon become night, the sun will as surely rise again tomorrow. Continuing on this trajectory but at perhaps a different level of wisdom, one comes to the valuation of "truth" as higher than personal *khepets*: if transient (i.e., *hebel*) things are not what I desire and thus "bad," they may also be perceived as "good" because of the reality principle: that is what we have to work with. Both of these levels are operative "under the sun or heavens" and are of real benefit in dealing with opposites as part of a unified (not yet a larger) picture wherein negativity is accommodated and the conceptual reality

---

[13] Emmanuel Levinas, TI, 9.

[14] Henry David Thoreau, *Walden, or Life in the Woods* (New York: New American Library, 1999), 108.

[15] See Appendix 1, "Hebel Repetition."

(fiction?) of unity (totality) provides a level of satisfaction. Such accommodation of our complex lives and bewildering realities do provide orientation and a level of happiness, and its principles can be derived from concrete experience within the totality itself – without the help of revelation or prophecy or even clergy.

Is there then no reality "above" (beyond, outside of) the sun or cosmos? Is there no infinity beyond the totalities? To approach this perplexing zone, let us take a simple example from the Book of Beginnings itself. At the end of Day One of the Genesis account we have day and night (or two twilights....), and we are told that this merism arises from the creation of light. Fine and good, but what has happened to the primeval darkness itself (1:2), the one that preceded the first act of creation? It has been humanized, so to speak; it has been pictured or conceptualized by the familiar experiential modality "night," even though the sun that produced the day/night is not created until the fourth day! This gives a richer spin to the dictum of Rabbi Ishmael that "The Torah speaks the language of human beings."[16] Not only does it speak in a human language (Hebrew in this case) and use literary figures like repetition and polysemy; it also uses the concepts of daily human experience.

Well, a day totally without sun is surely a distant but fit companion to a primeval darkness. This primeval "Night" (let us humanize it as well) must be of a totally different nature from our usual night that arises only on day four along with the sun. Maurice Blanchot, in a stunning essay, attempts to distinguish these two nights: today's night and the night from the outside.[17] To approach this distinction Blanchot takes the example of sleeping. For most of us, sleeping occurs at night, and night becomes the servant of the day, just as sleep is required to "get us through the (next) day." Night and day thus work in dialectical partnership, just as, in the Genesis account, they together make one *day* (rather than, say, one night or something else). Thus, for example, when I sleep it is the "I" that sleeps, the self that rises to action and activity the next day. Not that the "I" thereby loses its identity, on the contrary: through this restoration the "I" retains and strengthens itself, just as this nighttime negation of the world "preserves us to the world and affirms the world."[18]

---

[16] Maimonides (*Guide for the Perplexed,* 1:26) refers this dictum to anthropomorphisms in the Bible, whereby God is said to behave like humans.

[17] Maurice Blanchot, *L'Espace littéraire* (Paris: Gallimard, 1955), 357–62.

[18] Ibid., 358.

In dreams, however, something else can happen, since they are closer to the nocturnal region:

> If the day survives into the night, goes beyond its boundary, becomes something that cannot be interrupted, it is no longer the day, it is the un-interrupted and the incessant; it is, along with events which seem to belong to time, and people who seem to be of the world, the approach of the absence of time, the threat of the Outside (*dehors*) where the world is absent.... The dream is ... a dangerous summons ... to the neutrality of that which is compacted (*ce qui se presse*) behind the beginning. The dream seems to awaken – in everyone, not only in children – the being of those first times and beyond that, to the most distant: the mythical, the emptiness and the vagueness of the archaic (*l'antérieur*).[19]

The Outside is thus notoriously difficult to conceptualize, since it evades all existent concepts. As seen above, its approach is strewn with negatives: not this, not that, certainly not "under the sun/heavens." Construed positively, the following areas may be appropriate:

1. what preceded creation of this world: that is, the darkness or *khoshek* of Genesis 1:2, perhaps a correlate of Blanchot's Night.
2. the infinite time expanse that traverses our cosmos and exceeds its totalities from all sides.
3. the fear of God,[20] which may well be its most radical religious and psychological formulation.
4. the non-anthropomorphic, including things located "under the sun" but remaining outside the human point of reference (e.g., animals, the environment).[21]

There are also transitional categories that stand at the border and allow participation in both perspectives. These include twilight perceptions to be studied below: the Sabbath, revelatory signs. Also included in this category are hybrid personalities, those that join ego or individual interests with the Outside. Examples include Moses, both king and prophet, or the tragic case of King Saul, who could not simultaneously be both except by temporarily becoming another person, an *'ish*

---

[19] Ibid., 361.

[20] See Chapter 13.

[21] Examples of animals in wisdom writing would include mythical beasts such as Job's Behemot (40:15) and Leviathan (40:25). For the radically non-anthropomorphic thrust of God's speeches in Job, see especially Kathryn Schifferdecker, *Out of the Whirlwind: Creation Theology in the Book of Job* (Cambridge, MA: Harvard Theological Studies, 2008), 82–95.

'akher.[22] This lesson was learned by Qohelet, who became a scholar and man of words only after setting his kingship aside.

When all (totalities, the All) has been *hebelized* and removed, what profit remains: *mah yitron?* If everything becomes nothing, does nothing become everything, does the reversal of language apply or is it only a rhetorical trick masking as deep thought?[23] There are two answers. In the dialectical mode, wisdom conclusions can indeed be generated by such reversals; whereas, from the Outside, such language tricks may be only that. However, both expressions, through their paradoxical combination of opposites, enable us to navigate the instantaneous flip of perception from "everything is breath" to "breath is Everything," meaning not that breath is every thing but rather that the all of human life is indeed *hebel* if grasped only as a fictional totality. For such a dialectical formulation, while valid under the sun, does not account for what lies beyond the totality, where a void or *hebel*-perception is accessed through other kinds of consciousness entirely.

When the entire universe of things has been reduced to no-thing, there remains an awareness, but of what? Of awareness itself, perhaps; like Blanchot's hero,

> ... capable only, leaning upon the endless tranquility of the outside, to interrogate, from the other side of a glass partition, silently, the world.[24]

This brings the concept of passivity and patience to a point beyond the dialectal binary of active/passive. Equally interesting is the status of what is perceived, once its human interest has been removed and worldly values suspended by their being viewed from outside the box. This "neutral" (neither positive nor negative, thus aside from the dialectic) status was described by Santob de Carrión (fourteenth century), one of Qohelet's most incisive continuators and perhaps exegetes. Here is how Don Santob described the axiological status of the world (*mundo*):

> We speak ill of the world, but there is no evil in it except ourselves: neither monsters nor any such thing. The world does not seek or intend to harm one man and please another.
>
> Each man judges it according to the state of his own affairs;
>
> but it bears neither friendship nor enmity toward anyone....

---

[22] See T. A. Perry, *Wisdom in the Hebrew Bible: God's Twilight Zone* (Peabody, MA: Hendrickson, 2014), 77–91.

[23] For the *renversement de langage* see Chapter 10, "Mortal Remains."

[24] Maurice Blanchot, *Au Moment voulu* (Paris: Gallimard, 1979), 95.

It is always the same [Él es uno],

as much when it is blamed as on the day when it is highly praised.

The sages attribute no change to it: its changes are only

according to those who receive it as such,

It is the celestial sphere that causes us to move,

but it itself has neither love nor desire for any thing.

(ll. 2485–92)[25]

Striking here is both the cosmos' (*mundo*) indifference to human concerns and also its *lack* of change, both expressed by the world's oneness (*él es uno*), that is, its sameness, and these characteristics apply both to the totality "under the heavens" and to all particulars: time and its basic unit of creation (the day), and even to the human body:

Under one same heaven we always lie enclosed....

Time is always the same....

And the world is at all times in equality with itself,

and man also is one in his body.

And the day is one and the same, it did not change

when one man received the opposite of the other.

(ll. 2529–32)[26]

Again, the crucial point is the radically non-anthropomorphic nature of the world, its indifference and total neutrality with respect to human values and their motivating subjectivity and interests and desires.

This axiological neutrality or indifference of the world, I think, is also captured by Qohelet's *hebel* refrain, its cumulative judgment of the world being in fact just the opposite: a non-judgment, a removal of the world as a possible source of either grief or happiness. This does not mean that *hebel* is nothing, rather that its standards are simply not ours. Whence Montaigne's observation concerning the human body's judicial indifference, its ability to see things with a single, indifferent eye:

The body receives the loads that are placed upon it justly, according as they are; the mind often extends them and makes them heavier to its [the body's] cost, giving them the measure that it sees fit.[27]

---

[25] T. A. Perry, *The Moral Proverbs of Santob de Carrión* (Princeton, NJ: Princeton University Press, 1987), 55, 112–14.

[26] Ibid. and p. 56. See also Jankélévitch, Appendix 3, "*Vivere* and *Bene Vivere*," and "Quotationals."

[27] Montaigne, *Les Essais*, 1007 (III:10).

The world out there is thus, in Qohelet's thought, neither good or bad in itself (but always "good" or "bad" for us, dialectically speaking), and thus open for fresh and creative evaluations. Camus, for instance, sees this difference as a relief, as an escape from human-driven tensions and anxieties, opening himself to "la tendre indifférence du monde," the world's *tender indifference.*[28]

---

[28] See Albert Camus's moving conclusion to *L'Étranger* (Paris: Gallimard, 1942).

8

Living "Under the Sun" and with Transience

There are three things that can be likened to the world to come: the Sabbath, the sun, and sexual intercourse.

BT Ber 57b

This remarkable midrash considers and modifies the distinction between dialectical reality – the one of this world "under the sun" – and the Outside, here called the "world to come." It proposes that these domains are not hermetically opposed and offers experiential models or perhaps modes of transition and encounter among them. In terms of the Genesis account of the universe's creation, the Sabbath both concludes and summarizes the All totality. That is to say, its cessation or rest from creative work – its dialectical negation if you will – is precisely what constitutes the week as a totality or an "All."[1] Yet the Sabbath also both intimates a space beyond – a worldly domain not quite of this world – and launches a new secular week. So too sexuality, the epitome of interpersonal relations. By producing offspring, coitus perpetuates the ongoing generation of our human world, yet it also projects an experience of transcendence wherein sundered beings can recover or at least imagine an original edenic unity.[2]

---

[1] Without a creative cessation, the work of creation would continue its rush forward, with no end in sight. I see a meaningful pun in the summarizing verse on the word *all* (*KoL*): "And the heavens and the earth and ALL (*KoL*) their multitudes were completed (*va-yeKuLu*). And by the seventh day God finished (*va-yeKaL*) the work which he had done" (Gen 2:1–2).

[2] See Rashi's interpretation of "becoming one flesh" (Genesis 2:24) as the making of a child. The preferred modern and sentimental reading refers to the physical union of coitus. Thus, in the second reading, 1+1=1; in the first reading 1+1=3; or possibly 4, as per Gen 4:1 ("with the help of the Lord").

105

The third crossover concept is the topic of this chapter:

The light is sweet,

and it is good for the eyes to see the sun.

Even if a person lives for many years,

he should rejoice in them all.

And let him remember that the days of darkness will be many: All that dies
is *hebel.*

11:7–8

It is seldom noticed that, after the word "*hebel,*" which appears thirty-six times in the text, the sun (*shemesh*) is Qohelet's favorite word (thirty-four appearances). For in Qohelet, as in Psalm 19, the sun scans the entire horizon of discourse, its light forms a sharp contrast to the death of breath, and the "days" that are the sun's particular dominion are, each one of them, a space for rejoicing. Dante's "dolce lome" recaptures the spirit, but for Qohelet, as we shall see, the sun's light is also a way of expressing the most basic fact and enjoyment of being alive, indeed the centrality of life itself. What better metaphor to translate what for many scholars is an important focus of the wisdom movement?[3]

The theme is introduced at the very start, and in a phrase that, because of its constant recurrence throughout the book, comes to be viewed as a simple tag and thus disregarded.

What profit for a man from all the toil that he toils *under the sun?"*

1:3

When we then come, almost immediately (1:5), to a description of the sun's activity, we allow it to get lost in the enveloping cosmology and thus, again, miss what is particular and important. But let us not lose Qohelet's own focus and, for what happens "under the sun," let us hear what he has to say immediately about the sun:

The sun rises and the sun sets,

Panting to its place

Where it rises again,

Going to the south and turning to the north,

Turning, turning goes the wind,

And upon its turnings the wind returns.

1:5–6

---

[3] See Appendix 3, "To Lives!"

In this crucial opening cosmology, wedged in between the sun and the wind there is a hanging descriptor, the verbal phrase "Going to the south and turning to the north," which can be attached either "above" or "below," making it either an attribute of the sun or the wind. Now, whereas ancient interpreters strongly favored the first,[4] more recent commentators (with the exception of Rashi) and all modern commentators attach the italicized clause to what follows, and this preference is reflected in what has come to be the accepted division of verses. The logic, presumably – since, as a rule, the matter is rarely discussed – is that the sole characteristic of the wind is to "turn," and it is somehow felt that, much like the excessive repetition-for-emphasis of verse 1:2, even the fourfold stress of turning/returning in the rest of the verse is hardly sufficient. The problem with this stylistic explanation is that it introduces a contradiction. For now, in addition to the wind's arbitrary turnings, sensitive only to its own movements, one is asked to posit a determinate direction *outside* its aimless course, a circuit from south to north (and, according to this reading, back to the south in order to renew the circuit). One would like to know from meteorologists whether the wind is regularly known to behave is such ordered fashion; and, even if this were the case, whether the point would have any relevance whatever to the rest of the book.[5]

It appears that Rashi reacted to both these problems: the stylistic over-determination of "turning" and, even more serious, the concept of a wind driven by a regularity external to its own capriciousness. But there is a compelling positive reason as well, one that has to do with Qohelet's focus on the fact that the sun has not one but two movements. Here is how the sun's *two* movements are presented:

The sun rises and the sun sets,[6]

Panting to its place

4　Septuagint, Targum Jonathan, Vulgate, the Babylonian Talmud (Baba Bathra 25b, Erubin 55a), the Jerusalem Talmud (Erubin 7:1), and the Tosefta (Erubin, ch. 5).

5　One intriguing possibility is the frequent combination of *hebel* with *re'ut ruakh*, stressing the ambivalence of *ruakh* as "wind" and also as human "spirit" (see Appendix 2, "*Hebel* and Friendship with the Ruakh").Thus, just as those who pursue *hebel* become hebelized themselves, so too, measure for measure, those human spirits or minds who pursue the wind become windy themselves. Yet, just as the sun's transience is framed or regulated by a pattern, so too is the spirit of inquiry, which goes around and around endlessly, but always on a bound trajectory ("north to south"). No wonder, then, that Qohelet concludes with the warning of 12:12: "There is no end to the making of books."

6　From the explicit repetition of "sun" – the normal formula would be: "the sun rises and sets" – this mild form of *antanaclasis* makes the point that there are in fact *two* different

> Where it rises again,
> Going to the south and turning to the north...
>
> 1:5-6a

From this we are reminded both that the sun moves from east to west and back to east, and also that it moves to the south and then to the north, again so that it can repeat the circuit. As is well known, these two movements delimit distinct periods: the day and the year. Both are necessary to describe those functions of time most appropriate to human labor: "the work that we do under the sun."[7]

It might be said that in the Bible the day is the minimum measure of human work time and perhaps also the limits of one's normal physical endurance, whereas the annual yield gauges the cooperation of "the elements." Of the two, in the Bible as among us, human longevity is typically measured by years, and this is the case in Qohelet as well (6:3, 6; 11:8). When asked one's age, the usual answer is x years and not x months or days. In fact, however, Qohelet does use a rather rare combination of the two to describe longevity:

> And as many as the days of his years will be...
>
> Qoh 6:3

From this one infers that days as well as years figured heavily in the counting of longevity: the days of one's life as well as the years of one's life. The joining of the two may of course be seen as a compression, when the intent is to stress life's brevity. The point here is that both are needed to account for the sun's activities under its hegemony.

A verse in Psalms (90:4) allows a more positive perspective, however, namely that a day can seem as a thousand years. A hint of this is present in its occurrence in Qohelet:

> If a man should live many years: as many as the days of his years will be, if he does not take satisfaction in the good things...
>
> 6:3

---

suns. We have seen how this repetitive figure opened the cosmology (1:4), to stress that the explicit doubling *dor/dor* (generation/generation) is needed in order to refer to two distinct and different sequential generations (see Crenshaw, cited above, p. 73, n. 11. Here too the sun is seen as having not one but two lives or domains. A close parallel is Ps 19:6, where the sun is a warrior by day and a lover by night.

7　The synonymy wherein *yom*, day, also means *shanah*, year, is pervasive in Hebrew Scripture.

The joining of days into years is now seen as an expansion in which each single day takes on the importance of years, indeed appears to be the very basic measures (sic) of all human time:

> The very longest space of time possesses no element which cannot be found in a single day – namely light and darkness, – and even to eternity day makes these alternations [of night and day] more numerous, not different...
>
> Seneca[8]

Thoreau's notion of the reinvigoration of the world "each day," the true sign of the world's "everlasting vigor and fertility,"[9] finds kindred echoes in Qohelet's sun, which "pants to the place where he can shine forth again," which can only be the "place" of perpetual rebirth. Levinas:

> Time is not the limitation of being but rather its relation with the infinite. Death is not annihilation but a necessary question so that this relation with the infinite or time can be implemented.[10]

Let us now return to the epigraph with which we began, but with a fuller reading:

> The light is sweet,
>
> and it is good for the eyes to see the sun.
>
> Even if a person lives for many *years*,
>
> he should *take joy in* them all.
>
> And let him remember that the *days* of darkness will be many.
>
> 11:7–8

The mention of both years and days is not accidental but rather a deliberate allusion to the sun's *two* domains. And one should rejoice not only in them, as a simple designation of time (for when else would one rejoice?) but of object as well: one should take one's principle delight not only *during* those times so much as *in* those times, in their full extent but especially in the perpetual renewal of both the dawn and the spring.[11]

---

8 Seneca, *Letters*, Letter 12 (I:69).

9 Henry David Thoreau, *Walden, or Life in the Woods* (New York: New American Library, 1999), 72.

10 Emmanuel Levinas, *Dieu, la mort et le temps* (Paris: Grasset, 1993), 28.

11 One usually reads *b-* as a temporal preposition, but it is commonly construed with the verb *samakh* to indicate the object of enjoyment, as in Qoh 5:18; Deut 26:11; and often. For the enjoyment of light as the supreme pleasure of esthetics, see Conclusion, "Primary or Transitional Experiences under the Sun."

Returning to the Talmudic passage, then: like the Sabbath, the sun is a Janus concept, it has both a beneath and a beyond, thus serving as an eternal *'ot* or "sign of eternity" (Exod 31:17). It is now apparent that the three Talmudic hints to the world to come – the Sabbath, sexual intercourse, the sun – are brought together under the aegis of the sun in Qohelet's remarkable verse:

> Enjoy life with a woman you love all the days of your *hebel* life that he [God] has given you under the sun all the days of your *hebel.* For this is your portion in this life and in your toil that you toil under the sun.
>
> 9:9

It is all given "under the sun": all the days that the sun delineates (1:5), the life and sweetness and warmth that it proliferates, the daily toil that you toil toward Shabbat, and the joy of companionship and procreation.[12]

And all this is *hebel*!? From what perspective? What then is *hebel*?

---

[12] This text seems to favor companionship, whereas Rashi (see n. 248) and Qohelet on 3:2 (see n. 201 and Appendix 3, "Giving Birth.") stress procreation: "A time to bring a child into the world."

9

Breath of Breaths: Qohelet's Motto and Theme and Refrain

A Levinassian Exegesis

My method in this chapter is standard exegesis – what we used to call close reading – enriched by recently published philosophical and linguistic meditations of Emmanuel Levinas.[1] Each topic will refer to one of his guiding principles of exegesis. The goal is to uncover the rich polysemy of Qohelet's defining concept, *hebel* ("vanity"), moving from its literal or concrete meaning (*peshat*) of breath and through its various metaphoric interpretations.[2]

The Effects of Poetic Language

Qohelet opens with an image: *habel habalim*. It is some kind of metaphor, but of a very peculiar sort. Along with others, I will for convenience call it a motto, one that introduces a main theme. But it is, in the first instance, not a thesis,[3] as all current translations would have it (e.g., "Vanity of vanities"), because then we are held captive by the abstract interpretation imposed upon it.

Before any meaning can be imposed on a fact of discourse, however, there is the pure or direct artistic physicality of the text itself. Levinas notes it as follows:

Principle 1

The expression of thought is always something other than the objective content of thought... It is in language, in this "matter" of thought, that art

---

[1] I am referring to Emmanuel Levinas, *Carnets de captivité et autres inédits* (Paris: Grasset, 2009), here abbreviated as CC.

[2] For further development see CC, 236ff.

[3] In disagreement with Michael V. Fox, approvingly quoted by Douglas B. Miller, 437, n. 4: "The book's motto is a thesis that we can expect to see validated in the following monologue." *Qohelet and His Contradictions* (Sheffield: Almond, 1989), 168.

111

operates. The final form of this play of the matter of language is the poem with its rhythm and rime… The poem is a collaboration of intelligence and art cutting into language, playing with language as matter, creating its own effects.

Levinas, CC, 116[4]

It is quite surprising that the Book of Qohelet – this long collection of wisdom sayings sponsored and somewhat unified by a confessional perspective – should be introduced by a verse that is strikingly, even blatantly poetic:

> *Habel habalim /*
> *habel habalim /*
> *ha-kol habel*

The rime and rhythmic repetition – sound-words that turn upon themselves in the same form – have their own peculiar artistic effects. My approach in this literary matter is suggested by the title of Henri Meschonnic's remarkable theoretical essay, *La Rime et la vie*, Rime and Life.[5]

Almost immediately the surprise is intensified, as we are plunged into verses that again produce the same effects of sound repetition:

> *a generation* comes and *a generation* goes
> *the sun* shines forth and *the sun* sets.

1:4–5

Normal prose syntax, of course, would simply avoid the repetition through a pronoun, here implied: "A generation comes and goes; the sun shines forth and sets." The most stunning effects of pure sound repetition, however, are reserved for the *ruakh*, the cosmic winds:

> Going to the south and *turning* to the north,
> *turning, turning* goes the wind (*ruakh*),
> and upon its *turnings* the wind (*ruakh*) re*turns*.

1:6

The superlative intensity of the motto repetitions – five *hebels* in a single verse – is now echoed in the multiple repetitions of turning. Even before thinking about meanings, the pure physical forms of the language have oriented our thought. Levinas may offer an initial perspective when he

---

4 Levinas thus typifies poetry as both "thinking without knowing what one is thinking, and thinking this not-knowing in order to bring it forward" CC, 307.
5 Paris: Verdier, 2006.

speaks of "the difference between sensibility and intelligence. Music and painting: they do not reach you through translation, they flow into you like eating. But thought involves signs to translate, it passes through the head."[6] In terms of thought content, the poetic repetitions in the opening verses (1:1–6) intimate a solution to the opening All question ("All is *hebel*").[7] For the text first points to an anthropological reference (what benefit to *humans*?) and then proceeds without transition to a universal and *cosmological* focus. Rather than the disjunction advanced by most critics, the motto's sound repetitions, reverberating throughout the entire opening poetic passage, argue a continuity between human and cosmological levels of being. Microcosm and macrocosm: both are in some connected sense *hebel*. This reading goes against the usual either/or choice common among critics.[8]

The Book of Qohelet is dominated from start to finish by its motto metaphor. *Hebel*, which recurs as a refrain some thirty-seven times in Qohelet and thirty-five times in all the rest of the Hebrew Bible, is variously rendered as vanity, as something absurd, insubstantial, futile, ephemeral, incomprehensible, frustrating, ironic, or, in a somewhat more positive vein, enigmatic and mysterious. While there is no consensus as to which meaning is the right or intended one, there *is* broad agreement that it is only one of these. Levinas's view of the Bible as a polysemic text, however, allows the possibility of several different meanings of the same word in a given work.[9] And, when it was finally observed, in a long overdue article, that such high levels of abstraction[10] could not singly account for all occurrences of *hebel* in Qohelet, it was proposed that the number of acceptable renditions be bumped up to three; and

[6] Levinas, CC, 338.

[7] In our text "all" quite frequently has the meaning of "both" (7:15, 18; 2:14; 3:19). Thus, "breath of breaths, breath of breaths, BOTH are breath." While the exact reference is yet to be presented, we are warned at the start that two kinds or levels of breath are to be discussed: human and cosmic. In terms of the omnipresence of binaries in Qohelet's thought, this interesting possibility must be considered. For the possible reading of this statement as a question, see Appendix 5, "Is *All* vanity?."

[8] As epitomized in the title of Lohfink's article, "Koh 1,2 'Alles ist Windhauch' – universale oder anthropologishe Aussage?" in *Der Weg zum Menschen*, ed. R. Mosis and L. Ruppert (Freiburg: Herder, 1989), 201–16.

[9] And when two or more of the same word with different meanings occur in close proximity, then we have the figure of *antanaclasis*. Krüger comes close to this possibility when he translates *habel habalim* by two distinct concepts: "futile and fleeting." See Appendix 6, "Antanaclasis," for an extended discussion of this figure and how it may apply to Qohelet's motto and refrain.

[10] This danger is companion to wandering too far from the *peshat*, and it requires what Meschonnic has called a "state of watchfulness against abstractions." *Rime et vie*, 129.

these are: insubstantiality, transience, and foulness.[11] In terms of our previous discussion, I am arguing that Qohelet's favorite word (*hebel*) is indeed king doublet, and in the grand manner already set out: acting as an enigma, it posits a trajectory from negative valuations (vanity) to more neutral one such as transience and change, finally to positive ones more congenial to wisdom perspectives such as life and discourse.

Toward the Peshat *or Concrete Literal Meaning* of Hebel: *Is Breath "Vanity"?*

With this we can pass from what Levinas called "the poetry of philosophical aphorism" and turn to direct and immediate content. This is the second step preliminary to interpretation as usually construed.[12]

Principle #2:

> To read an archaic text and be able to take it literally without adapting an interpretation to it, without searching for it a symbolical or metaphorical sense.
>
> Levinas[13]

Speaking of his friend Jean Wahl's thinking as an effort to reanimate questions, comparable to a dart penetrating into the organic body of thought:

> The lance both isolates and reduces to its simple meaning – to its value of experience and sensation – to its pain or its problem – the attacked articulation, tearing it away from the totality (*l'ensemble*) where it was already becoming the possession (*avoir*) of a philosophy and private game reserve of a philosopher, but where it also was in danger of getting stuck. *Towards the concrete*: that is to say, above all, outside the protective enclosure of a system.[14]

All current translations of the *hebel* image are only interpretative abstractions, pale metaphors that, at great expense, neglect the first

---

[11] Douglas B. Miller, "Qohelet's Symbolic Use of Hebel," *JBL* 117 (1998): 443. "Insubstantiality" and "transience" were already in circulation; "foulness" is Miller's own contribution. As I argue above, Qohelet uses *hebel* in at least three different and graded senses: the first as a negative marker, the second in a neutral sense, and a third to project creativity and transcendence. Krüger (p. 42) also sees the first two levels: a negative one ("worthless, futile"), stopping short of the more serious negativity of "sinful" proposed above), and a neutral one ("transitory," "fleeting").

[12] Emmanuel Levinas, discussing Jean Wahl's poetics, in *Hors sujet* (Paris: Fata Morgana, 1987), 95.

[13] CC, 214.

[14] Levinas, *Hors sujet*, 97.

requirement of metaphorical expression. I mean that, while Levinas champions metaphorical extensions, he also insists, as did the rabbis, that a term never entirely departs from its concrete literal sense, what I refer to elsewhere as *peshat*-metaphors. Curiously, its literal meaning is typically put forth as "vapor."[15] If this were the case, however, readers would be constantly drawn to the kitchen oven or the boiler room, and one might wonder why vapor would have seemed of such importance as to characterize all of human – and indeed universal – life. No indeed. Vapor can acquire that breadth of existential reach only by being briskly transformed from its material trace and into one or more of the mere abstractions that dominate our interpretations. And, in fact, *hebel* cannot be shown to mean vapor in any of its appearances in the Hebrew Bible, including Qohelet. Yet it is routinely selected as *peshat* – while never perceived as such – by nearly all major critics today, and as the only *peshat* by some.[16]

To introduce *hebel*'s only other possible concrete meaning – the correct one – I ask you to conduct a quick experiment:

PROMPT: "Inhale; exhale. One breath; two breaths: It is all breath."

There! You have just performed Qohelet's motto at its most literal level. The translation is:

A breath of breaths; a breath of breaths: it is all breath.[17]

If this only available *peshat* is unfamiliar, this may be due to habit. Of course, this translation does itself require clarification, since it still, as Lohfink observed, "throws readers into a world whose conceptual system invites them, and yet remains cloaked in darkness."[18] To be

---

[15] None of the four texts cited by Fox 27–28 is conclusive: Isa 57:13; Prov 13:11, 21:6; Ps 144:4. This tradition seems to be rabbinic in origin. See, for example, Kohelet Rabba ad loc.

[16] The only support for this position is in cognate languages, never in the Hebrew Bible or in Qohelet. Douglas Miller (443, n. 25) uses only "vapor," which is defined as "a quantity of visible matter, such as gaseous water, diffused through or suspended in the air." What seems important here is the stress on "visible," since we like our metaphors to be concrete or at least somewhat substantial in some primitive sense. To his credit, Krüger does not include "vapor" as a literal rendering of *hebel* but, correctly and creatively, restricts its meaning to a "breath (of wind)."

[17] Alternatively, the final sentence can be rendered either as "The All is breath" or as "They are both breath."

[18] Lohfink is the only major exegete to retain "breath" (Ger. *Hauch*) as the correct rendering of *hebel*. Norbert Lohfink, *Qoheleth: A Continental Commentary* (Minneapolis: Fortress, 2003).

sure, even when an abstract sense of a metaphor imposes itself on a translator, either because of context or because the original meaning has been worn out or occluded, the intent of etymological research is to sense the trace of the concrete reference below the surface. This typically uncovers a new depth and poignancy of focus: "The woman that God has given you under the sun all the days of your breaths" (9:9). Life is measured out in years and days and, most intimately, in breaths.

At the very least and before all-embracing interpretations and abstractions and metaphors take over, readers of Qohelet now have a concrete point of departure and reference. Let's now enter our text with a concrete *fact*, what Levinas states rather cryptically as "*le fait de respirer*," the *fact* of breathing.[19]

The Dynamism and Transcendence of Metaphor: Cosmology

Principle #3

> A metaphor is the very participation of an object in something other than itself.[20]

Principle #4

> A metaphor enables the various orders and levels of being to communicate with one another.[21]

We now examine the dynamism and transcendence of metaphor, extending the range of *peshat*, through the methods of polysemy and textual analysis, with particular relevance to the Cosmology in Qoh 1:4–7 and, with Levinas's help, all the way to God.

How do we read a metaphor? As we said, after seeking to recover the true *peshat*, often through etymological research, and lingering in its concrete, lived physicality, we then follow Levinas's requirement that texts be "solicited" (an erotic metaphor). In our text we allow the reference of *hebel* to deepen and expand in the direction of its possible synonyms,

---

[19] Levinas, CC, 56. This notation is introduced as a reflection, with no apparent context that might clarify it, except that breathing is asserted as a fact, both a fact of life in a very pregnant sense (see below) and a fact as opposed to a metaphoric interpretation.
[20] CC, 231.
[21] CC, 241.

such as they exist both in Qohelet itself and in the Hebrew Bible.[22] In the
Hebrew Bible, for example:

> When you cry, let the collection of idols deliver you. All of them a wind [*ruakh*]
> will carry off, a breath [*hebel*] will take them away.
>
> Isa 57:13

This verse seems to be constructed on the principle of guilt by association known as parallelism, but with what Levinas might term a metaphoric
extension. The "parallelism" of this verse advances two possibilities: the
semantic synonymy of *hebel / ruakh,* and the resemblance (Levinas) of two
objects that establish a relationship between different levels of reality, here
the microcosm and the macrocosm.[23]

The synonymy or "resemblance" of *hebel* and *ruakh* is quite common in
the Hebrew Bible:

> Ordinary humans are breath [*hebel*], and important men are a lie. In a balance
> they are all lighter than air [*ruakh*].
>
> Ps 62:10[24]

Ruakh and *hebel* can thus be used interchangeably. Again:

> Put not your trust in princes or in humans, in whom there is no help: his
> breath [*ruakh*] goes forth, he returns to the earth.
>
> Ps 146:3–4

In Qohelet, *ruakh* is, of course, the air surrounding us:

> No man has power over the wind (*ruakh*), to restrain the *ruakh.*
>
> 8:8

But the verse's conclusion also authorizes this reading of *ruakh* as also the
air we *breathe,* the breath of life:

---

[22] In his discussion of Qohelet's literary dexterity as a writer, Douglas Miller (p. 445)
focuses on the use of synonyms as one way to both protect and expand the inherent
ambivalence of live metaphors such as *hebel.*

[23] The precise relation is left vague. There may be "resemblances "between realities of
the same order. But are these only resemblances or also correspondences? "Metaphor
pulverizes those structures of meaning which do not always go from the human to the
material in order to humanize the material but which go in reverse." (CC, 228).

[24] This translation is Harold Fisch's, in *The Holy Scriptures: English Text Revised and Edited*
(Jerusalem: Koren, 1992). JPS is even more telling concerning the synonymy of *hebel* and
ruakh, both of which are rendered by the single "breath." For *ruakh* as "breath" see also
Job 15:30, "the *ruakh* of his mouth."

> ... to restrain the breath (*ruakh*) [from departing];
> – he has no power over the day of death.[25]

This ambivalence should remind us always to recall the *peshat* of *hebel* before jumping too quickly into interpretation such as "fleeting" or "absurd":

> The fate of humans and the fate of animals is one fate: as one dies, so dies the other. They all have one life-breath (*ruakh*), and humans have no advantage over the animals, for all is *hebel*, breath.
>
> 3:19, also 21

Similarly, God's *ruakh* or breath issues from his mouth (Ps 104:29; Job 12:10).

The synonymy of *hebel* and *ruakh* is important lexically also because, through metaphorical extension or overlap, one's individual breath can now be seen as continuous with the universal air that surrounds us and is indeed one of the four constitutive elements of this universe under the sun, as per the Cosmology of 1:4–7. This notion may be further expanded by its association with *re'ut ruakh* and *ra'yon ruakh*, which Fox takes as having a single meaning in their combination with *hebel*.[26] Beyond the precise meaning of these expressions, however, the crucial point of this discussion is again the focus on *ruakh*, wind, as a core reference of *hebel*, and vice-versa as well.

> All is breath (*hebel*) and a chasing after the wind (*re'ut ruakh*).
>
> 1:14

And, of course, at the very conclusion of Qohelet:

> The dust will return to the earth as it was,
>
> And the life-breath (*ruakh*) will return to the God who gave it.
>
> A breath of breaths (*hebel* of *hebels*) said Qohelet: It is all wind/breath (*hebel*).
>
> 12:7–8; also Ps 104:29

---

[25] Consider the repetition of *ruakh* in Qoh 8:8: "No man has control over the *ruakh*, to hold back the *ruakh*." As I once pointed out, the repetition is suspicious, since the second *ruakh* could have simply been an object pronoun: to control it." Thus many commentators (Lohfink, Fox, Perry) read "no control over the wind, to hold back the breath." This reading speaks, of course, to the close synonymy and interchangeability of wind and breath in Qohelet. For the rich polysemy of *ruakh* in Qohelet see Scott B. Noegel, "Word Play in Qoheleth," *Journal of Hebrew Scriptures* 7 (2007): 19.

[26] Michael V. Fox, *A Time to Tear Down and a Time to Build Up: a Rereading of Ecclesiastes* (Grand Rapids, MI: Eerdmans, 1999), 43. For Thomas Bolin's reading, "all is mortal but strives for immortality," see my discussion in Appendix 2, "*Hebel* and Friendship with the *Ruakh*."

Let us state the matter as simply as we can. We typically rush to interpretation and abstraction before attending to the word's *peshat*. However, the text does not repetitively assert that "this too is vanity" but rather "this too is *hebel*, a breath." The question then becomes: what is a breath? where? In life but especially in the text before us, the one that wants to talk so much about *hebel*? It is the *hebel-ruakh*, both the air that I breathe in order to live, and also the winds that circulate through the universe and through me. The poet Edmond Jabès puts it nicely:

> There is the wind that blows outside
> and the wind that blows in us.[27]

Semantic synonymy, in its expansive ambiguity, sponsors reflection on possible relationships between two orders of reality, the human and the cosmic, and if one can discover or posit a level of interdependence or indeed coincidence, then the absurdity argument is compromised.[28] To be sure, when the going gets tough Camus can lead us to ponder the possibility that our situation is intrinsically absurd and learn to deal with it. Levinas can perhaps be of greater service, however, and at two levels. On the one hand, the focus is not on the absurdity of the universe (or the whimsicality of God), but rather on the act of breathing as constant and life-sustaining. Then, at a second level, the focus moves from the surface *peshat* to its inner meaning: What does it mean to breathe? And, as a further stage of this meditation, what then is a *habel habalim*, a Breath of breaths? As I have been proposing, we must ask whether *hebel* is only a poetic synonym of *ruakh*, thus a mere esthetic appurtenance, or whether this figure of speech is also a figure of thought, whether it does not also foster a meditation on the relationship between macrocosm and microcosm, in particular on humanity's place within the cosmos. And vice-versa.

The Peshat *as Metaphor: The Breath of Life*

We thus come to a paradox. If what transcends the *peshat* or literal sense is, in Levinas's language, a metaphor, have we then not compromised, even abolished, the consecrated opposition between the literal and the figurative? On the one hand, as Levinas stresses, "there is the necessity to

---

[27] "Il y a le vent qui souffle à l'extérieur et le vent qui souffle en nous." *Le Livre des questions* (Paris: Gallimard, 1963), 178.

[28] The argument wherein *hebel* is translated as "absurdity" is derived by Michael V. Fox from Camus's dualistic definition. See Chapters 3 and 4.

have recourse to the literal sense"; yet, on the other, "the literal sense is like swollen with meanings that transcend it but which it cannot be without."[29] Indeed, "is the literal sense not already metaphorical?"[30]

It would seem that this feat, starting with the literal meaning, can occur in two opposite directions: (1) reaching outward and beyond or above, transcending it; (2) going deeper within, to more intrinsic levels of meaning. Metaphors that go beyond the *peshat* can occur, as we have just seen, as ways for different levels of being to communicate with one another. Thus, for example, an accident could be viewed as a "test"; a being could be described as a "creature" (CC, 240). In this way metaphors are ways in which "anthropological meanings are inscribed into things" (ibid), ways of attaching or lending a human meaning ("prêter un sens") to a thing or fact.

At a related and more obvious level, metaphors typically occur as comparisons. To say that something or someone is a "breath" (Ps 144:4) means a comparison: *like* a breath in some respect. Yet, the phrase "breath of life" or "life-breath" is different; it is not a comparison but rather a kind of pleonasm or tautology. I mean that each could be used independently, since you cannot have one without the other: when you are alive you have breath; when you don't you die. At the very least, there is no comparison here; rather, a definition. Just as "the blood is the life-soul" (Deut 12:23; Lev 17:14), so too, perhaps: *ha-hebel hu' ha-khayim*, *hebel* is life.

It is true, of course, that such a figure – that breath suggests brevity and emptiness – is characteristic of many of the uses of *hebel* in the Hebrew Bible, including Qohelet:[31]

Only in Qohelet, however, is this typical phrase glossed with a significant addition:

> Enjoy life with the woman you love *all the days of the life of your hebel,* which he [God] has given you all the days of your *hebel.*
>
> 9:9

> Indeed, who knows what is good for humans in life, the number of *the days of the life of his hebel* which he passes like a shadow?
>
> 6:12[32]

Only in Qohelet is the word attached to life itself.

---

[29] CC, 242.

[30] CC, 330.

[31] For further discussion with more examples, see Appendix 2, "Counting the Breaths."

[32] He passes his life like a shadow and leaves no trace (Fox), thus denoting transience and brevity rather than futility (Whybray). For other things that leave no trace and yet are

Thus, *hebel*, the breath, is Qohelet's *peshat*-metaphor for life. We said at the start that it is a very special kind of metaphor. *Hebel* is the inclusive metaphor or symbol for human life because it is the breath that marks the arrival and the departure of life. Thus, everything that dies is *hebel* (*kol she ba' hebel*, 11:8), referring precisely to everything that first lives.[33]

This is the point: *hebel* is the fact of life-breath; its first *peshat*-metaphoric level, therefore, is life itself.

The All as the **Hebel** of Hebels: *God as the Metaphor of Metaphors*

Principle #5

> To think beyond the givens of our world. What does it mean to go beyond one's experience? It means to think God.

> Levinas[34]

There is another reaching beyond or above *peshat* that is also, paradoxically, turned within: the kind of hyperbole that occurs in the phrase "breath of breaths." Such figures, normally classified as superlatives, occur frequently in the Hebrew Bible: Song of songs (Cant 1:1) = the best [song, *shir*] of songs [*shirim*].[35] For the superlative sense to apply, however, there must be a construct particle: *shir **ha**-shirim*, literally "song of [all **the**] songs."[36] The sense is that this one song is the best in quality of all the songs.

This is clearly not the case of *habel habalim*, which is not in construct and therefore not a superlative (GKC 133). For this to be possible, the literal level must be skipped, if only because "the best of all breaths" makes no sense, and one is required to jump (prematurely) to interpretation: "utterly senseless or absurd" (Fox JPS 3). Literally our phrase means "[a] breath [of] breaths," where, rather than any kind of

signs of transcendence – just as breath is perhaps a sign of life, its revealed essence – see Chapter 5.

[33] As in v. 3:2. Fox interprets (as I do) that the reference is to death, either generally or to come, and gives it the usual Epicurean twist: because death is on the way, enjoy what you have now. What dies, however, is the breath, as per 12:7.

[34] CC, 231.

[35] Also: holy of holies (Exod) 26:33; 29:37. Heaven of heavens (Deut 10:14; 1 Kgs 8:27). Lord of lords (Deut 10:17; Ps 136:2,3).

[36] Possible exceptions: a servant of servants (Gen 9:25); chief of the chiefs (Num 3:32); *netsakh netsakhim* (Isa 34:10). Or, as in the phrase "holy of holies" (Exod 29:37, see Ibn Ezra), the meaning might be superior but not superlative (Sarna, JPS Commentary ad loc).

superlative quality, the stress may be on equal quantity, implying that all breaths are the same.[37]

Levinas's hyperbolic figure "metaphor of metaphors" reflects a more general approach to what he calls language's dynamism or transcendence at another level. For example, Levinas speaks of the soul of a soul, the earth of the earth.[38] He also makes a distinction between a place and a location in that space, perhaps mirroring the rabbinic explanation as to why God is called The Place: theologically God is not in a place, things are in God, *The Place* of everything and of other places.[39]

Perhaps even more pertinent to our subject is Levinas's distinction between the *Dit* and the *Dire*: whereas the former indicates what is actually said, the "pre-original" *Dire* is defined as "l'emphase" of signification, its expressive force of exaggeration, "la signifiance même de la signification," the very significance [the very fact of having meaning] of signification." Levinas refers this to the very function of metaphor in its etymological sense of taking beyond, thus "an excessive thinking that goes beyond language" but that finds meaning there. And in fact, and as Levinas never tires of repeating, transcendence is built in to language even in its common use. Speaking *(Dire) is the* very possibility of exegesis, of constantly undoing and going beyond the *Dit, what has already been said.*

What then is a "breath of breath," the saying that allows the said? Here we go beyond the manifestations and to the root reality. For if *hebel* is life itself, and a *hebel of hebels* is the very possibility of life; and if a metaphor is defined as a way of reaching beyond experience, then a metaphor of metaphors is the very possibility of transcendence. Our so-called hyperboles thus converge: Just as a metaphor of metaphors is the very possibility of thinking about God, *Habel habalim* is a working definition of God's work as the creator of life, already figured, perhaps, as the divine *ruakh* or spirit hovering over the face of the deep at the very start of creation (Gen 1:2).

---

[37] For this reason Ellermeier's suggestion (quoted in Fox, *A Time to Tear Down,* 162) of an iterative use is appropriate: "again and again Qohelet said *hebel.*" Indeed, this is *hebel*'s use as a refrain.

[38] "L'Ame de son âme" (CC, 179), "terre de la terre" (244ff). On hyperbole see Jacques Rolland, *Éthique comme philosophie première,* p. 17

[39] See also p. 229, n. 107.

PART FOUR

THE *HEBEL* OF WORDS

Bible – book; that is to say – nothing: words.

Levinas[1]

---

[1] "Bible – livre c'est-à-dire – rien: paroles." CC, 186. Montaigne begins his essay "On Vanity" with an allusion to the word-vanity as a vanity of vanities: "There is perhaps no more obvious vanity than to write of it so vainly" (trans. Donald Frame), 721.

10

Nothing Remains (1:3)? Nothing New (1:9; 12:8–12)?

Students are sitting in meditative positions at the foot of their guru.

A bearded young man raises his hand and asks: "Exactly what is this nothin' I've been hearing so much about?"[1]

Qohelet complains, it is often argued, that there is nothing new under the sun and that everything is circular, repetitious, and thus monotonous or even "absurd." But do critics themselves believe this as a sustainable argument based on real life? What would be, to take Qohelet's own example, if the sun just decided NOT to rise tomorrow, or chose to rise only randomly, say a few times a year? That would certainly relieve monotony, but would it also bring a sense of celebration? Is it possible to imagine the sunlight's daily appearance as boring, its perpetual renewal as monotonous? Would one not rather Goethe's sense of a primeval truth?

"Die Sonne tönt nach *alte* Weise."[2]

True, the sun rises only to set, because it has a distinct and limited goal, but it will renew the race tomorrow and tomorrow. And when the sun does indeed rise every morning, we may still, with Qohelet's help, recover the sense, a hint of eternity perhaps, that there is nothing new: Thank God! Or rather, that everything is new precisely because nothing is. It was clear to the ancients that lack of newness is an advantage.[3] The person who

---

[1] A cartoon in *The New Yorker*, July 31, 2000, p. 25 (by Cipress).

[2] "The sun intones, in its *ancient* way." Faust, part 1, v. 243.

[3] Michael V. Fox argues that "circularity is felt to show futility and thus absurdity" (*A Time to Tear Down and a Time to Build Up: a Rereading of Ecclesiastes* [Grand Rapids, MI: Eerdmans, 1999], 332). Lohfink argues, as I do, to the contrary, that "'new' here is a negative word. In a world of unending duration and return, what is 'new' could only be worse – but then there is no such thing" (*Qohelet*, 41). Emmanuel Levinas refers to the liturgical year

plays a Beethoven sonata forty times is nothing like the person who plays it only thirty-nine! This performance passes, but the tune remains, and the sense changes, deepens perhaps. And along with it, again in Thoreau's memorable phrase, the infinite expectation of the dawn.

In the dialectical world, of course, everything has a flip side. It is known that fools also believe in newness (1:9–10), but their belief is based on sheer inexperience and naïveté. Seneca again gets it right:

> If an evil has been pondered beforehand, the blow is gentle
> when it comes. To the fool, however, and to him who trusts in fortune, each
> event as it arrives "comes in a new and sudden form" (*Aeneid* 6:103ff), and a
> large part of the evil, to the inexperienced, consists in its novelty.[4]

From living we of course know and must abide the tawdriness of the everyday, which will not go away for our convenience. But must we settle?

The Great Inclusio *(1:2–3; 12:8–9)*

Concerning the brackets that encapsulate virtually the entire book, Michael V. Fox has observed that the opening *hebel* theme, repeated at the end, can be considered "the most memorable *inclusio* in the Bible."[5]

> Breath of breath said Qohelet
> All is breath.
>
> > Qoh 1:2; 12:8

Fox is surely correct but does not tell the whole story, since the repeated text makes two adjustments:

> breath of breath said Qohelet
>
> breath of breath.
>
> All is breath.
>
> What remains....? [The implied answer: "nothing."]
>
> > Qohelet 1:2–3

> Breath of breath said the Qohelet.[6]

and our awareness of its circularity as "anticipating eternity" and as "anterior in truth to historical time." *Difficile liberté* (Paris: Albin Michel, 1976), 280.

4   Seneca, Letter 76 (II:167).

5   Fox regularly renders *hebel* as "absurd" (*A Time to Tear Down*, 332). Throughout this study I discuss my preference for the literal sense of *hebel*, which is "breath."

6   Most commentaries simply skip over the definite article: *the* Qohelet. R. N. Whybray (*Ecclesiastes.* New Century Bible Commentary [Grand Rapids, MI: Eerdmans, 1989],

> All is breath.
> Yet *this* remains....
>   12:8–9

I offer three remarks. First of all, *inclusio* is not merely a stylistic device; its appearance, especially in such dramatic form – the great distance between its components – has a crucial effect of meaning, here the isolation or removal of the entire bracketed material from the general plot or argument. Since in this case we are referring to virtually the entire book, no better illustration could be found to Qohelet's dominant point that it (the entire book!) is *all hebel.*[7] In other words, what reflects the totality could only be a false infinity, a totality-book.

The second point to be noted is that the elements of the *inclusio* are extended by an appended notion of crucial import: the revision of the opening hypothesis (projected there as a negative) that nothing remains. At the end it now seems that, indeed, something *does* remain:

> "Breath of breath," said the Qohelet.
> "All is breath."
> Yet this remains:
>
>   12:8–9

Just a minute! Since the opening expressed the strong, totalizing hypothesis that *nothing* remains, what could it possibly mean to now assert the *more of...* nothing? Has it now become possible to contradict the ironic adage about "an absence that cannot be counted" (1:15)? As the students in the cartoon put it to their guru, "what exactly is this 'nothing' that everyone has been talking about?" Does it indeed leave traces? Traditional exegesis of the "Yet" does not do full justice to the introductory particle "*we-yoter she,*" glossed either as an additive conjunction ("Qohelet was not only a sage but also taught") or an adverb (furthermore). Both are consistent with the meaning, and the first has the advantage of stressing an important rabbinic pedagogical principle, that of a "high regard for a wise man who does not keep his wisdom to himself but instructs others."[8] The alternative ("moreover") seems closer to the point

---

169) refers back to 7:27, where the verbal feminine ending can plausibly be attached to the following subject, so that we now have not one but two designations of the author or character as *ha-Qohelet, the* Qohelet.

[7] For a somewhat parallel example, the bracketing of the first two chapters of the Book of Jonah makes the point of removing the entire first half of the book from the plot. See T. A. Perry, *Jonah's Arguments with God: The Honeymoon Is Over!* (Peabody, MA: Hendrickson, 2014), xxxiii–xxxv.

[8] Whybray, *Ecclesiastes,* 170.

(so Michael V. Fox), but the strong return of the argument to the very initial point of departure and after the extraordinary bracketing, must be rendered more forcefully in the translation, thus "Yet *this* remains."[9]

There is yet a third point. At the very start, the *hebel* argument is compounded by its verbal excess, the performative repetition of "breath of breaths." But at the book's other extremity the repetition is withheld. No surprise, then, that the loss of one of the "breath of breaths" is reinforced by the admission that, well, at least *something* does remain, even if that something is a *hebel,* a nothing. Well almost. It rather evokes, to use Jankélévitch's elegant expression, "la pudeur de la litote," *hebel* is not a nothing.

We now have a deeper view of the opening repetition of 1:2, especially in its linkage with 1:3: it is a *khidah* or riddle, given not as an explanation but rather, through its rhetoric of exaggeration and negation, as a challenge to be explored and solved. The breath repetition is no longer seen as a preacher's attempt at winning a point, nor the negative formulation ("what benefit?") as emphatic. If indeed universal transience means that no-thing remains (1:2) and there is thus no *yitron*; when indeed everything has been said (12:13) and we have reached the stage of disaster, what then? Instead of the obligatory negative answer "what remains?" "Nothing!" we are redirected to an exploration: "Yet *this* remains:"

Im-mortal Remains: The Great Void or the Nothing That Is

When everything has been said, what remains to be said is the disaster, the ruin of speech, the breakdown [enacted] through writing, the murmuring mumble: what remains without remains (the fragmentary).

Blanchot[10]

The end of the matter: When everything has been said.

Qoh 12:13

Before considering Qohelet's worldly gains – arising from his multiple forms of "gathering" – proposed by the book's ending (12:9–11), we must first attempt to conceptualize the residue of the omnipresent *hebel* theme itself, the sense that *hebel,* understood as no-thing, does not

---

9 This "*we-yoter*" is repeated at the start of 12:12, thus forming its own *inclusio,* this one being a parenthetical explanation of Qohelet's own personal contributions or spiritual remains left to the ongoing human community.

10 Maurice Blanchot, *L'Écriture du désastre* (Paris: Gallimard, 1980), 58.

means absolutely nothing.[11] Levinas's meditations offer an interesting approach:

> Let us imagine the return to nothingness of all things and persons. Shall we encounter pure nothingness? After the imaginary destruction of all things there remains not something but the fact that *there is.*[12]

Stated in Qohelet's terms, a paraphrase might well be: If everything is *hebel*, then *hebel* is everything. Levinas goes on to speak of a "residual existant," an "atmosphere of presence":

> Like a density of the void, like a murmur of silence. There is nothing, but there is some kind of being, like a field of forces … the existential density of the void itself, the void of every being, or the emptiness of the void.[13]

It is hard to speak of such things, which strike us either as warmed-over attempts to revive ontology or, in a more positive but mysterious vein yet, forms of prophetic consciousness. Witness how a "murmur of silence" evokes the "thin silent sound" present to Elijah (1 Kings 19:5).[14] Our author clings to the notion of personal experience, but of an experiential awareness of what lies *outside* our world of normal activity and beyond its categories.

The goal of language, even here viewed in its (but non-dialectical) negativity, is not at all a withdrawal into some mystical or other-worldly realm, some spiritual replacement. Of a piece with the truth criterion that is operative in the world of dialectic, its goal is to reach "a direct experience of existence as such."[15] Poulet continues:

> Consciousness for Blanchot, being irremediably separated from every object and even from itself, could never be anything else than the infinite separation from everything that is, if there were not in the very single fact of existence an irreducible witness of presence, an incessant affirmation

---

[11] The paradox of a "nothing that is" is the title of an interesting book by Robert Kaplan, *The Nothing that Is: A Natural History of Zero* (New York: Oxford University Press, 1999). Rami Shapiro's works are a good introduction to the Tao aspect of Qohelet. See his *The Way of Solomon: Finding Joy and Contentment in the Wisdom of Ecclesiastes* (San Francisco: Harper, 2000). Also *Ecclesiastes Annotated and Explained* (Woodstock, VT: Skylight Paths, 2011).

[12] Emmanuel Levinas, *Le Temps et l'autre* (Paris: Arthaud, 1947), 27.

[13] Emmanuel Levinas speaks of an "étant résiduel," "l'atmosphère de présence," "like a density of the void, like a murmur of silence. There is nothing, but there is some being, like a force-field … the existential density of the void itself, the void of each being, or the emptiness of the void (the *vide du vide*)." *L'Intrigue de l'infini* (Paris: Flammarion, 1994), 112.

[14] See my discussion in Perry, *Jonah's Arguments with God: The Honeymoon Is Over!*, 64–69.

[15] "Une expérience directe, fondamentale, positive, de 'l'existence comme telle'," Georges Poulet, *Critique*, "Maurice Blanchot, Critique et romancier," June 1966, 493. For the truth criterion, see the Introduction to this book.

which surges forth beneath all particular negations, a unique place, a point without extension or duration, where "there are no longer any contradictory terms," where the subjective and objective meet, thus an eminently privileged place, and the only one where the true can be located and our assent to that truth.[16]

This is the true function of language, its access to the indifferent *hebel* zone of the Outside.

Clearly there is a shift here from dialectical activities and their *hebel* removal to more passive and patient forms of awareness. Through a constant word- or conceptual play between *attente* and *attention* (waiting and attention), Blanchot describes a quality of reflective consciousness, one that focuses only on its own activity, what Simone Weil called "attention without object":

> When had he started waiting? From the time when he had freed himself for waiting by losing the desire for particular things, even the desire for the end of things.... Whatever the importance of the object of waiting, it is always infinitely exceeded by the movement of waiting itself. Waiting renders all equally important things equally de-void of value.[17]

There are two related results from such a refocusing. The first is an intuition of things in themselves, stripped of their daily configurations of usefulness and pursuit, those "things" that Francis Ponge attempted to describe. The second, Levinas's *il y a*, is the impersonal residue of being (the *en-soi*) that Sartre described in *La Nauseé*.[18]

Of even greater import for the wisdom project is, along with a withdrawal from things, a journey inward, toward both a keener sense of reflexive self-awareness and also a much broader projection of time, a time that spills over the normal confines of mortal life and toward the *'olam*, that Outside that Qohelet and Levinas call the Infinite (3:11). Whereas our accustomed point of reference – as in Qohelet's own context of worldly, dialectical wisdom – is what is termed this life (the "days of our years" under the sun, between birth and death), the sudden injection of infinity projects or jettisons the problem outside this time frame. Job, for example, undergoes a divine put-down by God's question: "Where were you when etc.?" (chs. 38–39). The presumed answer is "Nowhere, you weren't even born yet!" But the relevance question

---

[16] Ibid., 493–94.

[17] Maurice Blanchot, *L'Attente l'oubli* (Paris: Gallimard, 1962), 51. "Equally de-void of value" renders the French "également vaines." For Simone Weil, see p. 170, n. 35.

[18] For a probing discussion of Sartre's relation to Blanchot on this issue, see Poulet, "Maurice Blanchot, Critique et romancier," 494–97.

remains, and it is huge: God's question is all the more probing if it assumes that, indeed, Job *was* somewhere and indeed is somehow aware of it. Whence Blanchot's remark:

> Dying means: dead, you already are, in an immemorial past, of a death which was not yours, which you therefore neither knew nor lived.[19]

Having already died, in a mode beyond memory and experience, seems to tap into the negations by now familiar: Nothing? Nowhere? But no-thing is not nothing, no-where is not nowhere. Behind the ego "I" stands the *I*. Beyond the totality of time (*ha-kol*) stands, and in both directions, infinity, Pascal's "infini de grandeur et infini de petitesse." And if the infinity possibility expresses only an Outside, this indicates that the experiential "I" is now doubled as a "he": I-Qohelet is also He-Qohelet, and both may be operative at all times. As Arthur Rimbaud mysteriously put it, "Je est un autre."[20]

Mortal Remains: Writing Fragments, Collecting Students, Righting Proverbs (12:9–11)

> For true language to begin, it is necessary that the life that is to carry that language have experienced its own nothingness.
>
> Blanchot[21]

> There would still remain the never-resting mind,
>
> So that one would want to escape, come back
>
> To what had been so long composed.
>
> The imperfect is our paradise.
>
> Note that, in this bitterness, delight,
>
> Since the imperfect is so hot with us,
>
> Lies in flawed words and stubborn sounds.
>
> Wallace Stevens[22]

Something remains, then, in the world out there, beyond (but not under) the sun, surely beyond our powers of understanding. That domain or entity is designated as the deeds or works of God (*ma'aseh Elohim*), a

---

[19] Blanchot, *L'Écriture du désastre*, 108.

[20] "I is another." See T. A. Perry, *Wisdom in the Hebrew Bible: God's Twilight Zone* (Peabody, MA: Hendrickson, 2014), 84, 90.

[21] Blanchot, 327; quoted in Poulet, *Critique*, June 1966, 437.

[22] "The Poems of Our Climate," in *The Collected Poems of Wallace Stevens* (New York: Alfred A. Knopf, 1954, 1982), p. 194.

pervasive topic from the start to finish, as we shall see in Chapters 11 and 12. We apprehend – but not in any traditional sense – that something exceeds the human totality, through no fault or input from our toil, and this Outside is also, in its third and ultimate meaning, a *hebel*, an *almost nothing*.

We have seen how Qohelet's philosophical meditations are based on and doubled by a literary plot that is an autobiographical account of a radical change of life, a conversion of sorts:

> I am Qohelet. I was king...
>
> (1:12)

Qohelet's demise from kingship, the fragmentation of an existence signaled by the cumulative nausea of *hebel*, finds its expression and its required discourse in the literary fragments that he will set about co(he)llecting. Stated differently, a king – representing the height of worldly power – is no longer king. Rather than a bit of history (can one retire from being king?), these words stress the project of a person who has passed from a man of power to one of words.[23] And, in fact, it is precisely his vain or empty or *hebel* words that best describe his decision to turn from power.[24] Of all *hebel* statements the most assertive is the opening repetition, now seen not only as a performative[25] and thus the ultimate of pessimistic valuations. For *hebel* now reveals a further ambivalence, it signals the case of "repetition as non-power,"[26] indeed as a "guarantee that forbids a man of words from becoming a man of power."[27] What possibilities could then emerge, once this transformation becomes socialized, indeed the foundation stone of a new society? Michael V. Fox formulated it in this way:

> The Rabbis called Torah study the "foundation of the world," crucial to the cosmic economy. In Pharisaic and rabbinic Judaism, revelation is no longer direct or via prophecy but must be mediated through Torah. But Torah itself must be mediated exegetically, through scholars who are called "the wise" or "students of the wise" in rabbinic usage. Book-learning (which is

---

[23] Blanchot states the reverse; see n. 325. A touching biblical parallel is King Saul's episodic departure from kingship to the practice of prophecy. See T. A. Perry, *Wisdom in the Hebrew Bible*, 125–56.

[24] See Blanchot, *L'Écriture du désastre*, 20–21.

[25] See Chapter 2.

[26] "La répétition comme non-pouvoir," *L'Écriture du désastre*, 20.

[27] Ibid., 22: "La garantie qui interdit à l'homme de parole de devenir homme de pouvoir."

included in the Hebrew concept of "wisdom") thus becomes an intrinsically religious virtue and duty, whose fulfillment is a realization of a transcendent potential.[28]

Qohelet as a Foundational Myth

Are the true books nothing but books? Aren't they also the embers that sleep under the ashes, like the words of the Sages, according to Rabbi Eliezer? In this way the flame traverses history without being consumed in it. But truth illumines the one who revives with his breath (*souffle*) the sleeping flame. More or less. It is a question of breath. To admit the action of literature on humans, that is perhaps the ultimate wisdom of the West in which the people of the Bible will recognize itself. It was from an old lost book recovered by his clerks that King Osias set up a kingdom. It is this figure of life that gives itself up to the mastery [*emprise*] of texts.

Levinas[29]

This would indeed be breathing life into old bones, perhaps as generational recovery and renewal. The Sages of Israel knew such an explosive reading of Qohelet's *hebel*:

There is nothing stronger than the *hebel*-breath of children studying Torah.[30]

Such cultural recovery was in fact experienced by the West. Levinas concludes: "[Such is] the myth of our Europe descended from an analogous discovery that is called the Renaissance." The work's conclusion carries Qohelet's personal transformation to social levels, serving as a foundational myth for the Wisdom movement itself. Further, it may be seen as a meta-wisdom text as well, arguing not only the transfer from power to discourse, but also modeling how wisdom discourse is supposed to work in a world addicted to power.

The question then becomes: How can one find a way to live in a world known to be transient and based on power, indeed violence? The collector (of things) has now become a member of a society of gatherers: *ba'alei 'asupot*, masters of collections. They collect anecdotal notations (such as the so-called autobiography), not solid conclusions

---

[28] Michael V. Fox, *Proverbs 1–9: A Commentary.* http://www.bibleinterp.com/articles/proverbs.htm

[29] Levinas, *Difficile liberté*, 81–82. For King Josias (640–10 BCE), see 2 Kgs 22. The reference is to an old copy, recently recovered, of the Torah. In his translation Sean Hand understands and translates Levinas's Sages as Prophets (*Difficult Freedom*, 53).

[30] BT Shabbat 119.

or the closures of knowledge and grandiose concepts (e.g., the All). Rather, traces, literary fragments, gestures: experiences, but ones that wish to move forward and thus serve as "experiments" as well: experiments in living, pursuing knowledge of how to *live* in a human sense. Collages. A writer who says "I" is standing outside herself as a "she" and thus already on a path of turning around and starting over. An apt parallel might be Noah emerging from the ark, *dum conderet urbem*,[31] escaping with mere shards of a previous existence, starting from scratch and patiently putting the pieces (fragments) together into the creation of a new community. Noah building the ark of salvation, from which will emerge what *remains* of a previous existence and now constitutes the raw materials of this new creation: the *debarim*, inchoate things that emerge from the ark, words that rename and goad[32] to greater wisdom, nails that hammer them together into a different collage. At the end of the book we can now return to its beginning with a new understanding of the author's wanderings and trials and mistakes and tribulations and vanity complaints. So too Job, taken by God back to the universe's very origins so that he can imagine the uncharted mysteries and danger and excitement of the creative enterprise. And every day the one Pastor ushers in a new creature (ostrich, leviathan), all strange things of speech over which to be puzzled and challenged to relocate in a context of teeming void and new meanings. For God does not annihilate Job from the whirlwind. Rather, He takes him to Calvino's moon, where Job can again see himself as the original dust and ashes from which all new creation emerges.[33] Like Qohelet's sun, Job is reabsorbed into the night, only to shine forth again and again on the next day. And, indeed, his new daughters are even prettier than the former ones.

Job and Qohelet: God's put-down of Job at the end is like a Qohelet meditation on what Neher called "the MYSTERY of the world's suffering."[34] Its perspective is from a point "out of the box," thus accessible only

---

[31] "Until he should found a city," Virgil's Aeneid, Book 1, describing Aeneas' departure after the fall of Troy and referring to the future founding of Rome.

[32] "Goad," *darbon* (12:11), is a possible pun on *dabar*, "words."

[33] Lyn M. Bechtel calls death in the Genesis depiction a "return to an original state, a return to the earth, a return to the source of new life," "Rethinking the Interpretation of Genesis 2.4B-3.24," in *A Feminist Companion to Genesis*, ed. Athalya Brenner (Sheffield: Sheffield Academic Press, 1993), 100. For Calvino's moon see the Introduction to this book.

[34] See the Introduction.

in fragmented outline, which by the end of the dialogues the Book of Job has provided. But its perspective from death's threshold offers intriguing parallels with Qohelet's concluding "Elegy on Death and Dying" (Qoh 12:1–8), which focuses, rather than on death, on the aging process that has to be managed at whatever age and that involves constant withdrawal from life as "normally" lived and stripped to the essentials. In this regard Levinas manages to extract extraordinary benefits from the atrocious captivity of internment:

> As paradoxical as it might seem, [the prisoners] experienced, in the enclosed spread of the camps, a wider amplitude of life and, under the watchful eye of the guards, an unsuspected liberty... We had [few] possessions, but property was not our master, was no longer sacred... We learned the difference between having and being. We learned how little space and how few things are needed to live. We learned freedom.
>
> These were the true experiences of captivity: suffering, despair, mourning, to be sure. But above all this, a new rhythm of life. We had set our feet on another planet, breathing an atmosphere of unknown composition and handling a material that no longer had weight.[35]

To be sure, such conditions uncover the macabre of the human body, involve suffering and a death, which may even be anonymous, the dissolution/resolution of human duality into dust and spirit,[36] but perhaps also the locus of communal ingathering and assistance.

The comparison between the conclusions of Job and Qohelet puts into high relief that virtue so celebrated: Job's patience. As traditionally understood, Job's motto focuses on acceptance: "God has given and God has taken," and so forth. The dialogues certainly document his extreme suffering, but describing his complaints and diatribes pushes the boundaries of what we would call patience, for what else could he do (except commit suicide, I suppose)? Job's embrace of true patience, however, is in both his *silent* acceptance of God's creation as being beyond his comprehension (Job 42:1–6), and also his ensuing decision to live out his life within those borders. So too Qohelet – demoted from power and influence, aware of the purely contingent nature of everything including wisdom itself and the burdens of study and writing many

---

[35] CC, 202–03.

[36] For an upbeat exegesis of Qohelet's "Elegy" on death and dying, see Perry, *Wisdom in the Hebrew Bible: God's Twilight Zone*, 125–56. Also Harold Fisch, *Poetry with a Purpose* (Bloomington: Indiana University Press, 1990), 177–78.

books (1:18; 12:12), who nevertheless modestly and vigorously puts his energies to the task:

> He listened[37] and pondered,[38] he composed [alt: righted] many proverbs. Qohelet sought to discover pleasing words, recorded straight talk, words of truth.
>
> 12:9–10

But only empty words upon words, and "as long as there is ink and paper in the world," as Montaigne put it with deep irony, playfully but patiently.[39]

The inspection and experience of *hebel* has now run its course and its hypothesis confirmed. What remains is the recording of these experiences as, yes, positive, and this, despite Montaigne's ironic remark that writing about breath is itself breath. But surely at another level, since he adds:

> What the Divinity has so divinely expressed to us about it [i.e., in Qohelet 1:2] ought to be carefully and continually meditated by people of understanding.[40]

That mere, weak words can prove capable of keeping power at a distance is one of wisdom's deepest paradoxes. To speak of the power of words would seem contrary to Qohelet's intentions, although worthy of wisdom's devices at a dialectical level. For we would then have a case of "power vs. weakness," with the typical reversal wherein "(worldly) power is weak, and word-y weakness is strong." It seems more likely, however, that in Qohelet's thinking "weakness" is not to be seen as power's dialectical opposite but rather beyond both, as resident in the Outside, as the equivalent of vulnerability and thinking. But thinking about what? About further *words*?

---

[37] *'Izzen*, related to the ear. This could have been the habitual pose of the (now deposed) king/judge, or the submissive critical listening of the scholar critic. This notion measures the distance between the *roi/savant* Solomon of 1 Kings and his demoted Qohelet replacement, thus a possible parallel with Foucault's reading of Oedipus, who no longer has that "royal knowledge … capable of resolving enigmas and saving cities without help from anyone." All his knowledge was only a *savoir excessif*. See Michel Foucault, *Leçons sur la volonté de savoir: Cours au Collège de France, 1970–71* (Paris: Gallimard/Seuil, 2011), 250.

[38] This word is used of in-depth inquiry of things hidden (Deut 13:15), and in the rabbinic period was characteristic of the judge who interrogates witnesses. See *Ethics of the Fathers* 1:9: "Be very diligent in questioning witnesses."

[39] Michel de Montaigne, Essais III: 9, "De la Vanité,"start (Paris: PUF, 1965), 945.

[40] Montaigne, *Les Essais*, 945 (III:9).

Yes, but the words of *sages*. We return to a verbal ambivalence central to the wisdom tradition and in need of further meditation: *debarim*, words but also things, or perhaps: power-things and word-things. Such a state of affairs could lead to misunderstanding, not unlike the one Paulhan experienced in his efforts to crack the secret of proverbs:

I had taken for words what the Malgaches understood as things.[41]

Paulhan attempts to clarify:

Certain words must also be considered as things. And that is not all: they are also singular things which it is urgent to speak, and to speak as precisely as possible: so that, concerning these things or these words, an entire part of language finds itself at work establishing that speech is possible.

Jean Paulhan[42]

This ends up, for Qohelet, being the burden of wisdom: collecting and writing and righting its word-things, thus, perhaps, in Mallarmé's sense, giving a purer sense to the words of the human tribe.

[41] Jean Paulhan, *L'Expérience du proverbe* (Paris: L'Echoppe, 1993), 60.
[42] Ibid., 58.

PART FIVE

THEOLOGICAL CONCLUSIONS

The next two chapters focus mainly on God in Qohelet, or, more precisely, how Qohelet can serve as a prolegomenon to modern reflections on the divine. The Dutch theologian and writer Klaas Smelik has framed the problem nicely:

> The book [Qohelet] has a very significant message for the world. It prevents us from using Biblical prophecy as a kind of fortune telling. It prevents us from a too-easy explanation of the riddles of our life in the light of the Bible. Reading Qohelet makes it clear to us how limited our knowledge of God still is – notwithstanding the work of 50 generations of theologians and all the libraries they have filled.[1]

---

[1] Klaas Smelik, "God in the Book of Qoheleth," in *The Language of Qohelet in Its Context: Essays in Honour of Prof. A. Schoors on the Occasion of His Seventieth Birthday*, ed. A. Berlejung and P. Van Hecke (Leuven: Peeters, 2007), 177–81 at 180–81.

11

Qohelet's Very Final Words

A Judging God, or Judging God? (12:13–14)

The end of the matter; all has been heard.
Fear God and keep his commandments, for that is the whole duty of everyone.
For God will bring every deed unto judgment, including every secret thing,
whether good or evil.

12:13–14, NRSV Translation[1]

Judging God: a favorite pastime, to be sure. For when "bad things happen to good people" – as well as, for some at least, when good things happen to bad people – Whom else can we blame? The urge to do so is clearly put forth in the Book of Job, and most provocatively, for there God not only allows his advisor Satan to inflict pain upon a perfectly righteous person but even assists in the operation. As readers we share both Job's pain and his sense of injustice; but, for all that, should we blame God? The Book of Qohelet allows such reactive judgments to arise, and from the very start:

> I set my mind, through wisdom, to investigate and explore all the things that happen under the heavens: it is an evil business that God has given to humans to be busied with.[2]

1:13

[1] As against the NRSV and similar versions, I shall propose the following reading of Qohelet's two final verses:

The end of the matter, when all is said and done: Fear God but also keep His commandments, for that is the whole [duty] of man. For [otherwise] *he [i.e., man] will bring all of God's works to judgment,* whether it be good or whether it be evil.

12:13–14

[2] "To be busied with" is a usual translation of *la'anot b-.* I distance myself from this understanding at the end of this chapter.

141

The clear reading of this sweeping statement is that God is at the origin
of the bad things that happen in this world. Some exegetes have clev-
erly explained the "it" ("it" is an evil business) as referring not to God's
doing but rather to the human attempt at wisdom itself.[3] This perception is correct but premature in that it anticipates a major argument
that requires the entire book to establish. We thus, in the course of reading, indulge the theory of God's plot upon mankind, while retaining
the alternate theory of human complicity embedded in the ambivalent
"it." For while the Book of Qohelet will allow pained reactions against
the Creator-God to arise, and most notably in the mouth of Qohelet
himself in his pre-confessional phase, it will not – again like the Book
of Job – allow them to prevail as attitudes. The proof is in the text's very
final words, which summarize and stress a sustained argument to the
contrary.

Qohelet's closing verses, as Roland Murphy has pointed out, have
"exercised great influence in the history of the exegesis of Ecclesiastes."[4]
As interpreted by all major commentaries and translations, 12:14
advances the notion of a judging God, a notion we wish to call into question. It must be granted that the standard interpretation is not without
its difficulties, even at the grammatical level.[5] It is especially on interpretative grounds, however, that such a reading must be challenged.

For one thing, the thought had already been expressed, to be repeated
and in virtually the same language:

> God will judge the righteous and the wicked…,
> and He will bring judgment upon every deed.…

3:17

And, more proximately:

> Follow the desires of your heart and the wishes of your eyes. And know that
> for all these things God will call you to justice.

11:9

Moreover, the radical message of this earlier text – that God will visit
his judgment upon us *not* for following heart and eyes but rather for

---

3 See, for example, R. N. Whybray, *Ecclesiastes.* New Century Bible Commentary (Grand
Rapids, MI: Eerdmans, 1989), 49.
4 Roland E. Murphy, *Ecclesiastes* (WBC 23A; Dallas: Word Books, 1992), 127.
5 Notably the absence of the definite article *ha-* after the direct object particle *'et*; this is
discussed further in this chapter.

denying them their pleasures! – is not quite in sync with the concluding verse as currently interpreted, as Murphy was quick to point out:

> The emphasis on divine judgment is not strictly contradictory to Qoheleth's views, but it is hardly possible that he would have expressed himself in this way. He recognized God as judge but nowhere does he attempt to explain this, much less to motivate human action on the basis of divine judgment.[6]

For his part, James Crenshaw does hold to such a strict contradiction ("totally alien to Qohelet's thinking"), since, in his view, Qohelet finds God remiss in the matter of reward and punishment.[7] Both critics agree, however, on the strange location of this notion at the book's very conclusion.

Murphy's analysis continues by noting that for Qohelet "the judgment of God is a total mystery," as perhaps suggested in the phrase "all that is hidden." He goes on to observe that "the word for every 'deed' is *ma'aseh*, which is used in the book to indicate the inscrutable *divine* action."[8] This emphasis is crucial to our reassessment:

> I have seen the task which God has given to the sons of men to be exercised with. He has made everything beautiful in its time [alt: in His time].[9] He has also given eternity in their hearts; except that it is not given to humans to understand,[10] from beginning to end, the *work that God has made.*

> 3:10–11

> Consider *God's works*: for who can make straight what he has made crooked. If your fortune is good, enjoy it! And when it is bad, consider [this]: God has made the one as well as the other, so that humans might not find out (i.e., understand)[11] anything of His motives.

> 7:13–14

---

[6] Murphy, *Ecclesiastes*, 126. Thomas Krüger (*Qoheleth, A Commentary* [Minneapolis: Fortress Press, 2004], 213–14) also questions the usual opinion that 12:14 refers to God's eschatological judgment and instead refocuses – as we do here – on the "accidents and 'strokes of fate' to which life subjects a person." He goes on to speculate, citing 9:1, that it is human fear (i.e., awe) of God expressed in the preceding verse (12:13) that motivates the usual thesis of God's forthcoming judgment. However, the argument that divine judgments are hidden from human beings, as in 9:1 cited by Krüger, argues more forcefully for the necessity for *humans* to suspend their judgment of God, as we argue here.

[7] James L. Crenshaw, *Ecclesiastes: A Commentary* (OTL, Philadelphia: Westminster, 1987), 192.

[8] Murphy, *Ecclesiastes*, 126, italics added.

[9] For an explanation of this possible ambivalence, see p. 147, n. 17.

[10] For *matsa'* meaning "to understand" see 7:24: "What is deep who can understand (*matsa'*)," as well as in the two following passages (7:14; 8:17). See also Appendix 5, "'Finding' a Good Woman."

[11] See the previous note.

I considered all of *God's works*. But a [mere] human cannot understand all the works that are done under the sun. And no matter how much a human labors to seek it out, s/he will not be able to find it out. And even if the sage says that he knows it, he will be unable to understand.

8:17

Just as you do not know the ways of the wind, like the powers hidden in the pregnant womb you cannot know *the works of God*, who makes everything.

11:5

Michael V. Fox perceptively extends the emphasis to include Qohelet's programmatic focus at the very start:[12]

> I set my mind to investigate and explore *all the things that happen under the heavens… that God has given to men* to wrangle over. I saw *all the deeds [those of God] that are done under the sun.* Look they are all breath and chasing after the wind.

1:13–14

If, then, "all the deeds/works that happen" in this world focus on divine rather than human agency, the appearance of this notion in the very final words is hardly surprising. For, in addition to its cumulative focus throughout the text, the ending reference reaches back to the very start, forming an *inclusio* that unifies Qohelet's entire enterprise.

It is now possible to read our text according to its plain grammar, producing an emphasis quite different from that usually put forth:[13]

> Now fear God and keep His commandments. For this is man's usual pursuit: namely, to pass judgment upon *every one of God's deeds*, even all the hidden ones,[14] whether it be good or whether it be evil.

12:13–14

Such a refocusing now allows a more satisfactory resolution of the grammatical problem of *'et kol ma'aseh ha-'elohim"* by positioning *ma'aseh* in construct with *'elohim* and thus part of the direct object.[15] What then is

---

[12] Michael V. Fox, *Qohelet and His Contradictions* (Sheffield: Almond, 1989), 175.

[13] I retain the reading made earlier in my *Dialogues with Koheleth: The Book of Ecclesiastes: Translation and Commentary* (University Park: Penn State Press, 1993), 171.

[14] Norbert Lohfink, *Qoheleth: A Continental Commentary* (Minneapolis: Fortress, 2003), 144, observes that this notation "seizes on an important aspect of Qoheleth's teaching: that we humans do not see to the bottom of things." Indeed, as Qohelet argues, it is precisely because the bottom of things is hidden from humans that we should not venture to see. See also 3:11; 9:1.

[15] This would require repointing the final syllable of *ma'aseh* from *segol* to *tsere*, as H. L. Ginsberg offers, but without explaining his hypothesis (*Koheleth* [Tel Aviv-Jerusalem: Newman, 1961], 136 [Hebrew]).

the subject of the verbal expression "to pass judgment?" The only available and more likely one, the man (*ha-'adam*) at the end of the previous verse. This also averts the difficult absence of the definite article *ha-ma'aseh*, usually required after the particle *'et*.

> *Whether it be good or whether it be evil.*

These very final words of the Book of Qohelet are rarely commented upon or even noticed. From the point of view of traditional readings this neglect is reasonable, since the need to insist on God's attention to both good and bad actions seems trite at this juncture. Yet, as their concluding position suggests, they serve to reinforce one of the book's most crucial arguments. Their only duplicate in Tanakh points in an important direction:

> *Whether it be good or whether it be evil,* we will obey the voice of the Lord our God... That it may be well with us, when we obey the voice of the Lord our God.
>
> Jer 42:6

Obedient acceptance is the recommended path to follow, and it must be *non-judgmental*, at the levels of both attitude (fearing God) and performance (keeping His commandments). Whether God's actions *seem* to us good or not, consent and obedience and trust are required:

> He is the Lord. May He do what is good in *His* eyes!
>
> 1 Sam 3:18

Since Eli had just received the worst possible news, one can hear the echo of Qohelet's conclusion:

> *Whether for good or for evil.*

It may even be that this closing phrase is meant to evoke that merism through which human life and maturation is symbolized at the very start of human existence on earth: the tree of the knowledge of good and evil. The message: while the knowledge of good and evil is requisite for our total existence as creatures "under the sun," such knowledge cannot have as their object a God who is beyond both good and evil and thus beyond our earth-bound judgments as creatures. In our revised reading, "what this verse pronounces is confidence in the ultimate justice of God with regard to every human endeavour."[16] Although Ogden uses this

---

[16] Graham Ogden, *Qoheleth* (Sheffield: JSOT Press, 1987), 212.

summation to bolster the traditional view, it in fact is better used for the latter, which argues for justice rather than (final) judgment, and trusting confidence rather than fear. Indeed, such trust has more kinship with love, but it is hardly a motivating factor of human behavior.

In sum, on the basis of these considerations I propose the following revised reading:

> The end of the matter, when all is said and done:
> Fear God and keep His commandments, for that is the whole [duty] of man.
> For [otherwise] he [i.e., man] will bring all of God's works to judgment,
> Whether it be good or whether it be evil.

Qohelet's concept of not criticizing God receives further elaboration in the extended Catalog of the Times (3:1–11), which is structured as an elaborate chiasm (ABBA):

a1) To the ALL there is a *zeman* (3:1a)

b1) and "all" things/desires (desirable or undesirable things) under the heavens (i.e., in their human totality) have their *'et* or appropriate time (3:1b)

We normally experience b) piecemeal. This is the realm of good and bad, either morally or what is "good" or "bad" for me (my human *khepets*, the things that I desire) at this particular time

b2) continues the subject of b1) with the Catalog of the Times (3:2–8)

a2) returns to the opening topic: the "All" (3:11a)

Just as each individual desire has its time (*'et*), so too does the All have its own time (*zeman*);

> God has made everything beautiful in its time. He has also placed eternity
> in their minds, except that the human being will not be able to grasp, from
> start to finish, all the things that God has made.
>
> Qoh 3:11; also 8:17

This complex summarizing verse refers to not one but two interconnected levels or perspectives. The first is from within the dialectic, under the sun. It means that even within this totality realm everything cannot be known. Obviously this is not to discourage empiricists and rational investigation from extending the limits of knowledge, but it is also a disclaimer from any failures to reach absolute knowledge by such results. For experiments and experiences are only that, always tentative and open to further discovery and revision. And what guarantees both the value and the limitations of such an approach is the intuition of endless openness (infinity, *'olam*), the intrinsic sense we have of being able to stand outside because there is an outside: unknown but present. This suggests that any totality is infinitely expandable and thus, always and as such, a fiction. That is to say, a scientific hypothesis only.

Note that, in this reading, an alternate reference becomes possible:

He has made the All beautiful in its / His time.[17]

Qoh 3:11

Reading the reference as His (God's) time in fact solves the difficulty of ascribing an *'et* (restricted to the human realm "under the heavens") to the "All," which above (3:1a) has only a *zeman*! The answer is that, like humans, God too has, from the point of view of His own desire or *khepets*, an *'et* for His creation of the All. Since God's All-creation refers to both under the heavens and also beyond, its evaluation is more general: *yapeh*, beautiful. Like esthetic objects, this broader reality can be felt but not grasped as a totality and totally understood by humans.

[17] For similar wisdom ambivalences on reading both God and something else, see T. A. Perry, *Wisdom in the Hebrew Bible: God's Twilight Zone* (Peabody, MA: Hendrickson, 2014), 116–17.

12

Qohelet's Very First Words

Testifying against God and His "Evil" (1:13)

O my people, what wrong have I done to you?
What hardship have I caused you?
Testify against me!

Mica 6:3

One of the most perplexing verses in the Book of Qohelet is the author/
character's autobiographical statement of purpose at the very outset of his
first-person discourse, immediately following upon his self-presentation
("I, Qohelet, was king") (1:12):

> I applied my mind to all that is done under the heavens:
> it is an unhappy business that God has given to human beings to be
> busy with.

1:13, as per NRSV

Lohfink, always sensitive to undercurrents in the text, interprets the
verse as presenting, rather than an assertion concerning God's gover-
nance of things, a rejected possibility: "Qohelet has a thesis in mind with
which he disputes."[1] Thus,

> to examine and to explore… *whether* all that is carried out under the heavens
> is really a bad business.

Judging only from the point of view of syntax, Krüger finds this reading
to be "rather improbable."[2] It is improbable, to be sure, but not impossible. And, as we shall see from the content and the vocabulary, it is by far
the most correct orientation of this verse.

---

[1] Norbert Lohfink, *Qoheleth: A Continental Commentary* (Minneapolis: Fortress, 2003), 47.
[2] Krüger, 56.

Lohfink's observations deserve to be quoted *in extenso*, especially for the notation that, at the programmatic start of his text, Qohelet is already introducing "the discourse about God":[3]

> What is new is that here ... the sphere of "god" (*'elohim*) is introduced. That happens here for the first time in the book, and not yet as a formulation of Qohelet himself. Because of the passive formulation "all that is carried out under the heavens," the original readers could come to the question whether human enterprise, which was clearly meant, was not to be understood at the same time as something with which God too was involved. It may not be by accident that Qoheleth does not say "under the sun" here, but rather "under the heavens." He is already drawing the reader toward God, about whom the text will immediately speak. See 5:1: "God is in heaven, and you are on the earth."

Recall that the very last verse of the Book of Qohelet (12:14) has the same focus. Now if, as seen in the preceding chapter, Qohelet's concluding words argued not God's active judgment against humans, as traditionally interpreted, but rather the reverse, the human propensity to judge God, one is moved to ask whether the broader *inclusio* of God-discourse does not also argue the same. Such a rereading would refocus the message of the entire book.

Here is my proposed reading, followed by its exegesis and rationale:

> I set my mind to investigate and explore all that is done under the heavens: [to see whether] it is an "evil" business that God has given to human beings so that they may bring charges against Him.

> 1:13

investigate, *drsh*, to inquire of God, "often appears in a liturgical context for seeking the divine will or presence."[4] The word often has a legal context, directed either at the accused or at the witnesses who testify in support or refutation of the charges.

explore, *tur*, famously evokes the Israelites' confrontation with God concerning the divine plan to send them into the land. They want to test and see whether the divine plan was a good or a bad one. They did this by sending spies. Thus, perhaps, "spy out."

all that is done under the heavens, *ma'aseh*, as referring to God's actions.[5] If so, its opening position forms a nice conceptual *inclusio* with Qohelet's

---

[3] Lohfink, *Qoheleth: A Continental Commentary*, 47.
[4] James L. Crenshaw, *Ecclesiastes: A Commentary* (OTL, Philadelphia: Westminster, 1987), 72.
[5] See p. 143, n. 8.

very final words, the focus of which was on the "deeds of God" (12:14) as put forth above. Does this totalizing focus ("*all* that is done") also include the notion that in both cases (thus in the entire enclosed text) the issue is one of judging God?

It is an "evil"business, *It* refers both to "all that happens in this world, God's doing," and also to the (human) desire and power to investigate those charges, so as to clear or, preferably, impugn God's purposes.

The word "evil" is quotational here, designating not an absolute value but rather one's opinion or judgment of what befits him or her, as in 12:1: "of which one would say."[6] Qohelet's most general term for this is *khepets*, the varying human motivations that all have their own time or *'et*: "for each and every desire there is a time" (3:1). A parallel case can be seen in the Book of Jonah. Observing that the word evil (*ra'*) occurs frequently in Jonah, Daniel Sibony continues:

> Jonas' trajectory is beyond good and evil because the two terms – good and evil – both necessary, pass easily from one to the other. Good and evil communicate by unexpected or unpredictable returns. In this area of "in-between" goods and evils are intertwined.[7]

that God has given cf. 3:10 There may be a projected touch of irony in pointing to God's "gifts." 1:13 is repeated in 3:10, in a context that evokes, as a response, a favorable judgment concerning God, who makes everything *yapeh*, perfect in its/His time.

to testify against Him *la'anot bo,* The most curious aspect of this minor exegetical drama may well be the universal misinterpretation of the Hebrew expression. Someone long ago observed that the verb *'anah* has several meanings, constituting a grab bag of possibilities, none of which really fits our text. What has been overlooked is that this verb can occur with the preposition *b–*, yielding an expression that occurs no less than seventeen times in the Hebrew Bible, all with the same meaning, and this is the key to understanding this verse, one that has escaped the inspection of all major commentaries. The expression *'anah b–* means, often in a legal context: to bring charges of wrongdoing against someone so that one can be cleared of guilt, testifying in an attempt to prove someone's

---

6 See T. A. Perry, *Wisdom in the Hebrew Bible: God's Twilight Zone* (Peabody, MA: Hendrickson, 2014), 135; also Lohfink, *Qoheleth*, 57. The Stoics referred to such particular judgments or opinions as *dogmata* (Epictetus, *Encheiridion* #5). For further discussion see Appendix 3, "Quotationals."

7 Daniel Sibony, *Lectures bibliques* (Paris: Odile Jacob, 2006), 285.

guilt (or innocence). Here are the major texts, the first of which sets the tone of the Qohelet discussion, since God himself is the defender against the charges of the people:

> "O my people, what wrong have I done to you?
> What hardship have I caused you?
> Testify against me [*'aneh bi*]!"
>
> Mica 6:3

The legal context is common:

> If a false witness rise up against any person, to testify against him [*la'anot bo*] that which is wrong....
>
> Deut 19:16

The judge is understood, often explicitly, to be God, as when Samuel wants to clear his name of false suspicions and possibly accusations:

> Here I am: bring your charges against me [*'anu bi*] in the presence of the Lord and his anointed: whose ox have I taken...?
>
> 1 Sam 12:3

However, suspicions can be held even against the ultimate judge. In the Book of Ruth, Naomi expresses her misfortune as a complaint against God:

> The Almighty has dealt very bitterly with me ... the Lord has testified against me [*'anah bi*], and the Almighty has brought evil [*hera'*] upon me.
>
> Ruth 1:20–21

As in Qohelet, this "evil" (*ra'*), momentarily felt and certainly real enough, will, from a later perspective, actually be the condition of her complete restoral, thus not really evil, except quotationally.

Job complains of his wretched physical state in these words:

> "You have shriveled me; My gauntness serves as a witness, And testifies against me [*be-panai ya'aneh*]."
>
> Job 16:8, JPS

Although the context leaves no doubt that it is God himself who is pulling the strings and thus, in Job's eyes, responsible for the evil brought upon him, the view that the witness against him is actually his own gauntness somewhat diverts the complaint against God while affirming it.

What has misled critics – aside from a brief suspension of dictionary skills – is the pronominal reference at the end of the verse. Although all critics attach *bo* – "to it" – to the preceding "unhappy business," its more proximate and correct antecedent is Elohim, "to or against Him," yielding a neat chiastic structure:

God has given to / **humans** // so that **they** / may testify against **Him**.

The question as to why would God make "evil" available to humans is of course *the* question that the Bible and probably most humans try to come to grips with. Qohelet's contribution is to formulate and perspectivise the question as a totality within an infinity (recalling the title of Levinas's major work): Humans cannot understand God's deeds in their entirety. Secondly, even within the totality (e.g., 3:1–8) something seen as "good" or "bad" today may tomorrow be just the reverse. That's the way the world (under the heavens) spins, and God's actions are exempt from such evaluations, seen as good or evil only from human perspectives, but in themselves, and in their time, *yapeh*, perfect.

Of course, traditionalists may still read the antecedent of *bo* as "man" rather than God, and that is not only possible but perhaps intended as well, if guided by the principle of both/and rather than either/or:

That He/he might bring charges against him/Him.

Such double or, as I have argued throughout, doublet reading is quite common in poetic texts such as Psalms.[8] For both possibilities, however, usual readings of *'anah* must yield to its true meaning here, as attached to the preposition: *'anah b-*, "to testify against." As the cited examples show, in the Hebrew Bible humans do in fact bring the Holy One to court, as well as the other way around.

Rashbam's comment on this theme in 3:14 favors our reading and, moreover, can serve both as a résumé of our thesis and a transition to the subject of fear in the previous verse (12:13):

[I know that] *whatever He does*: "All the times are in the power of the Holy One Blessed be He."

and God has made [that He should be feared] : "God has made the good times and the bad times in order that humans should fear Him and repent. For they will say: 'Whatever already existed in former days, namely that times were alternating, that same behavior and pattern exists now also, to this very day.' "[9]

---

8 See Perry, *Wisdom in the Hebrew Bible*, 118–21.

9 Rashbam (Samuel ben Meir, 1085–ca. 1158). See Sara Japhet and Robert B. Salters, *The Commentary of R. Samuel Ben Meir Rashbam on Qoheleth* (Jerusalem: Magnes, 1985), 117.

Clearly, the focus is not on God's judgment of humans but rather on human reaction to the times, both good and bad, as in the hands of God and therefore to be accepted as such and negative judgments toward God to be either removed through repentance, or avoided through skepticism and pious fear.[10] Let's look at each of these recommendations in the next chapter.

[10] In order to preserve the more popular reading without doing violence to the grammar, one could of course appeal to the method of reading "above and below," here by repeating *ha-'elohim* so that it can serve as both subject and object-in-construct: 'et kol ma'aseh ha-'elohim [ha-'elohim] yabi' be-mishpat": "God will bring all the deeds of God to justice" (literally: "all the deeds of God, God [alone, and not humans] will bring to justice"). For another example of this mode of reading, see Perry, *Wisdom in the Hebrew Bible*, 38.

13

The "All" of Humans

Fear God but Also Keep the Commandments (12:13)

Qohelet's very final words are framed, if that is the right word, from one side only, stressing the concept of fear. Here are his penultimate very final words:

> The end of the matter, when ALL is said and done: Fear God and keep His commandments, for that is the ALL of mankind.

12:13

The traditional reading of the following verse regarding impending divine judgment sees a natural connection with this verse: "Why fear and obey God? Because God will judge you."[1] An equally intriguing issue is the linkage itself, of fear with observance of the commandments, since, as commentators ritually note, only Sirach joins the two.[2] Such a dual program admittedly does make sense, for it can be assumed, not unreasonably, that fear and the observance of the divine commandments work in harmonious relation, and this generally along two lines:

a) fear God *by* keeping the commandments
Here God moves to center stage of the entire enterprise of living, since fear is seen as the motivating factor of ethical behavior. In this reading the retributive aspect of God has regained full sway: observe the commandments or fear his punishment. Additionally, observance is seen as

---

[1] Tremper Longman III, *The Book of Ecclesiastes* (Grand Rapids, MI: Eerdmans, 1998), 283. However, this argument would also apply to the version proposed above: fear God and don't always try to judge him.

[2] In so noting, they find confirmed one of their pet suspicions – that these are after all only words of a pious glossator, whose epilogue is meant to take its distance from Qohelet's own often heterodox opinions.

the content and proof of respect for God, respect being seen as a derivative of fear.

b) fear God *and also* keep the commandments
That is, give to God what is God's and to Caesar what is Caesar's. Here ethical behavior is viewed from within the dialectic and operates on its own set of principles, advocating balance and moderation.[3]

Both a) and b) readings are supported by the text and argue, at different levels to be sure, the cordial *convivencia* – if not dependence – of fear and observance.

However, the connective *waw* also supports a more puzzling claim as well, suggesting that fear's meaning may be not only distinct but oppositional:

c) fear God *but also* keep His commandments.
The concept here involves the rigid demarcation already outlined between inside and Outside. Now, whereas the commandments offer the dialectical perspective, from within the ethical world under the sun, of wisdom's way, the view from the Outside asserts "the numinous element of fear before God."[4] And whereas the former refers to the world of power and action, the latter is a quality of consciousness and attention to what? Exclusive love for God is the only goal, and the result (*not* the purpose) is to deserve God's blessings: of worldly existence and the precepts that make it meaningful and joyful.

To grasp the radical nature of Qohelet's text we must recapture the radical nature of fearing God as presented in its very first occurrence in the Bible, its most terrifying example and perhaps also its clearest definition. Abraham and Sarah, immigrants and childless, have received the divine promise of a numerous progeny. Yet Abraham's entire hope is now canceled by the command to kill the very son through whom this promise is to be fulfilled. In brief, what Abraham has refused is his future. Or, as the midrash formulates it, his All.[5]

How then does Abraham come to exemplify his virtue of Fear?

> For now I know that you are a God-Fearing person, seeing that you have not withheld your son, your only son from me.
>
> Gen 22:12

---

3 See 7:18 and Whybray ad loc.
4 Thomas Krüger, *Qoheleth, a Commentary* (Minneapolis: Fortress Press, 2004), 213.
5 "Now the Lord had blessed Abraham with all things [*ba-kol*] (Gen 24:1)." Rashi: "The numerical value of the word *ba-kol* is equal to that of the word *ben*, a son."

The condition of blessings – of any successful future in *this* world – is, paradoxically, to refuse them, relying totally on God's superior trust and wisdom. Carried to its contemplative extreme, this would smack of escapism; or, to remain within the fideistic tradition (e.g., quietism), to abandon any form of self-reliance on one's active potential. What then of the directives to live life in *this* world, as exemplified in Qohelet by the commandments? These too are important, the other part of the human All or totality. Thus,

> Fear God, but ALSO keep the commandments,
> since these are given to you on this condition.

Fearing God would then mean neither fear of divine judgment, whether imminent or final, nor a dutiful respect for God's honor on the analogy of what is due to Caesar. The issue, rather, is divine transcendence. Neher cites Jeremiah and Job on the dangers of bringing God too close to human perspectives:

> By equating the Divine and the human we eliminate the unknown.[6]

He goes on to observe that this is the strategy of those who follow a middle path such as the ethic proposed by Qohelet for the conduct of our normal business-day lives. Such an opposition signals a strong paradox, since the fear that Abraham initially shows – in his carrying out the command to offer up his only son – signals not an acceptance of this world but the exact opposite: a renouncement of the All of this world (under the sun) in favor of absolute transcendence. But God, the lord of paradoxes, returns the favor: Abraham's future (his son) is returned because the All was forfeited in favor of an unknown Outside. Thus, Gen 22 uses the argument of fear to sanction release back into the world.

A linguistic detail of Qohelet's formula can further sharpen this notion:

> Fear God but also OBEY (*shmor*) the commandments.

So reads a standard theology of obedience. Rabbinic tradition, however, attaches the verb *shmor* to the performance of the *negative* precepts, the ones stressing what *not* to do, and this leads to a second paradigmatic

---

[6] André Neher, *Jérémie* (Paris: Seuil, 1998), 134.

example of God fearing, this one all the more interesting to Qohelet in that it comes from the wisdom tradition itself:

> Job … feared God and turned from evil.
>
> 1:1, 8; 2:3

> The fear of the Lord is wisdom,
> and to depart from evil is understanding.
>
> Job 28:28

Thus, Krüger can refer to the Torah's "common human core" as exemplified "by the ethical maxims of fearing God and keeping away from evil, as advocated by the book of Job."[7]

There are, however, not one but two levels of fearing God, both accessible to humanity in general (Job was not an Israelite). The first is the observance of the negative precepts of turning away from evil that Job exemplified from the start. This beginning level could be illustrated by the important motto of Proverbs:

> The fear of the Lord is the beginning of knowledge.
>
> Prov 1:7; also 9:10; Ps 111:10[8]

The second level is the one we are now presenting, the awareness of God's awesome distance and of a subsequent refusal to judge God, one that Job acknowledges emerging from the whirlwind and Qohelet from the daily *hebel* or wind of the cosmos. At the start of his tribulations he saw himself and his entire world as *hebel*; at the end, his concluding summation of *hebel* (12:8) is preceded by the description of universal physical demise (12:1–7): he too is dust and ashes. Job especially, in his admirable closing formula, adds a crucial theological explanation: his unworthiness is in the context of God's transcendent Otherness or Outside.

The foundational theological concepts of these very final verses are broadly expressed in Scripture. The first is the recognition of the essential difference between the Creator God and His creatures, described above, by analogy, as the difference between totalities and infinity. Thus,

---

[7] Krüger, *Qoheleth, a Commentary*, 215.
[8] See Michael V. Fox's admirable commentary in his *Proverbs 1–9* (AB18A; New York: Doubleday, 2000), 67–71.

Whybray, in his summarizing exegesis of 3:14 ("God has made it so that men should fear before him"):

> God rightly demands "fear" from men in the sense of recognition of his essential difference from his creatures.[9]

Qohelet similarly observes:

> Keep your mouth from being rash, and let your throat not be quick to bring forth speech in God's presence. For God is in heaven and you are on earth.
>
> 5:2

Commenting on the expression "in God's presence," Rashi cites Isaiah 55:9:

> For as the heavens are higher than the earth, so too are my ways higher than your ways and my thoughts than your thoughts.

The conclusion of section 5:1–6 ("Fear God!" 5:6) can now be seen as based on divine transcendence or Outsideness, here linked with an appeal to repentance and return to God.

We have noticed Qohelet's fondness for those literary brackets labeled *inclusio*. This is the occasion to take note of yet another, more conceptual than literal.[10] According to Psalms, fear of God has outstanding longevity:

> The Fear of the Lord is pure, it endures forever.
>
> Ps 19:10 [9]

Recall that Qohelet opens with a similar claim:

> The earth [people of the earth] endures forever.
>
> Qoh 1:4

What both have in common – a comparison powered by the shared verb "to stand, endure" *'amad* – may be suggested by the Rabbinic dictum, according to which "everything is in the power of Heaven except the fear of Heaven."[11] In a world in which All is under the suspicion of *hebel*, Qohelet nevertheless began by noting the permanency of the earth and

---

[9] Whybray, ad loc. As confirmation of Qohelet's stress on God's Otherness, he further cites 5:2: "God is in heaven, and you upon earth." See also the cited works by Bolin, Sneed, Soggin, Eunny P. Lee, 85.

[10] Actually, all such *inclusios* are strongly conceptual necessities as well as structural conveniences. See my *Jonah's Arguments with God: The Honeymoon is Over!* (Peabody, MA: Hendrickson, 2014), xxxiii–xxxv.

[11] BT Ber 33.

its people, as enduring forever. At the very end of his inquiry and as if forming an elegant conceptual *inclusio*, Qohelet advises the fear of the Lord, since this is the All of humankind. Thus the enduring cycles of natural existence are linked to that human quality capable of outlasting the ups and downs of outrageous fortune.[12]

[12] Eunny P. Lee has evoked the largely unexplored interplay between fear and joy in Qohelet; see her p. 86.

Conclusions

Singing in Truth

In Wahrheit singen, ist ein andrer Hauch.
Ein Hauch um nichts. Ein Wehn im Gott. Ein Wind.
Rilke

To sing in truth is quite another breath:
A breath around/about nothing, a breeze in God, a wind.[1]

The poet sings in truth, the truth of time, the dimension of music, and also of God's judgment on the works of time. Rilke's exquisite couplet is the perfect summary of Qohelet's philosophy and practice of *hebel*: the human life-breath about no-thing but itself, the air that pervades and invigorates the cosmos, the metaphorical breeze of creation that points to transcendence, the *souffle poétique* that sings it to us. An egregious aspect of *hebel* is that, at all times, its four semantic dimensions may be relevant. As in the opening mnemonic *habel habalim* (1+2=3), repeated to stress its circularity: All of human existence works according to these principles: human breath, the creative and nurturing breeze of the God of creation, and the cosmic wind that connects and negotiates the two. Other readings may be proposed, but the basis is the same: the tripartite structure of God, humans, and the cosmos; or, under the sun/heavens (cosmos), above and beyond the cosmos (God, the infinite, the other), and humans, who partake of both.[2]

---

[1] For an alternative translation: "It is another breath that sings the truth. / A breath round nothing. A gust in the god. A wind." Rainer Maria Rilke, *Sonnets to Orpheus* #3, trans. C. F. MacIntyre (Berkeley: University of California Press, 1960), 6.

[2] Jacques Rolland, referring to Rosenzweig, evokes these three as "the last as well as the first elements of the real and therefore of philosophy: God, world, humanity" in his introduction to Emmanuel Levinas, *Éthique comme philosophie première*. Préface par Jacques Rolland (Paris: Payot et Rivages, 1998), 14.

160

All the pursuits and collections elaborated in Qohelet survive and reach us through the *presque rien*, the almost nothingness of words. Arising as both personal a-spiration and poetic in-spiration, they replay the two movements of breathing; and, perhaps like the breath, they will also suffer (patiently, one would hope) ex-spiration. But not entirely. Such, at least, is Qohelet's general message, now seen as a foundational narrative of a humanism and word culture. Of such vanity-strength, so thought the rabbis, is the strength of schoolchildren learning to grow up as decent human beings. We thus have, at the exegetical center of the entire work, a mere breath, an almost "nothing that is an everything." The joy of learning and teaching thus focusses on a question: What is a *hebel* (breath)? Is it not through such magnificent enigmas that wisdom, like a child playing on God's lap, is pleased to challenge our lives?

Qohelet the Poet and the Practice of Language

It is now appropriate to consider further the poet's project to sing in truth, both his method of transformative self-discovery and teaching others, bequeathing to future generations. This pedagogical project is fraught with the pregnant emptiness of *hebel* itself. For if time itself is cast in its conceptual origin as also a possession, it is one devoid of content, as if time were its own content:[3]

> This is the situation of consciousness. To have consciousness is to have time, it is to be on this side of nature, in a certain sense to be not yet born. Such an uprooting is not a lesser form of being but rather the *manner* of the [human] subject. It is the power of rupture, a refusal of neuter and impersonal principles, a refusal of Hegelian totality and politics, a refusal of the bewitching rhythms of art. It is the power to speak, the liberty of words… Whence the power to judge history instead of waiting upon its impersonal verdict.
>
> But time and language and subjectivity presuppose not only a being capable of uprooting itself from the totality but also a being which does not englobe that totality. Time, language, and subjectivity outline a pluralism and consequently, in the strongest sense of the term, an experience: the reception of a being absolutely Other.
>
> Levinas[4]

---

[3] See "Primary or Transitional Experiences under the Sun" in this Conclusion.

[4] Emmanuel Levinas, *Difficile liberté* (Paris: Albin Michel, 1976), 407–08. For an exegesis of this concept of not-yet being born in its possible relevance to Qohelet (4:2–3), see Appendix 5, "Praising the Not-Yet Born."

Qohelet's way out of the dilemma of a worthless existence is neither through religion nor philosophy but rather through the regular exercises of daily thinking and discourse: thinking dialectically to get through the day; thinking "out of the box" to locate the day within broader perspectives, using thinking as transcendence and metaphors as hints that transcendence might take.

To raise the question of the worth of human effort cannot automatically be termed renouncement, and there is an important distinction between detachment and simply giving up the ship. Retirement is not resignation; indeed it is the attitude that allows us to hang in under circumstances that would seem to warrant severance and withdrawal. Some of Qohelet's literary and intellectual methods can be outlined in this regard.

Discussion

The horror of existence for one of the greatest pessimists of literature, Cioran, is the paradox of being something, however infinitesimal, and being worth nothing.[5] The paradox can be reversed for Qohelet, since for this book "all is breath" and yet, we are somehow deeply convinced, worth something. Start with life's greatest evils, the relentless destructiveness of time and the inevitability and universality of death – one fate for all, righteous and wicked, wise and foolish. Yet it is asked whether death is the worst form of nonexistence, for is not the fear of dying upstaged by the fear of committing murder?[6] Moreover, it is noticed that time can produce maturity and healing as well as destruction. Thus, things can be worse and they can often be better as well, and if there are then degrees of "vanity," this means that vanity is not uniformly a "vanity of vanities." As we say in English, there seems to be still and always room for discussion.

Debate

Pessimism is regularly checked and even neutralized (but surely not discarded) in Qohelet by contradictory arguments. "The sun rises only to

---

[5] For Cioran see Clément Rosset, "Le Mécontentement d'E. M. Cioran," *Critique*, April 1987: 92–98 at 93.

[6] Levinas, often. While there is no explicit mention of homicide in Qohelet, does not the dialectic of "a time *to beget* and a time to die" (3:2) an indirect reference to withholding paternity, as put forth in the command to be fruitful and multiply, as one of its perhaps mitigated forms? See my discussion of Tamar's contrivance to have a child from Judah in Genesis 38 as such an argument (*Wisdom in the Hebrew Bible*, ch. 1). See also Appendix 3, "Giving Birth versus Being Born."

set," says the pessimist. Yes, the voice of eschatology could reply at the other extreme of the spectrum, but a time will come when "thy sun shall no more go down" (Isa 60:20). To this latter extreme, the person of experience would still want to ask: "but when?" To the voice of pessimism Qohelet offers an alternative answer (note that he does not reject either position, simply keeps the questions open), this one based less on historical reality than on psychology, on the old conundrum of a glass being half full or half empty: you say that the sun always sets, but I notice that the setting sun always rises, and my model is just as true to reality as yours (note: not more true, yours also is valid). Take another example of the habit of looking at all sides, or at least both sides, of a question: If you complain that God takes, must we not also say that He also gives? And, I suppose, if you notice that God gives, don't worry: He'll take soon enough! The entire list that starts Qohelet's chapter 3, the famous Catalogue of the Times, is built on a perfectly regular and balanced debate between pessimism and optimism.[7] Such a solution would have pleased the Stoics, concerned with the binds that language and its models can impose on life's meaning.

Judgment and Evaluation (e.g., "Better-Than" Statements)

Take another apparent human necessity, than of evaluation, of regularly, even compulsively, deciding what things are worth, usually in terms of personal utility or pleasure, statements to the effect that "this is good, this is bad." In wisdom writing one of the stylistic devices for carrying this out is through better-than statements.[8] This suggests that evaluations are typically comparative. Now if something is judged "vain" or insignificant, then we must ask with respect to what? For example, wisdom is (somewhat) better than its opposite because it gives life to its possessors. The most sweeping example is of course "the All," and again we are entitled to ask "more vain than what?" If we answer that the All has intrinsic insignificance, that it is vain with respect to itself, then we have not made a comparison. If we answer, with the rabbis, that the seven days of creation are value-less with respect to infinity, since, as Pascal observed, the more and the less are indiscernible in the infinite,[9] then Qohelet's decision to persist in discussing the more and the less (i.e., "better than") indicates

---

7   See T. A. Perry, *Dialogues with Kohelet: The Book of Ecclesiastes: Translation and Commentary* (University Park: Penn State Press, 1993).

8   See T. A. Perry, *Wisdom Literature and the Structure of Proverbs* (University Park: Penn State Press, 1993), 40–44.

9   Rosset, "Le Mécontentement," 96.

the abandonment of an absolutist (some would say a "religious") perspective on daily living, which consists precisely in the ominous sense of living always under the gaze of eternity. The key word here is "always" as implying exclusively, since to be sure such a gaze is ... helpful?

With our sights set firmly on ethical issues in this world under the sun, on the one hand, and with an awareness of an Outside on the other, we come to the threshold of the infinite, which also resides in the practice of language. For Blanchot adds writing to the concept of the infinite (i.e., of an escape from totalities): "the infinite of language which no totality can bring to closure."[10] This clarifies Qohelet's notion of skepticism, meaning his reservations concerning knowledge, especially authority, systems, obedience. That is to say, "philosophy is also reason's battle against what seems reasonable."[11]

Skepticism and Piety

Thy Path, the Purposes conceal
From our beleaguered realm,
Lest any shattering whisper steal
Upon us and o'erwhelm.
Kipling, "Prayer of Miriam Cohen"

Le langage est déjà scepticisme.[12]

Skepticism is one of Qohelet's intellectual habits most broadly acknowledged by critics, but it is usually ascribed to an antireligious tendency in his thinking and therefore, somehow, inauthentic. Despite the long subsequent alliance between skepticism and relativism, Qohelet uses skepticism as a powerful intellectual and religious weapon (Kipling's prayer for skepticism raises the possibility of their compatibility). And, indeed, the old critical canard, according to which the Book of Qohelet is to be interpreted as preaching either piety *or* skepticism, is a false start, since Qohelet countenances both, and as mutually supportive. Equally distracting is the theory upon which the false dichotomy is based, that

---

[10] Maurice Blanchot, *L'Écriture du désastre* (Paris: Gallimard, 1980), 201–02. This comes to affirm, in response to the opening thesis (there is nothing left over, no *yitron*), that there is no closure and always something left over and ongoing. It may be of something we don't like and find profoundly contrary to our desire for closure. Yet, "there is always something to say when everything has been said [e.g., Qoh 12:13]: "Saying ... is always in excess of the 'everything has been said'" (ibid., 208).

[11] Ibid., 202.

[12] Blanchot, quoting Levinas, ibid., 123.

of a sharp difference between an "orthodox" epilogue, very attractive to the religious among us, and a skeptical character, too often the object of the religious crowd's irony – which is thought to be caught up in a messy and undignified accommodation with this world.

Because language predates my existence, my initial point of view as I enter the world will be that of someone else. Thus, another's language becomes the mirror through which I see and understand myself. The only way to alter and possibly improve that image is through further words and points of view, and the only chance I have at "truth" is through a perspective that is always outside the one under which I am currently operating. The essay (the literary form of experience and experiment), dialogic in its very nature through its open-ended form, offers the possibility of comparing points of view even when – and because – their purely relative nature is perceived. Dialogue is thus a permanent, concrete challenge to obstinacy and orthodoxy, but also to the "world the way it is." It should be added that Qohelet's skepticism is a lack of confidence not in the modest methods of observation and experience/experiment but rather in the certitude of the results.

A sly and notorious danger of going beyond or around skepticism is the tendency of hypotheses to harden and become absolute perspectives, transformed into contents of their own, so that remaining partial points of view lose any validity whatsoever. To return to an earlier discussion, take the ambivalence of *dabar*: things, words. Trying to think beyond the limits of the skeptical method allows "things of discourse" (words) to take on the hardness of things, imposing their slick surface of stability and "truth." Thus, to take a simple example, the value of detachment is usually taken as applicable to all attachments. Yet, as Blanchot cautions, this includes the necessity of detachment from detachment itself, which can harden into a dogmatism as unproductive as any other.

Back to Our Place: This World of Death and Rebirth

I had eyes only for the infinite, I had a tendency to let the days pass by. They punished me.

Edmond Jabès[13]

---

[13] "Je n'avais de regard que pour l'infini. J'avais tendance à laisser passer les jours. Ils m'ont puni." "La Chute de l'exil," in Paul Auster, ed., *The Random House Book of Twentieth Century French Poetry* (New York: Vintage, 1984), 406.

The Outside is everywhere, like infinite space engulfing our little globe on all sides and dimensions, the "eternal silence of these infinite spaces," which so terrified Pascal. Given, along with its heightened risks, the apparent pervasive superiority of the Outside, one must still wonder whether our daily world of dialectic – the world "under the sun" of All, things both human and natural – can ever be totally left behind. Qohelet's answer is in the negative; that this dis-aster-ous, cosmic totality has to be lived through and not around, and on a daily basis. Here is how Blanchot formulates such a decision:

> There must *always* be at least two languages or two exigencies, one dialectic and the other non-dialectic, one where negativity is the task, the other where the neuter sets itself off from both being and non-being; just as one should *both* be a free and speaking subject "I" *and also* disappear like the patient-passive one whom dying traverses and who doesn't show himself.[14]

Moreover, this decision must be renewed each and every instant, due to the inevitable ambiguity: on the one hand, the power of the Outside to live in a time without present; and, on the side of the dialectic, to live out "a history able to exhaust (in order to accede to the contentment of presence), all the possibilities of time."[15] To be avoided are both those who live only in the Other world, but also those whose unique ambition is "under the sun." How then is one to negotiate both perspectives? Can Caesar and God be both accommodated; or, alternatively, can they be hermetically sequestered?

Primary or Transitional Experiences under the Sun

Returning to Blanchot's essay on dreams as an access to night, regular nighttime sleep is characterized by a stasis and fixity:

> I am not dispersed but rather gathered up altogether where I am, at that point where my position is and where the world, thanks to the firmness of my attachment, is localised… The place where I sleep is not only where it is situated, my person IS that very place; and the fact of sleep is now the fact that, now, my place of abode is my very being.
>
> Blanchot[16]

The language of site or place is also, we recall, the focal point of the sun's desire in Qohelet's opening cosmology, where this concept, too,

---

[14] Blanchot, *L'Écriture du désastre*, 38, italics added.
[15] Ibid., 48.
[16] Maurice Blanchot, *L'Espace littéraire* (Paris: Gallimard, 1955), 359–60.

is typically understood statically, its temporal, dynamic motion is spatialized and end-stopped at the end of the day, at sunset. Like the wind and the waters, however, the sun turns upon itself, and this element of *retour* injects a permanence that stands outside the cycle of rise and fall – or rather sets this transience into a ceaseless (ongoing, perhaps also infinite?) phenomenon, wherein the wonderment is generated less from the sun itself than from the interminable repetition of the repetition! All this, returning to Blanchot's essay, is like a dream of the night, where "the form of the dream becomes its sole content."[17] Similarly, as we have proposed, to experience breath as breath (*habel habalim*) is an instance of *peshat* as both imminence and metaphor.[18]

Examples of such reflexivity, wherein a particular experience is reduced to its essence through an intuition of void, is difficult to localize. Where are we, for instance, once the *hebel* litany has worked the magic of its focused destruction and we are left with nothing (no-thing)? In our normal perception and practice of living, things are seen privately and primarily as they serve our *khepets* (desires), in terms of their use and enjoyment. Thus, even such basics as health, freedom, light itself are conceptualized as mere *conditions* of enjoyment and are usually perceived (if that is the right word) either by their absence or as mere subsidiary background. For we think and experience through opposites, dialectically: we think of health only when we are sick, it takes servitude to teach freedom, and so forth.

However, such things can also be viewed, more deeply, as primary experiences and enjoyments in themselves. Here are a few examples, along with literary parallels, presented in stark outline and to be pondered further:

existence

Normally we exist for something or someone, and we think of it only against nonexistence or death. Jean-Jacques Rousseau, in his rêveries on the Lac de Bienne, taught us to focus on the pure sentiment of existence, Qohelet's equivalent for which may well be "to see the sun" (11:7). Or Levinas, stated as a question: "Happiness – the joy of existing?"[19]

---

[17] Ibid., 362.
[18] See Chapter 9.
[19] Emmanuel Levinas, CC, 56. Jean-Jacques Rousseau, *Rêveries du promeneur solitaire* (Genève: Droz, 1967), "Fifth Promenade." See my discussion in T. A. Perry, *Jonah's Arguments with God: The Honeymoon Is Over!* (Peabody, MA: Hendrickson, 2014), 130–31.

breath (*hebel*)

We have discussed at length the notion of a *hebel of hebels*, like a metaphor of metaphors, as an awareness of the very possibility of life and God.[20]

light

Esthetically speaking, light can be thought not merely as the background or conduit of the visual perception of beauty but rather, more fundamentally, as the very essence and content of the esthetic experience.[21]

health

Typically, we think of health only in its absence rather than as a presence of joyous vitality.

freedom

We normally seek freedom *from* something (tyranny, hard labor), consistent with dialectical thinking. Qohelet's is metaphysical and epistemological, grounded on the positive openness of his skepticism. Its watchword is "perhaps," as in "Perhaps both will succeed" (11:6).[22]

time

This refers not to the time for this or that (e.g., "time is money") but to the time that is integrated in the infinite. Like freedom, it is an awareness of the future's openness, its riskiness and indeterminacy.[23] And just as time *is* not this or that, neither is it to be experienced as an activity but rather as a patience.[24] Levinas highlights its absence of content by Bergson's word *durée*, hoping thus "to avoid confusion between what flows *in* time and time itself."[25]

More darkly, Levinas sees this as the realm of the *il y a*, much akin to the experience of the excessive quality (*de trop*) of bare existence in Sartre's *La Nausée*.

[20] See Chapter 9.

[21] According to the principle that "prima substantiarum est lux." See, for example, Leone Ebreo's *Dialoghi d'amore*, and my discussion in *Erotic Spirituality: The Integrative Tradition from Leone Ebreo to John Donne* (Tuscaloosa: University of Alabama Press, 1980), 23, 93.

[22] See T. A. Perry, *Wisdom in the Hebrew Bible: God's Twilight Zone* (Peabody, MA: Hendrickson, 2014), 173. This notion is theologized in Jonah as the "God of perhaps." See Perry, *Jonah's Arguments with God*, 122–25.

[23] I permit myself to quote once again Emmanuel Levinas's extraordinary remark: "Time is not the limitation of being but rather its relation with the infinite," *Dieu, la mort et le temps* (Paris: Grasset, 1993), 28.

[24] "There is no action in the passivity of time, which is patience itself, " ibid., 15.

[25] Ibid.

Time's epicurean possibility focuses on a more daily (and perhaps also more rare) sense, one related to the joy of lack of constraint that allows Levinas to wax poetic:

> The goodness of time, to have time... Time is not only the possibility to repair something – consequently something dead – but also the positive joy of leisure. It is more than the possibility to avoid alternatives; it is to have rich possibilities instead of definite and poor realities. It is the very happiness of living, of making and living a history.[26]

In terms of the normal dialectic of living opposites – that is, things we pursue or avoid, things that happen and that we like or dislike: all are included under the rubric of *khepets*, as we have seen. Such binaries, in their totality, are called a personal history, a life lived through in all its positives and negatives. Thus, "the happiness of living is not the happiness of being. Being is a cadaver."[27] Time is thus both the possibility to change the bad into good, and also the sheer enjoyment of enjoying the good things, which is stated in its most general form here as simply "having the time." The surplus arising from such an imminent practice is, surprisingly, the possibility of turning things around:

> "Time" initially comes from the notion "to have time," and that is the condition of reflection for intelligence itself. It is the possibility to grasp and understand one's self.[28]

night, darkness
This refers not to the night that serves the day and ego purposes but rather to a level of consciousness, an awareness without object that is grounded in the Outside and exceeds dialectical thinking.[29]

silence
Not the silence from disturbing noise but rather Blanchot's "silence of silence." A parallel might be a song of songs, referring not to one of the songs (the best) but rather to the pure song or musical aspect of all the

---

[26] Levinas, CC, 69.
[27] Ibid.
[28] Ibid., 71.
[29] See Blanchot's irreplaceable essay, "Le sommeil, la nuit," in *L'Espace littéraire*, 357–62.

songs.[30] Or, more likely, this is a silence that speaks "after all has been said" (12:13), the very possibility of silence.[31]

the human face?

Levinas meditates on metaphor's "mystifying moment": "Does it arise in the passage from the literal to the figurative sense? But is the literal sense not already metaphorical?"[32] Levinas proposes the human face as having meaning anterior to both language and culture and thus a universal conductor of human meaning.[33]

It could be thought that such primary experiences are forms of detachment from "real" or daily life, what Bergson, referring to sleep, called *désintéressement*. Using the same point of reference, Blanchot explains their importance for daily living: "Sleep may perhaps be a lack of attention to the world, but this negation of the world preserves us in the world and affirms the world."[34]

That meaning arises from (temporal) context is a central teaching of the Catalog of the Times. Once beyond or outside of the "normal" or natural context of daily life, however, we enter the domain of the "exterior," the possibility of a "signification without context" (Levinas), of an "attention without object" (Simone Weil), of a "négativité sans emploi" (Georges Bataille).[35] In all these examples, both the accustomed contexts and concepts have been hebel-ized, leaving only a (creative) void and the barest trace of their dialectical structures. Levinas applies this notion to the deepest meaning of events:

> The meaning of events is in their instant, in their "dead time" and not in their temporal context. In their instant: their initiation to being, the *manner* in which they receive the adventure of existence.[36]

---

[30] Henri Meschonnic, for example, focusses on poetic rhyme and rhythm as primary signifiers in their own right. See his *La Rime et la vie* (Paris: Gallimard, Folio, 2006). See also Chapter 9, "The Effects of Poetic Language."

[31] See Chapter 9, "The All as the *Hebel* of *Hebels*; God as the Metaphor of Metaphors."

[32] Jill Robbins, "Circumcising Confession: Derrida, Autobiography, Judaism," *Diacritics* 25 (1995): 25.

[33] CC, 330. Claire Elise Katz, noting Levinas's theory of love as "an event situated at the limit of immanence and transcendence" (TI 254), comments that "the face of the other, of the beloved, reveals within it what it is not yet" (*Levinas, Judaism, and the Feminine: The Silent Footsteps of Rebecca* [Bloomington: Indiana University Press, 2003], 62).

[34] Blanchot, *L'Éspace littéraire*, 358.

[35] Emmanuel Levinas, TI, 8. Simone Weil, quoted in Alfred Kazin, *Writing Was Everything* (Cambridge, MA: Harvard University Press, 1995), 101.

[36] CC, 306, italics added. For the importance of adverbs in the interpretation of meaning, see also Appendix 3, "The Reign of the Adverb."

How then does a writer gain access to such primary experiences – primary because they afford perceptions of the outside and of the world-as-outside? Referring to Camus's literary art, Blanchot writes:

> The life of a civilized writer, a witness to his times, begins with the poverty of things without history: facing their naked presence.[37]

Although things' naked presence has social and economic implications, of course, they typically navigate their existence below the radar of history and public attention, as well as this side of the "wealth of nations." For Camus, the comeuppance offered adequate compensation:

> Poverty has never been a misfortune for me: the light of day poured over it its riches.[38]

Blanchot immediately expands this beautiful personal remark in the direction of what Qohelet called *hebel*:

> Light brightens poverty, but poverty opens to light, gives it as the truth of destitution and also as the naked appearance which is the characteristic of truth.[39]

Qohelet's opening question ("What profit?") could easily have been posed without the tag "under the sun." Our reading to this point has clarified one of his intentions, namely, to establish the cosmic dimension as a moral analogy, suggesting not only that humans are subject to nature's rhythms but especially that these are a safe guide for negotiating human existence. Pursuing the metaphor of sleep as a primary experience, Blanchot sees sleep as an "act of fidelity and union. I entrust myself to the great natural rhythms, to the stability of order."[40] A second interpretation – both complementary and oppositional – is to reserve a space of consciousness above or beyond the sun. This reading focuses on that area of human access "in exchange for" the sun. Here the sun is also shorthand for the other major players of the nonhuman universe, those great presences about to be presented and seen not only as moral figures or teachers but also simply as presences that astonish by their repetition: the earth, the sun and light, night and day, the winds, rivers and sea. Here are movements that, paradoxically, *do not change*, whose mystery seems natural. If this has any reference to

---

[37] Maurice Blanchot, *L'Amitié* (Paris: Gallimard, 1971), 220.
[38] Quoted in ibid., 222.
[39] Ibid.
[40] Blanchot, *L'Espace littéraire*, 358.

humanity (which is questionable), it is to "an existence poor and root-less, naked nature bereft of lodging."[41] The upshot? "It makes us feel that, in this primary experience, there is something beyond the limited certitudes of an art of living, the likes of which it would not be difficult to find in the prosaic decorum of a certain antiquity."[42]

In Biblical tradition the exact parallel, of course, is the Exodus des-ert experience, combining exile and flight with the destitution of set-tled home and family traditions (the garlic, the leeks). It is Abraham's resettlement all over again, except that the extreme solitude is of a dif-ferent nature, for now Abraham's impoverishment and isolation are transmuted from the social – the Israelites journeyed with their entire society intact – to the desolation of nature's raw power: the desert land, an empty howling waste (Deut 32:10). It is here that the call of the wild is experienced, that arid and infertile desert (Jer 2:2) where the erotic encounter with the divine takes place.[43]

With this we return to the opening Cosmology, but now with an addi-tional perspective. Seen from a human point of view "under the sun," the four elements have important lessons for human behavior: how to negotiate time, how to reduce our interests and desires to manageable (circular) limits. Here individual matters (*khepets*) are typically seen as serving human desire (also *khepets*) and evaluated accordingly. Viewed globally *from the Outside*, however, this totally humanized world of ours loses any enduring valuation and takes on the Outside coloration of the neutral. From this perspective, which is accessible even from under the sun, the world becomes nonhumanized (which is anything but *de*human-ized), allowing room for such things as the environment and the animals (e.g., Job 40–41).

Living with and through Transience: Simple Joys, Simply Joy

There exists a tyranny of the universal and of the impersonal, an order that is inhuman though distinct from the brutish. Against it man affirms himself as an irreducible singularity, exterior to the totality into which he enters, and aspiring to the religious order where the recognition of the individual

---

[41] Blanchot, *L'Amitié*, 221.

[42] Ibid.

[43] For a moving variant of this theme see Albert Camus' "La Femme adultère," in *L'exil et le royaume* (Paris: Gallimard, 1957), 11–41 at 39–41. Here the desert is no longer the mere locus of erotic encounter but rather the very paramour of the adulteress. The paradox could not be more extreme: the most personal relationship of her life is consummated with nature in its most extreme otherness.

concerns him in his singularity, *an order of joy which is neither cessation not antithesis of pain, nor flight before it.*

Levinas[44]

We have seen both the omnipresence of totalities "under the sun" and also their nonhuman limitations and neutrality. What is at stake in such worldly transactions is whether totalities will be taken as the all of life or whether the "I," can survive and under what conditions. At ground level zero Julia Alvarez and Qohelet are one, by arguing that "cruel refinements interfere. And we forget the visceral first and truest response of our being to the world."[45] For, after all has been said, we are alive, we "see the sun," we have enough. We can gather together as communities when misfortune strikes. Even Job is not alone; even a corpse is accompanied and put to rest (Qoh 12:5). Where do these joys and strengths come from, and why? Do we turn away from joy because we cannot explain it?! Do we disdain it because it was not produced by our own efforts? Shall we receive the bad and not also the good?[46]

The presence of such joys against the void must have come as a surprise as much to Qohelet as to the modern reader. They recall the medieval adage cited by Karl Jaspers:

Je viens je ne sais d'où.	I come from I know not where.
Je suis je ne sais qui,	I am I know not who,
Je meurs je ne sais quand,	I die I know not when,
Je vais je ne sais où,	I go I know not where:
Je m'étonne d'être aussi joyeux.	I am astonished to be so joyful![47]

That this general and, within the context of universal breath, paradoxical joy comes also from God is not directly asserted by the text, but its subtle presence, acknowledging at the very center of our consciousness a strong desire to live life, is a good reason, by my lights, to have included Qohelet in the canon. It establishes what I have called, in another context, a theology of mere existence that moralists might refer to as (often

---

[44] Emmanuel Levinas, *Totality and Infinity* (trans. Alphonso Lingis; Pittsburgh: Duquesne University Press, 1969), 242.

[45] Julia Álvarez, in *You've Got to Read This*, ed. Ron Hansen (New York: HarperCollins, 2000), 349.

[46] See Job 2:10, with a slight reversal of language.

[47] Rosset, "Le Mécontentement..." One should add, with Jankélévitch, that such astonished surprise is anything but simple or spontaneous: "All of philosophy is already there, in this astonishment at being alive," *Quelque part dans l'inachevé*, 97. Levinas expressed it more modestly, as a question to be pondered: "Bonheur – joie d'exister?" CC, 56.

messy) dailiness.[48] Qohelet adds that this is a *joyous* theology. Although, as Levinas frequently observes, it is not heaven on earth, nor is it intended to be such. Nor does it exclude pain.

The truth is that the Book of Qohelet, like the texture of life itself, is rich with contradictions and inconsistencies and complexities, with fragments beyond knowledge and expectation. One of its most telling contradictions is Qohelet's inability to live out to its conclusion the logical consequences of universal vanity, namely the impossibility to have love for or even interest in any thing whatsoever. Yet listen to the so-called quietist/pessimist: the light is sweet, live out your life with the bride of your youth, enjoy life... God has made everything beautiful in its time (and you can read "His" time, if you wish: you do have a choice, but no obligation) – the stress here is not on the deterministic "in its time" but rather on the appreciative "beautiful." I wonder even whether there is not a close bond in Qohelet's mind between this esthetic criterion and transience, whether, in the words of the poet Wallace Stevens, "death is the mother of beauty."[49] In which case not only are nature's transient opposites beautiful "*in* their times" but also "*because* of their times."

There are few things so humanly moving in literature as this paradoxical, inconsistent, spontaneous revival of interest in living beyond quietism and despair. The surprise is that quietism and simple emptiness are themselves quite necessary in order to perceive the gifts that are there all the time. Further and related surprises:

– the intrusion of joy into the sheer *hebel*-breath of existence, totally unpredictable both in occurrence and in nature;

– the secret alliance between lucidity and joy: the lucidity of language and commentary, essayistic and aphoristic exercise. Michael V. Fox cites in this regard Kenneth James's understanding of the significance of joy for Qohelet:

> If the security of "conceptual knowledge" is taken away from us, we still have a center that feels strongly about life, and it is to this emotional center that Qohelet returns as a possible source of meaning in life.[50]

---

[48] On God's theology of mere existence, see Perry, *Jonah's Arguments with God*, 130–35. For dailiness, see Chapter 4, "Concepts of Time..." The concept is theologized in Ps 37:18: "For the Lord has regard (*yodea*) for the days of the innocent; and their inheritance will be forever."

[49] "Sunday Morning," in *The Collected Poems of Wallace Stevens* (New York: Alfred A. Knopf, 1954, 1982).

[50] Cited in Michael V. Fox, *Qohelet and His Contradictions* (Sheffield: Almond, 1989), 14.

I doubt whether this can be limited to pleasure, as some have argued, but it certainly includes the joy arising from the simple (some would say demeaning) acts of eating and drinking[51] – and, let us add, other radically simplistic activities such as breathing, or Montaigne's favorite: a robust healthfulness. It is of course misleading to term these simplistic, except to note that they are typically not even perceived except in their absence. Their philosophical interest consists in their being examples of perfect collusion between nature and art, or goodness and virtue. Moreover, there is the bonus joy of attributing such pleasures, in all their simplicity and gratuitousness, to God, what we would call the heartfelt joy of gratitude for unexpected and surely undeserved gifts. It is quite remarkable that in all seven major intervals in which enjoying life appears in the Book of Qohelet, usually in connection with eating and drinking, there is the explicit notation that these come from God, take it or leave it.[52] *Habel habalim,* inhale – exhale. And do enjoy your supper!

---

[51] Qohelet balances T. S. Eliot's "eating and drinking, dung and death" with "eating and drinking, joy and thanksgiving"; cf. Exod 24:11.

[52] See Perry, *Dialogues with Kohelet,* 29–32.

Appendix: Further Notes and Topics on Breath Research

The purpose of this study is to suggest philosophical perspectives appropriate to the exegesis of the Book of Qohelet as a reflection on life's spiritual possibilities as Qohelet imagined them. As such, it is a meditation on how like-minded thinkers such as Montaigne attempted to fathom his enigmatic teachings and embody them in human life and literature. In so doing I have bypassed the popular template of commentary, wherein each and every item is scrutinized for its philological and historical possibilities. Thanks to the work of Michael V. Fox and many others, the philological wealth is available enough, and if attempts to locate the Book historically have been stalled and remain unresolved, this may surely be ascribed in large part to the author's own desire for concealment.

It is of course undesirable to withdraw overmuch from local textual and literary problems, since these both must not only accommodate but also support the larger perspectives advanced here. In addition and no less important, there are broader rhetorical and conceptual issues that must be clarified and expanded, especially when they seem to appear on the horizon out of nowhere (I am thinking of such things as doublets and *peshat*-metaphors). The purpose of this Appendix is both to address some of these in greater depth and to suggest further topics of research, with the added advantage of keeping footnotes at reasonable length.

1. Hebel

Hebel *Repetition as a Terminus Technicus*
The interesting suggestion has been advanced by Lohfink that the excessive repetition of *hebel* at crucial points suggests the presence of a terminus technicus or sustained rhetorical device.[1] To some readers, its

[1] Norbert Lohfink, *Qoheleth: A Continental Commentary* (Minneapolis: Fortress, 2003), xiv.

performance throughout the entire work has a dramatic quality equal to that of the grand *inclusio* itself (1:2, 12:8). For a churchgoing individual like James Limburg, its recurrent "breath" theme "continues to sound throughout the entire book, like a sustained pedal point of an organ."[2] To my ears and in a pessimistic mood, it evokes Faust's calibrated series of curses, amounting to dismissal of things rejected, attempts to ward off all things that no longer seem to serve his life's purpose: *Fluch... Fluch*, and so forth.[3] One might also think of a mantra, adding the crucial point of the passage from a *hebel*-judgment to a *hebel*-meditation.[4] When, finally, we notice the three distinct and evolving *hebels* – a) the heat of *Fluch* and repentance; b) the coolness or maturity of a philosophical discovery; c) a spiritual distancing, from the *dehors* or Outside – then we must consider the possibility of an *antanaclastic* text, a single word or phrase repeated in close proximity and striking opposing valences.[5]

Such midrashic musings do not exhaust the attempts of readers to penetrate the elusive enigma of Qohelet's opening motto, formulaic repetition and gravitas. A recent study by Michael V. Fox, unrelated to this topic, may yet provide additional impressions and especially theoretical backing. Pointing to wisdom as a moral *esthetic*, Fox offers the following:

> To the modern ear, the long strings of righteous-wicked antitheses in Proverbs 10–15 may sound mechanical, if not tedious. But the back-and-forth, tick-tock quality of these series gives voice to the belief in the moral balance whereby God runs the world. The "tick" and the "tock" really say the same thing, count off the same pace, but the "tock" is necessary to complete the pair and tells us that things are right with world. The ideal of moral balance must have been aesthetically pleasing to the sages, and these proverbs give it literary form.[6]

To the church organ we can now add the clock ticking off the to and fro of events, much like the dialectical *va-et-vient* of the Catalog of Human Times in Chapter 6. Fox hedges his former pessimism even further when he sees wisdom as integrating what he calls "anomaly proverbs" (no justice

---

2 James Limburg, *Encountering Ecclesiastes: A Book for Our Time* (Grand Rapids, MI: Eerdmans, 2006), 20.

3 Goethe, *Faust* vv. 1591–1606. One can perhaps also detect (in 8:14, for example) the *mea culpa* of the former king, the one most responsible for justice in the kingdom.

4 Mark R. Sneed sees the mantra function of "all is vanity" as hyperbolic and rhetorical, "meant to shock the readers and radically disorient them." *The Politics of Pessimism in Ecclesiastes: A Social-Science Perspective* (Atlanta: Society of Biblical Literature, 2012), 172.

5 See Appendix 6, "Antanaclasis."

6 See Michael V. Fox, "The Epistemology of the Book of Proverbs," *JBL* 126 (2007): 669–84 at 680.

in the world, God is unfair, etc.) into a broader perspective of universal balance.[7] Fox's extraordinary conclusions are applied only to Proverbs and wisdom, not pointedly including Qohelet, but not excluding Qohelet either. I for one hear the *hebel/hebel* along with the tick-tock and would apply Fox's characterization of Proverbs to Qohelet as well. *Hebel* is thus both a conclusion and a method. What I see is *hebel* and so are the words that describe it. Like the breath that goes in and out, *hebel* mediates the outer and inner, it both takes a direct object and is reflexive.

Hebel *Pedagogy: Mr. "This Too Is* Hebel*"*

What do we do and think when bad things happen? At one end of the pedagogical scale would be one who walks a path with only carob seeds to eat and considers himself the most unhappy of mortals, until he looks behind him and notices a beggar following him and eating the rejected shells. The moral: there is always someone more unhappy than you, things can always be worse. At the other extreme would be the sage recorded by Jewish tradition named *'ish gam-zoo*, "Mr. this-too," since, when anything bad happened, his buoyant optimism would burst forth: "*This too* is for good." These two extremes provide a context within which Qohelet elaborates his advice on facing hardship. What they both have in common, of course, is the advice to accept and be content with what you have.

While the example of the carob seeds may be taken as an appropriate attitude against all the ills of fortune, the second actually has a pedagogical edge in at least two respects: the use of the positive concept "good" and its pedagogic tactic of repetition. As to the first, the evaluation of all things as "good" flies in the face of the obvious – as intended – and thus makes available two reflections: that "good" and its negative "bad" are **quotational** (q. v.) only and not ontological, and that either may easily turn into its opposite. Thus, one should never give up on change, either in the short run or at some point into the infinite future. The repetitive tactic may be of greater consequence, since in Qohelet the expression *gam zeh hebel*, "this too is hebel," occurs no fewer than ten times: 2:19, 21, 23, 26; 4:4, 8, 16; 5:9, 10; 6:9. As such, it functions as a kind of litany or mantra.

Returning to the carob seeds, Qohelet's method here is a tactic of leveling, of dummying down – to combat human presumption and vaunted superiority – familiar to Montaigne, who once noted that "kings defecate, and so do Ladies." Or perhaps Qohelet and Montaigne include the positive as well, once you start reflecting on the benefits of breathing.

---

[7] Ibid., 682–83.

But begin by dummying things down. Want to put human superiority in perspective? Look for what we all have in common:

> How can the sage die like the fool?
>
> 2:16, 15

> I know that one and the same fate will befall both.
>
> 2:14

Or, concerning our putative superiority over the animals:

> God has indeed chosen them [the sons of men] out, but only to see that they themselves are but beasts to one another.

> What befalls the sons of man befalls the beast; they have the same fate: as one dies, so dies the other; indeed, they all have the same breath [*hebel*].
>
> 3:18–19

The lesson in all cases is the commonality of life. It is not much, and it is everything; for without it we have nothing.

If you say that "this too is a breath," referring to a situation or result or experience, then you are indeed making a comparison = metaphor, since for instance the loss of a job is not literally a breath but rather *like* a bad breath or a breath of fresh air. If, however, through many experiences and repetitions the conclusion is the same, then the "all" comes forward ("it is *all* breath"), and the most likely referent is no longer local but rather cumulative and general. What do they *all* have in common? They are what characterize life, they are in fact what life is in its daily and repetitive reality: "*C'est la vie!* This too is *hebel*" has thus passed from being only descriptive and metaphorical to being definitional: that is what real concrete life is not only "like" but also what life under the sun literally and concretely "is" in its *peshat* and most general experiential nature.[8] And "merely" (the pessimists' favorite word) a breath pervades all possible ups and downs of human life under the sun.

The beauty of "This too is *hebel*" is that it can go all three ways: for the pessimists, for the optimists, and for the philosophicals who view all things as relative and prefer their peace of mind. Included here would be the Qohelet types, who aspire to both self-control and the reduction of trauma arising from possessions.[9] A rich palette of emotions and attitudes/evaluations rides on breathing, signals, like dreams and words, a

---

[8] See Appendix 3, "To Lives! C'est la Vie!"

[9] For, "Indeed, in *too many* dreams and breaths and word/things..." (5:6). See my commentary in Appendix 2, "Dreams."

state of mind. "This too is *hebel*"! Take some deep breaths, control your anger, be patient and joyful.

Elemental Hebel*: Making Something of Nothing*
> What did he fear? It was not fear or dread. It was nothing that he knew too well. It was all a nothing and a man was nothing too. It was only that and light was all it needed and a certain cleanness and order. Some lived in it and never felt it but he knew it all was nada y pues nada y nada y pues nada. Our nada who art in nada, nada be thy name thy kingdom nada thy will be nada in nada as it is in nada. Give us this nada our daily nada and nada us our nada as we nada our nadas and nada us not into nada but deliver us from nada; pues nada. Hail nothing full of nothing, nothing is with thee. He smiled and stood before a bar with a shining steam pressure coffee machine.
>
> "What's yours?" asked the barman.
>
> "Nada."
>
> "Otro loco más," said the barman and turned away.
>
> Hemingway, "A Clean, Well-Lighted Place"

Hemingway's *nada* is a *peshat*-metaphor, the most concrete of realities, without particular context because it includes them all as virtualities and thus a comprehensive metaphor for life itself, life as lived, the *il y a* or element background from which all arises and persists.[10] "It was all a nothing and a man was nothing too. It was only that and light was all it needed."

At least for Hemingway's client, *nada* is not totally nothing. But close. It speaks the minimalist presence of the All as absence of clutter and as air: clean and well-lighted. Like Levinas's element, it is the environmental basis for enjoyment itself. Here breath is likened to air, not the one that we breathe but rather the substance without substance, the existence without existent in which we bathe, to use Levinas's phrase. Whatever we do, whatever happens, circulates in the elemental *hebel*.

---

[10] The study of the four elements (fire, air, water, earth) became important in literary criticism thanks to Gaston Bachelard's groundbreaking studies, which devote a volume to each element. The subject has been philosophically explored in Emmanuel Levinas, *Totalité et infini* (Paris: Kluwer, 1987), especially pp. 137–51, to which the reader is referred for further study. Of possible interest, at least for Hemingway scholarship, is a Ladino (Judeo-Spanish) tradition that goes back to the Middle Ages and that resisted the Vulgate "vanity" tradition: *Nada de nadas nada de nadas, el todo nada.* See Thomas Krüger *The Ladino Bible of Ferrara* [1553], ed. Moshe Lazar (Culver City, CA: Labirinthos, 1992); *The Ladino Five Scrolls*, ed. Moshe Lazar (Culver City, CA: Labirinthos, 1992).

2. Breath Research

One fruitful and necessary direction for breath/*hebel* interpretation can begin by bracketing out the aggressive and dominant negative valences still currently in vogue (foulness, vanity, absurdity) in favor of neutral ones such as transience, emptiness, and more positive ones as well. One general watchword that might well carry the burden is Jankélévitch's *presque rien*, breath as an "almost nothing." We explore here some possibilities of thinking about *hebel* (breath of life, breathing) in other literary contexts that could be unlocked by Qohelet's initiative.

Hebel *as Life-Breath;* Ruakh *as Breath, Wind/Air, Spirit*
We started these reflections with Goethe's frustration over the inaccessibility of life using current methods of laboratory research. Similar problems arise when the topic is the concept of life as it is brought forth as *hebel* in Qohelet. Here I wish to gather and extend our observations above concerning the meaning of *hebel,* breath. The first point is that *hebel* has a *peshat,* a simple literal referent: breath. Breath and not vapor. While both have little substance, the differences are huge. On the one hand, a breath is ongoing, renewable; on the other, it does not arise from an oven but from a living being, thus synonymous with the breath of life, which in the Hebrew Bible comes not from the baker or a steamship but ultimately from God.

Once the *peshat,* the life-reality and so-called simple meaning of *hebel* independent of context is established, we can prepare to reread Qohelet from the ground up, so to speak. A prime pedagogical issue is that of translation, since seldom is the doublet translator/traitor more bothersome to open readings. The main problem is one of interpretation disguised as translation. *Hebel*'s correct translation is "breath"; heavy or ideological translation such as "vanity" is interpretation, which is also the case in a lighter but equally misleading form such as "merely breath." Why not, rather, either give a footnote indicating that this is (only) the translator's interpretation; or, better, why not Kathleen A. Farmer's option to "keep the matter open and let the reader decide the interpretation of "breath," which is what Qohelet wrote?[11] The initial choice, then, is not among the various available interpretations – all abstractions – but rather between such ready-made abstractions and the *peshat*

---

[11] Kathleen A. Farmer, *Who Knows What Is Good? Proverbs and Ecclesiastes* (Grand Rapids, MI: Eerdmans, 1991), 143–46.

itself. The interpreter should not prematurely foreclose on such highly polysemic terms.

One possible approach would be to explore the semantic fields in the Hebrew Bible that widen the possible interpretive contexts of breath and breathing. In so doing we bracket out the abstractions currently in vogue, focusing instead on the direct link between breath and life already mentioned. For life, of course, is already both a metaphor and anything but an abstraction. It seems to function as does the notion of face for Levinas, in that it is both the most concrete thing we have and the most distant one to explain.

THE PANTING SUN. To describe the sun's movement, Qohelet uses a term both highly anthropomorphic and dramatic, if not erotic:

> And the sun rises and the sun sets,
> And it pants to return to its place where it rises again
>
> 1:5

Sha'af, to pant for breath, can express a full range of desire in Tanak. At one extreme is the pain of thirst and hunger, as when animals, bereft of food and water, gasp for air:

> And the wild asses stand in the high places,
> They snuff up the wind [*sha'afu ruakh*] like jackals;
> Their eyes fail because there is no herbage.
>
> Jer 14:6

And, as for food, so too for love-lust and sexuality in the mating season:

> [You are] a wild ass used to the wilderness, that snuffs up the wind [*sha'afa ruakh*] in her desire [*a'wat nafsho*]; in her lust who can turn her away.
>
> Jer 2:24

Or, combining both longing and desire and at a more figurative level:

> With open mouth I pant [for breath], because I long for your commandments.
>
> Ps 119:131

> I will cry like a woman in travail; I will both gasp and pant [*esh'af,* breathe in].
>
> Isa 42:14

Do not desire [*tish'af*] [the quietness of] the night
Job 36:20

As a servant pants [*yish'af*] after the shade.
And a hireling looks for the reward for his work…

Job 7:2[12]

Returning to the panting sun as Qohelet may have imagined it, consider its complex figuration in Psalm 19:

> v. 5c   In them [the heavens] He [EL] has set a tent for the sun,[13]
> v. 6a-b   And he [the Sun] is like a bridegroom emerging from his chamber, rejoicing like a warrior eager to run his course.
> v. 7a-b   His [the Sun's] rising-place is from the very edge [*qetseh*] of the heavens, and his circuit to their [other] edges [*qetsotam*];

The latter verse establishes the sun's complete dominance over everything "under the sun," as Qohelet loved to say. It is verse 6, however, that presents a figure brimming with distinct and complementary energies and desires: those of a lover emerging from his nuptial chamber and a warrior joyously running to battle. In both texts the sun's focus is on that particular moment of transition and return, the morning twilight point or *entre-deux* where all projects are continued and desires renewed.

We can now return to Qohelet's solar circuit with a richer sense of its erotic aura:

> The sun goes forth [in the morning]
> and the sun comes in (*ba'*) [in the evening].

The verb that expresses the sun's setting also has strong overtones of sexually coming into a woman.[14] The next verb now does double duty:

> And to its place it pants with desire.

The bridegroom's desire occurs in his chamber and also, in the morning, propels him forward to shine again: *neue Liebe, neues Leben.*

[12] Job 5:5 is a most difficult verse to interpret. I propose to see an additional sense of *sha'af* here, one that yearns not for fulfillment of desire but rather for the desire itself: "One whose hunger famine eats up, and he pants for the thirsty, for their wealth." This would be in line with Bachelard's pun: "Give us this day our daily hunger"; Donnez-nous aujourd'hui notre pain/faim quotidien[ne]." For are we more alive by completion, which puts us to sleep, or absence and desire, which propel us forward to solutions and satisfaction?

[13] The sun lives in a house; so does God. See Ps 18:12, referring to the covering of clouds, here the entire firmament itself.

[14] For the verb *ba'*, to enter, as a doublet, see Appendix 6, "*Antanaclasis.*"

THE ORGANS OF BREATHING: NEFESH. The concept of *presque rien* or "almost nothing" is related by Daniel Sibony to the concept of *Entre Deux* ("Between Two"), referring to a point of transition such as the Sabbath, a no-man's land between two weeks or totalities.[15] At the conclusion of the six days of creation, the text states that the Creator "completed" his work. Sibony notices that the term has as its root the word *kol*,

> "All," a word that "totalizes work in a day without work" and the mark of this All is the Nothing of this empty day. This "nothing" punctuates the All of creation and the two extremities correspond: the all of creation and the emptiness (*vide*) on which it is completed. There is the breath which in-spires (*le souffle qui inspire*) and the one that ex-pires to mark off the repose. Creation lives and breathes, the seven days give the rhythm.[16]

The breath exegesis could be pushed even a step further, since it is stated that

> In six days the Lord made heaven and earth, and on the seventh day he rested and was refreshed (yiNaFaSH).

Exod 31:17

This unusual verbal form (the two other instances are 2 Sam 16:14 and Exod 23:12) is based on the word *nefesh*, typically translated as "soul, desire, neck, self." Here, however, the meaning "breath" is inescapable: And the Lord was refreshed, literally "recovered his-self by taking breath." But does God in fact "breathe?" Compare Qohelet's notion of a breathing, panting lord of his universe "under the sun." How are such associations of ideas related to the world of things, are they to be seen as only figures of speech?[17] May it not occur to us that we are alive only to the extent that the world itself is alive? Is this but a step down to animism, or is it rather an expansion of consciousness toward broader ontologies and encounters?

Hebel *and Friendship with the* Ruakh (re'ut ruakh)

Qohelet's expression *hebel u-re'ut ruakh*, which occurs no fewer than eight times in the first half of the text, presents a precious opportunity to refine our understanding of *hebel* itself;[18] indeed, it has been regarded by

---

[15] See his *Entre-deux* (Paris: Seuil, 1991).

[16] Daniel Sibony, *Lectures bibliques* (Paris: Odile Jacob, 2006), 31.

[17] For *nefesh* as an organ of breathing, see especially Hans Walter Wolff, *Anthropology of the Old Testament* (Mifflintown, PA: Sigler, 1996), 13.

[18] It occurs in 1:14; 2:11, 17, 26; 4:4, 6, 16; 6:9. This latter example presents the slight variant of *ra'yon* for *re'ut* but does not seem to alter the basic meaning.

Thomas Bolin as the critical focus of Qohelet's achievement: *hakol hebel u-re'ut ruakh*, "All is vanity and a chasing after wind" (NRSV).

Bolin, in an article that deserves close study, reads this gnomic phrase as a disjunctive parallelism denoting mortality (*hebel*) on the one hand, and living spirit (*ruakh*) on the other, yielding the sense that

> "all is mortal but strives for immortality."[19]

Bolin sees *re'ut ruakh* as humanity's windy pursuits of trivia that have been transfigured (wrongly, he thinks) into pursuit of the divine spirit. This thesis – that Qohelet argues for restraint against the human desire to be like God – produces a text much less radical and heterodox than often posited, aligning Qohelet with the Hebrew Bible from Genesis 3:5 and the Satan's temptation "to be like God."[20]

Although Bolin begins with his unfortunate choice of vapor as the *peshat* of *hebel*, guaranteeing a negative valence and leaving little room for the positive valences of the true *peshat*, breath (of life), this move is not fatal, since he later consistently attaches *hebel* to the life breath, citing Ps 39:6–7 as stressing the human being's nothingness *in comparison with God*, which is Bolin's main point and should be highlighted rather than put in a footnote:

> See, you have made my days few and brief; and my lifetime is as nothing *in your sight*. Surely all humanity stands as only a breath; surely each person walks like a shadow.[21]

Indeed, the view of *hebel* as referring to mortals parallels my own focus on human beings and their many life pursuits.

Bolin's really exciting innovation here is to identify *ruakh* as the divine spirit, universally understood as "wind," even in such texts as Genesis 1:2.[22] His notion, rather, sees *ruakh* as having "a figurative meaning that

---

[19] "Rivalry and Resignation: Girard and Qoheleth on the Divine-Human Relationship," *Biblica* 86 (2005): 245–59.

[20] Bolin's thesis (ibid.) is powerfully supported by recent scholarship such as J. A. Soggin, "And You Will Be like God and Know What Is Good and Bad," *The Moshe Weinfeld Jubilee Volume*, eds. Chaim Cohen, Avi Hurvitz and Shalom M. Paul (Eisenbrauns: Winona Lake, 2004), 191–93; also, Sneed, *The Politics of Pessimism in Ecclesiastes*. In Chapter 11, I also argue that this is the point of Qohelet's momentous conclusion.

[21] Bolin, p. 247, n. 10. He also cites 3:19 and 12:12 as further proof of the continuity between *ruakh* as both divine and human breath of life, while also taking note of the mention in the two passages of both *ruakh* and *hebel* (p. 250).

[22] See Nahum M. Sarna, *Genesis: The Traditional Hebrew Text with the JPS Translation* (Philadelphia: JPS, 1991), 6. Some de-theologize the phrase and read *ruakh Elohim* as "a mighty wind," and both are possibly intended.

denotes spirit, either as the agent of divine action or the animating principle of humanity" (p. 248).[23] No different from *hebel*, the polysemy of *ruakh* can now be seen as at the center of Qohelet's vision, as common to all three dimensions of being: appearing as God's spirit, as the cosmic wind or air, and the breath of creatures under the sun. In some contexts one of these is clearly intended; in others, the ambiguity is not only possible but undeniable. To opt for a single interpretation across the boards is to deny the poetic polysemy that is the work's literary glory, and also to limit its spiritual possibilities of universal unification.

I would like to extend Bolin's thesis by suggesting that, like its companion *ruakh*, *re'ut* is not limited to a single meaning. I mean that the double meaning of *re'ut* creates a central tension that both confirms and limits Bolin's thesis: *re'ut* as "pursuit," generally regarded as negative in Qohelet, on the one hand, and "friendship with," on the other.[24] Now, if "*friendship with* the divine spirit" is read, then no problem exists, since our human goal is precisely to enjoy and love what God has given, and we can revert to the usual reading of the *waw* as a connective:

All is life-breath *and* a friendship with the divine spirit.

I am proposing that Bolin's point may be enhanced by seeing *hebel* and *re'ut ruakh* as a hendiadys, meaning that the "all" of humankind is precisely to unify mortality, *hebel* as breath of life, through friendship with (*re'ut*) *ruakh*, both the cosmic winds and the divine spirit; and also gratefully to receive and accept God's gifts, beginning with the gift of life that imagines and enjoys transcendence through the sustaining gifts of cosmic and divine life. If the stress is on the negative valence of pursuit as opposed to friendly acceptance, however, then Bolin's strictures seem to apply.

But why would pursuit have a negative valence? Lohfink translates 1:14 as "all [the actions] are a breath, an inspiration of air."[25] While pursuing the wind seems fruitless and foolish because impossible, pursuing the breath, while possible, has a touch of impiety, since it is naturally given (and withdrawn…) only by God, as a gift (12:7). It thus requires no pursuit or striving. Can we then not pursue happiness? Lohfink's

---

[23] Job 32:8; 33:4; Ps 104:30. In Qoh 12:7 it refers to the life-breath. Bolin understands this term to mean "the source of life that comes from God" (p. 246).

[24] T. A. Perry, *Dialogues with Kohelet: The Book of Ecclesiastes: Translation and Commentary* (University Park: Penn State Press, 1993), 69, commentary on 1:14.

[25] Lohfink, *Qoheleth: A Continental Commentary*, ad loc.

formulation is elegant: one must "allow oneself to fall into the happiness offered us."[26]

An alternative interpretation of our phrase is suggested by the repetition of synonymous key words in all of its examples. The most frequent is the word *ma'aseh* (2:17, 4:4) and its plural *ma'asim* (1:14; 2:11), often understood as "deeds," the work of one's hands" (2:11) but with a documented meaning of "possessions" as well, which could be the result of the work of one's hands.[27] The next word in frequency is *'amal*, which also has a dual meaning: "labor," but also the results of labor, "wealth, possessions" (2:11; 4:4, 6). Verse 4:6, the only one without the mention of *hebel*, is also contextualized by both *'amal* and hands. The grand conclusion of Qohelet's confession in 2:26 brings these strands together by focusing on his sinful activities of collecting and gathering: *'asap* and *knas*, declared to be like all the other examples: "This too is *hebel* and *re'ut ruakh*."[28] In sum, all instances of our phrase *hebel u-re'ut ruakh* are closely contextualized by the collection of possessions. It is hardly surprising, therefore, that four of its eight instances lead up to the explicit confession of King Collector and that all of them are to be found in the first half of the book, where that issue predominates and is then dispatched.

Breathe in, Breathe out: The Balance Principle

> After four days of intense Zen learning and practice a student asks the master to summarize the teachings.
>
> The reply:
>
> > Breathe in breathe out;
> >
> > Breathe in breathe out.[29]
> >
> > Breath of breaths
> >
> > (said Qohelet)
> >
> > Breath of breaths.
> >
> > Breath is everything.
>
> Qoh 1:2

In our search for an explanation of the repetition "*hebel* of *hebels*" at the start of Qohelet, mention was made of its possible performative

---

[26] Ibid., p. 97.

[27] See above, p. 19, n. 11.

[28] Bolin highlights both the repetitions and the synonymy of its adjacent components as follows: "That Qoheleth is looking at the sum total of his entire existence is made clear in the redundant nature of the statement: 'All the deeds that my hands have done' is set in parallelism with 'the toil with which I toiled to do it'" (p. 247).

[29] The teacher was the Zen Buddhist poet and teacher Thich Nhat Hanh, as reported to me by Rachel Wizner of New Haven, Connecticut, with my thanks.

function.[30] Here I propose a more positive explanation, one grounded in the *peshat* and referring to the actual fact of breathing:

a) A breath (breathe in) of breaths (breathe out)
b) A breath (breathe in) of breaths (breathe out)

A complete breath-action would be a combined in-spiration and ex-piration, thus the minimum plural *habalim*, breaths.

There are two ways of explaining the repetition AB. The first is that each stands for a different level: the human and the cosmic, the two levels that immediately emerge in the text. The second is that human breathing cannot be established until the complete operation of in and out is repeated and thus confirmed, or that *both* a) and b) constitute a breathing being, whereas a single one would not (yet).

It is well known that attention to the breath is important to awareness and discipline in some spiritual practices. Here attention is directed to the simple *peshat*, actual breathing as a doublet, let us say, since its total meaning is not performed until its two parts converge into one. That is, until the concluding "breath is everything," where an almost nothing (a no-thing thing) becomes an everything and the *peshat* is rocketed to the highest level of universalizing metaphor.

Counting the Breaths: Longevity Formulas

While stressing the impossibility of counting the dust and the stars (Gen 13:16) and the danger of counting humans,[31] Scripture does advise that we count our days:

> So teach us to number our days,
> that we may get a heart of wisdom
>
> Ps 90:12

The formulas used for that purpose present variants that may shed further light on Qohelet's use of *hebel*.

A. LIFE-NUMBERING FORMULAS IN TANAK EXCLUDING QOHELET

#1 The days of one's life

Indeed, in Tanak the standard formula follows this advice to the letter: Life is counted in (the number of) days:

> Tell me, Lord, my end and the measure of my days, what it is.
>
> Ps 39:5

---

[30] See n. 93.

[31] See T. A. Perry, "Cain's Sin in Genesis 4:1–7: Oracular Ambiguity and How to Avoid It," *Prooftexts* 25 (2006): 258–75 at 269–70.

Other biblical examples also give this coloration of brevity and perhaps even disappointment and impending demise, as in the English expression "my days [not: 'my years'] are numbered!" When the formula is preceded by "all," the emphasis is on daily observance or performance (Deut 4:9).

#2 The years of one's life
Whereas the above formula is sometimes preceded by "the number of," specific numbers are never given. However, with the addition of *shenei* (*shanim*, years), the formula is different:

> Now the life of Sarah one hundred years and twenty years and seven years: [These were] *the years of Sarah's life.*
>
> Gen 23:1; also 25:17; Exod 6:16, 18, 20

#3 The days of the years
These two formulas can be joined:

> The days of our years are seventy years,
> And, with strength, eighty.
>
> Ps 90:10

#4 The days of the years of one's life
These preceding formulas can be conflated, and most of these occur in Genesis:

> Now these are the days of the years of the life of Abraham.
>
> Gen 25:7

> [Pharaoh to Jacob] How many are the days of the years of your life?
>
> Gen 47:8

> The days of the years of my sojournings .... Few and evil have been the days of the years of my life, and they have not reached the days of the years of the lives of my fathers.
>
> Gen 47:9

> And it was, the days of Jacob, the years of his life…
>
> Gen 47:28

The only example (other than Qohelet) outside Genesis projects the same tone of extreme age and disappointment. Barzillai excuses himself from accepting the king's invitation to live at court:

How many of the days of the years of my life [are left] that I should go up with the king to Jerusalem?

2 Sam 19:35[32]

The addition of "days" to the two preceding formulas adds nothing to the numbering, which is in years. English usage may be helpful here, in reflecting on the difference between "my years are numbered," with a perhaps merely neutral stress on longevity. "My days are numbered," however, shortens the expectation considerably, with also a hint of impending demise. The remarkable text of Ps 90:10 brings both outward valences and parameters into a single projection.

B. LIFE-NUMBERING FORMULAS IN QOHELET

#1 The number of days of one's life

There are four examples:

The sense of brooding detected in the mention of "days" in the last examples is also seen in the following advice to avoid such sour thoughts:

One should not brood too much over *the days of his life,*

because God keeps him busy enjoying himself.

5:19 JPS

The positive valence is also evident in the mention of life as a gift to be appreciated and enjoyed:

the days of life that God has granted him under the sun.

8:15

… during the *number of days of his life,* that God has given him under the heavens.

5.17

what good people can acquire during the number of days of their life.

2:3

Perhaps read "numbered" if a negative twist seems suggested by the catchphrase "under the heavens."

---

[32] For more on Barzillai the Gileadite see T. A. Perry, *Wisdom in the Hebrew Bible: God's Twilight Zone* (Peabody, MA: Hendrickson, 2014), 154–56.

#2 is absent in Qohelet, and #3 has a single example, both perhaps due to the brevity of the book:

#2 The days of one's years

If a man engenders a hundred and lives many years,
as many as will be the days of his years, if he is not
satisfied from the good things…

6:3[33]

#3 The days of my *hebel* (*yemei hebli*)

A most interesting variant on the usual Tanak formula #1 involves a telling substitution:

I have seen it all in *the days of my hebel.*

7:15

I will not live forever. Leave me alone, for my days are *hebel.*

Job 7:16

As in Deut 4:9 cited in this section, the valence shifts from negative to positive with the addition of "all":

Enjoy life with the woman you love **all** *the days* of the life *of your hebel* that [God] has given you under the sun **all** *the days of your hebel.* For this is your portion in life and through the means for which you toil under the sun.

9:9

Purported parallels of the phrase *yemei hebli* are the following:

beit tefilati, literally "the house of my prayer" and rendered in English as "my house of prayer," meaning "my house a house of prayer" (this is the standard way to express this in Biblical Hebrew)

har kodshi, literally "the mountain of my holiness" and rendered in English as "my holy mountain, meaning "my mountain the mountain of holiness."

On the basis of these parallels we are offered the following English translation: "The days of my *hebel,* my *hebelesque* days," explained to mean: my days are *hebel,* ephemeral, insubstantial, absurd.

This rendition is to be rejected on two related counts. First of all, in the two examples, the two members of the *semichut* or construct state are both nouns (house and prayer, mountain and holiness, and such is the case in *yemei hebli* as well (days and *hebel*). In the translation, however,

---

[33] Noteworthy is the unusual absence of the word "life"; see also Ps 90:10: "The days of our years are seventy."

hebli has morphed into an adjective "*hebelesque*," and this disqualifies the parallel. Secondly, this is an egregious example of injecting interpretation before following the direction of the simple *peshat*, the translation of which is primarily as follows: "my days days of breath, my breath days, the days of my life as counted in breaths (rather than years or indeed days)."

This explanation may help to interpret the intriguing addition of *khayei* to this formula:

#4 The days *of the life* [*khayei*] of one's hebel

Apparently riding on the strength of this substitution and patterned on the tripled structure of the Tanak formula #4, Qohelet twice takes a direction that is found only in that book:

> Who knows what is good for a person in life *the [total] number [= all] of the days of the **life** of his hebel?*
>
> 6:12

> Enjoy life with the woman you love *all the days of the **life** of your hebel* that [God] has given you under the sun all the days of your *hebel*. For this is your portion in life and through the means for which you toil under the sun.
>
> 9:9

To reread Qohelet from the perspective of "the days of the **life** of your breath(ing)" could lead in interesting directions. Even here, of course, we might still be as oblivious to our lives as we are to our breathing.

Or as conscious. Consider the paradigm:

> The days of your life = your life days, the days you are alive
>
> The days of your *hebel* = your breath days = the days that you breathe, have life.

It is true, of course, that such a figure – that breath suggests brevity and emptiness – is characteristic of many of the uses of *hebel* in the Hebrew Bible, including Qohelet:

> "I have seen it all in the days of my *hebel*" (Qoh 7:15; also 9:9).

Only in Qohelet, however, is the word attached to life itself. This particularly loaded formula poignantly reaches even further into life, its very beginning and end that we saw in 3:2, referring to the birth and death of the other, one's child.

Life is given out in days and years, the solar cycles. But it is ultimately (i.e., at the defining edges, those that constitute a totality) given also in breaths, witness a baby's first cry-breath, or the final breaths of the moribund. From personal experience I know the final "passing" of the breath of another, when the eyes that saw the sun-filled earth and the mouth that breathed the life-filled air are closed. Such an experience of death remains with one all the days of one's *hebel*-life. No memory is truer than this one, which looks both backward and forward, a "futured past," perhaps.

To be sure, even when an abstract sense of a metaphor imposes itself on a translator, either because of context or because the original meaning has been worn out or occluded, the intent of etymological research is to sense the trace of the concrete reference below the surface. This typically uncovers a new depth and poignancy of focus: "The woman that God has given you under the sun all the days of your breaths" (9:9). Life is measured out in years and days and, most intimately, in breaths. Full expanse of time and immanence as well, each moment measured by a breath of breaths (1:2; 12:8).

Dreams

> Let your words be few:
> Just as a dream come with too much busyness,
> So too a fool's voice with too many words.
>
> Qoh 5:1–2

Michael V. Fox raises the important question of cause and effect in the relationship between dreams and busyness, opting for the "probable" solution that dreams are accompanied by busyness rather than that busyness provokes dreams.[34] I suspect that Fox's hesitation points to deeper philosophical underpinnings here, what Levinas refers to as the identity of cause and effect or at least their perpetual ambivalence ("Do I love you because you are beautiful or are you beautiful because I love you?").

The problem of the excessive presence of dreams is evoked in another verse as well:

> When dreams multiply, and puffs of breath (*habalim*)
> and endless words, then fear God."
>
> 5:6

The parallelistic paradigm is as follows:

> dreams / much busyness/ too many words
> dreams / many puffs of breath/ too many words.

---

[34] Michael V. Fox, *A Time to Tear Down and a Time to Build: A Rereading of Ecclesiastes* (Grand Rapids, MI: Eerdmans, 1999), 231.

What we may have here is the anatomy of one's loss of control over the self, as evidenced by the random nature and content of dreams, on the one hand, and endless and pointless babble, on the other. The focus is even more precise, since the origin of uncontrolled words is plotted in the psyche. What is perhaps more to the point of our present inquiry, however, is the mediation between inner and outer: the "busyness" or unsettled mind in 5:1 and, more precisely, the multiple puffs of breath (*habalim*) in 5:6.[35] In this remarkably succinct verse, the love of excess is traced from inner preoccupations (dreams) to huff-puff overexcitement, to the words that express them. Here the gentle rhythmical flow of breathing in and out is disrupted, signaling inner turmoil, what occurs when the natural, rhythmical breathing in and out is disrupted. One popular antidote is simply to "take a deep breath."

On the model of the weaving of my body-flesh with the world-flesh,[36] so too my breath with the cosmic winds, my inspiration with the creative spirit. Are words only puffs of air? Is *hebel* only human breath, and does it necessarily have to be abstracted into vanity rather than toward the body that receives it and sends it back? Why do we always seek to disembody and eviscerate our metaphors? Why must our minds always lord it over our instincts, our philosophical abstractions over our polysemic outreach, "from the depths," as it were?

3. *To Lives!* C'est La Vie!

I have tried to take Nietzsche's observation seriously: "This concept of being, the only representation of it that we have is the fact of living." Philosophy can no longer hide itself from a reflection on the living, on respiration, on the breath. *Lehaim*: To life! Or rather: To lives! … *Life* is not a concept, it is only an entity through which we can lay claim to get to the bottom of things. *Lives.* I interpret in my own way this uncertain plural which gives room to thinking about the continuity and the diversity of the living.

Elisabeth de Fontenay[37]

---

[35] The traditional critical allergy to referring to the true *peshat* of *hebel* reaches an amusing point in Fox's rendition of *hebel* as "vapor," while conceding that this "straddles its literal sense, which comes from the mouth," (*A Time to Tear Down*, 233). Apparently, whatever reaches the interpretive goal of "absurdities" is rather tempting.

[36] Bettina Bergo, referring to Merleau-Ponty's "privileging the weaving of body-flesh and world-flesh" in his rejection of "pure" phenomenology. "The Face in Levinas," *Angelaki* 16 (2011): 17–38 at 33.

[37] *Actes de naissance* (Paris: Seuil, 2011), 71. The concept "life" in Hebrew is expressed in the plural: *khayim*, "lives."

Thirty-seven *hebels* in the thin Book of Qohelet: must we continue to think of a single level of *hebel,* as monochromatic readings insist ("vanity! Absurd!")? Are we not presented, rather, with a census or recording of encounters between breathing living beings and real life, viewed by some as the focus of the wisdom movement: to lives![38]

Giving Birth versus Being Born?: Qohelet 3:2
Misreading or emending a text in order to buttress a particular point of view can have serious consequences. Such is the tactic in interpreting the Catalog of the Times, where, it is claimed, "the time of being born and dying heads the list."[39]

> There is a time *to be born* and a time to die.
>
> 3:2, as emended in NRSV, Vulgate, Fox
>
> There is a time *to give birth* and a time to die.[40]

Commenting on the emended text rather than the received one, Alison Lo opines:

> Placing the life-death issue at the head of the catalogue of the times in fact alludes less to the life cycle than to the theme of fatalism that pervades the whole chapter. A person does not choose to be born or die.[41]

Lo continues by quoting Machinist:

> "So overwhelming in Qohelet's meditation is the presence of death as the divinely pre-determined point in all existence."[42]

---

[38] Qohelet is summoning the wisdom movement "to return to the central focus of wisdom itself and its chief referent – life" Robert K. Johnston, "'Confessions of a Workaholic': A Reappraisal," *CBQ* 38 (1976): 14–28 at 15. Johnston continues, citing Roland Murphy: "The kerygma of wisdom can be summed up in one word: life" ("The Kerygma of the Book of Proverbs," 9). See also the title of Roland E. Murphy's study of wisdom, *The Tree of Life. An Exploration of Biblical Wisdom Literature* (New York: Doubleday, 1990): "wisdom literature is exciting because it deals directly with life" (p. ix). See also Eunny P. Lee, *The Vitality of Enjoyment in Qohelet's Theological Rhetoric* (Berlin/New York: Walter de Gruyter, 2005), 62–72, also 35.

[39] Alison Lo, "Death in Qohelet," *Journal of the Ancient Near Eastern Society* 31 (2009): 85–98 at 89.

[40] Lohfink; Murphy; Krüger translates "bear, procreate," and notes crucially, as against the emendation, "the fact that active verbs are used exclusively in what follows." Thomas Krüger, *Qoheleth: A Commentary* (Minneapolis: Fortress, 2004), ad loc.

[41] See note 39 to this chapter.

[42] Peter Machinist, "Fate, *miqreh,* and Reason: Some Reflection of Qohelet and Biblical Thought," in *Solving Riddles and Untying Knots,* ed. Z. Zevit et al. *Festschrift for Shemaryahu Talmon* (Winnona Lake, IN: Eisenbrauns, 1995), 159–75 at 172.

What is here advanced as the extreme importance of the death theme – in this most popular of chapters and, by extension, in all of Qohelet – is now further reinforced by the theme of fate, which we will discuss below. While indeed one does not choose to be born, this becomes an issue only in the emended text, as we shall see. Moreover, this argumentative reading of 3:2 imposes a pall of fatality on a text that otherwise – in its original intention – does project real choices and positive activities for humans: planting, dancing, building. Beyond that, the alleged fatalism of death takes on an individual focus uncongenial to the general *social* orientation of the Catalog as a whole. The emendation, in short, is a self-fulfilling projection that has little bearing on Qohelet's text; and it would seem that, beyond the ritually advanced motivations of the emendation as based on reasons of parallelism and logic, deeper and ideological motivations also emerge, as we shall see. First, however, we must strive to interpret the MT.

In spite of the near universal translation of "to be born and die" – which would make this pair the only one in the series beyond human control – "to give birth," birthing or parenting, is not only the correct meaning of the received text but also the preferred one. The entire focus of this catalog is the alternation of opposites expressing human fortunes as a constant flux between joy and sadness, what is normally regarded as good and bad fortune or simply "good" and "evil" (not morally speaking, but rather what is conveyed by *yapeh* in 3:11), and which the author expresses by the word "time" (as the French *bon-heur*, happiness, that which happens in a good hour, and *mal-heur*, that which happens in a bad-hour).[43]

The first opposition is not between one's own life and death but rather those of others (loved ones) that we experience. Levinas explains that we do not suffer our own death since we are no longer there to suffer it. The real pain is the death of others, those we love and will never again have. The message: know that this child of yours that you bring into the world will also pass from it. The other verse that toggles life and death is 7:1, and there too the contrast is between one's self and one's progeny: "Better the day of [my] death than the day of *his* [the child's] birth." That is to say, my death is all the better in that I gave birth to a child. Gabriel Marcel offers a similar perspective. Though able to take head-on the horror of his own death,

---

[43] See Appendix 3, "Quotationals."

> It is not the same regarding the death of the other. If Gabriel Marcel's death
> holds no interest for Gabriel Marcel, if meditation on death quickly runs
> short, the death of a beloved person is a piercing preoccupation... I cannot
> speak *strictu sensu* of my own death. As soon as I speak of *my* death, I am
> doubled, I inevitably think of someone for whom *my* death would be *his*
> death ...[44]

The problem with this word, in the eyes of many readers, is that it devi-
ates from all other members of the oppositional series, and in two ways.
On the one hand, it is the only member of the series that has a passive
sense, since one is not born voluntarily; and, on the other, the true opposite of "to die," is not "to give birth" but rather "to be born." The common tactic here is thus to homogenize the verse by tampering with the
text, reading "to give birth" as a coordinate of "to die." Thus,

> There is a time to be born and a time to die.

The urge to homogenize can be honored, however, by respecting the
received text as it stands. For those who, in the spirit of parallelism, wish
to harmonize the text in the direction of perceived oppositions in the
remainder of the Catalog, death would indeed be the opposite of birth,
but this does not say whose death. Why assume that it is one's own death?
Indeed, to consider the "Catalog of the Times" (3:2–8) as a unified com-
position, the opening and closing verses give a clear and unusual picture
of Qohelet's true focus:

> A time to give birth to another / a time for that other to die
> A time for war / a time for peace.

This elegant chiasm birth/death // death/life that begins with the individual Other now ends with the death and survival of the entire community of Others, forming an *inclusio* that bears the weight of the book's
main argument: human life and its possible negation.

Pursuing the urge to homogenize, why not apply this tactic here as
well, especially since that is the *peshat* of the verb and does not require
any tampering. This would allow two additional possibilities to "a time
to die":

1) the death of my own child. The moral: have a child even though
   you know it will die.

---

[44] Reconstructed by Xavier Tilliette, "Gabriel Marcel et l'autre royaume," in *Jean Wahl et
Gabriel Marcel* (Paris: Beauchesne, 1976), 35.

2) stressing the active sense of the entire series, this adds the important possibility that I can commit murder. In Levinas's words, "The first death is the death of the Other."[45]

For the emendation "a time to be born," the problem, after being acknowledged, remains: that this is the only member of the series that does not have an active or causative sense. By retaining the received text, however, the harmonization can be carried forward to the latter part of the verse, yielding the balanced opposition between giving life and giving death, through murder. Levinas continues: "Death leads to the face of the Other, which expresses the commandment: Thou shalt not kill."[46] We must start with the concept of murder as suggesting the complete sense of death.

Rethinking Death: The Miqreh/*Fate Theory*
   Le vent se lève. Il faut tenter de vivre.
      Paul Valéry, "Le Cimetière marin"

Should we then think life from the point of view of death, or rather the reverse? Levinas raises the issue from the perspective of Bloch's utopianism: We should think death by starting with time, and not, as does Heidegger, to think time beginning with death.[47] For it makes all the difference between saying "death is part of life" and "life is part of death." Few would opt for the second formulation, yet many in fact think in these terms and would like to include Qohelet among them. Take as an example – perhaps unfair in terms of the brilliance of the paper – is Machinist's study of *miqreh*, understood as the abstract (and Greek) concept "fate," which he defines as an 'occurrence,' and "not just any occurrence but one that is predetermined and defines the life events of humans and animals. It becomes thus an abstract concept, and we are not wrong in translating it as 'fate'."[48] The irony is palpable, wherein DEATH is viewed as not only a life event but *the* life event, the one that "cuts across all moral categories of humans." Suddenly life has become a death event, one moreover to be understood in terms of an abstraction. Isn't that also what has happened to *hebel*, which also is typically treated only as an abstraction ("vanity, absurdity")?

[45] "Emmanuel Levinas, *Dieu la mort et le temps* (Paris: Grasset, 1993), 53, 121.
[46] Ibid., 122.
[47] Ibid., 133.
[48] Machinist, "Fate, *miqreh*, and Reason," 166.

Why then not start at the opposite end and think from birth, focusing on the live-ing rather than the mort-al? Because, Machinist posits, that would leave Qohelet "in an open-ended situation of intellectual chaos" (p. 167). The assumption seems to be that the intellect operates at maximum efficiency only when the data is already in and life's messiness and openness are not there to cloud up foregone conclusions. Can the intellect, however, not deal with the perhaps or the fluid or unpredictable openness? Or cannot critics formulate concepts such as *peshat*-metaphors to gather life data, abundantly available. Going to the Greeks will spell Greek; going to Scriptural traditions will generate, rather than abstractions, meaningful formulations and clues for dealing with real living. Rather than the abstractions that are the goal of thought, might not metaphor and polysemy lead in more fruitful directions? I for one follow Qohelet in preferring poetry and poetic meditation:

> Life's true form traverses the two domains [of life and death], the blood of the greater circuit rolls through both: there is neither a down here and beyond, but rather a great unity.
>
> Rilke[49]

Exegesis is slowly making this about-face as well, as when Alison Lo ventures that "life and death are mutually defining" (p. 96). And in choosing life (Deut 30:19), one should have in mind especially the life of the Other. This may be considered the main *mitzvah* or commandment, since without it there are no others. Or Others.

Vivere *and* BENE Vivere: *The Reign of the Adverb*

> There is no evil in itself. Independent of human intention, things are only indifferent, and these indifferent things become simply good or bad according to *the manner in which we wish them.*
>
> Vladimir Jankélévitch[50]

The sages were aware that, beyond doing and all its compulsions, there is a *manner* of doing. They observed that actions (and their results) are not always, if ever, within our power, but that the attitude and manner of their performance always is. The Stoics loved to think life through the metaphor of play-acting: we are given a role and a script, and that is the one we must perform, thus not what but how. Grammatically speaking,

---

49 Raina Maria Rilke, letter to Hulewicz, cited and studied by Maurice Blanchot, *L'Espace littéraire* (Paris: Gallimard, 1955), 169.

50 Vladimir Jankélévitch, *Le Sérieux de l'intention: Traité des vertus I* (Paris: Flammarion, 1983), 13, italics added. See also Santob de Carrión, p. 149, and Appendix 3, "Quotationals."

the part of speech that attracts the attention of the sage is not nouns and their adjectives, and not even verbs, but their adverbs.

Beneath or beyond the particular assigned script, however, there is the substratum of the performer herself, who still has the choice to perform or not. Such a withdrawal – beyond the radical one of suicide – would be a refusal to "say" the lines, to reject the script. A refusal to play the part of "doing" something refers the playacting metaphor back to its *peshat,* so to speak, for at the base of the actor is the person. The acting metaphor of course is founded on an ambiguity. On the one hand, its alliance with "action, activity" plays to the doer in myself; but when I withdraw from my role, am I necessarily "doing" nothing? This matter of negative morality or action ("Just say 'No'") is prominent in wisdom literature, beginning with Psalm 1, which opens the entire Psalter with a list of what *not* to do to be happy. Or Psalm 6, which, after listing six things that the righteous person does *not* do, concludes: "One who *does* these things will never be moved" (v. 5). For non-activity can be a supreme *action* – Montaigne gives chastity as an example of such passive-action. Such non-doing must be considered as a manner of "just" living, like "merely" breathing perhaps. On the other hand, there is a focused withdrawal in which living is both its own content and method: livingly. Unscripted but able to take on the required script according to the needs of the "times" (Chapter 3) and the will of the Author.

And also according to human input and wisdom. The matter came up with Montaigne, who, when asked what he did today, replied: "I lived!" Just as the goal of love is to "love lovingly," Qohelet's suggestion is to live livingly, taking life on its own terms, close to the breath and in rhythmical exchange with the outer worlds. For, asks the poet, why would one wish to play tennis with the net down? Life, in Qohelet's formulation, is given as a gift, but the manner is a human achievement: joyfully. In Lohfink's formulation, "people must appropriate happiness by being joyful," and "humans should be joyful as long as they can."[51]

Quotationals: "Good" and "Evil" Are What People Say
For a long time now critics have told us that Qohelet's contradictions can be explained as quotations of someone else with whom he disagrees.[52] According to this understanding, we have a mere rhetorical device whereby Qohelet distances himself from divergent opinions and there is

[51] Lohfink, *Qoheleth: A Continental Commentary,* pp. 134, 135.
[52] For a summary see Michael V. Fox, "The Identification of Quotations in Biblical Literature," *ZAW* 92 (1980): 416–30.

no contradiction in his own thought. Unless, as I have argued elsewhere, contradictions are themselves part of his thought, indeed intrinsic to the human condition of change and maturation, so that "I may happen to contradict myself, but ... I never contradict truth."[53] In the present study and at a deeper existential level, I have presented a reformed Qohelet, one who gives up the power game in favor of human culture, and both of these Qohelets are represented in the book. Thus Qohelet has two voices, and contradictions can be seen as natural expressions of his change of orientation. Disagreements of course remain; indeed, they are essential to his bipolar orientation. However, his change of direction refers constantly to his previous self; indeed, it is only in this way that his new orientation can be measured and remain firmly in place.

There is also a different level of quotationals in Qohelet's thinking, one that makes up the very fabric of human life. Its clearest, indeed definitional example occurs in the preface to the "Elegy on Dying":

> Remember your Creator in the days of your strength, before those "bad days" come, and years arrive *when you will say*: "I have no interest (*khepets*) in them."

12:1[54]

Recalling Roland Barthes's advice to always ask "who is speaking now?" we can distinguish the narrative voice ("Remember your Creator") from the one who will lose interest in life and refer to it as "bad days." Here the authorial voice is not giving her own opinion on old age but rather quoting what the listener will be saying and, more broadly, what people typically say as they deal with concrete living and aging. Theoretically speaking, things (and the human interests that pursue them) are indifferent, neither good nor bad in themselves. This means that "good" and "bad" and other such evaluative words *are always evaluative and quotational*, related only to the personal *khepets* that they express.[55] I would argue that this reading also applies to God in such a text as the following:

> If you are having a "good" day, enjoy it! And when it is "bad," consider [this]: God has made the one as well as the other, so that humans might not understand anything of His motives.

7:13–14

---

53 Montaigne, *Les Essais* III:2, 1991, 907–08.
54 For a discussion of the entire Elegy see Perry, *Wisdom in the Hebrew Bible*, 125–56.
55 See the texts by Jankélévitch and Santob de Carrión quoted in n. 50.

To state the matter boldly, God does not make things "good" or "bad": we do.

Such personal quotations are to be contextualized, from a wisdom perspective, as follows. We live in a world that hems us in on both sides: nature, which has its own way of doing things; and God who does the same. These are independent systems that do not respond to my ego wants and needs – they may of course correspond, but they also may not. Thus, for each thing (e.g., tomatoes) there is a *khepets*: the tomatoes will ripen according to their own rhythm, not mine. As represented in the Catalog of the Times, natural and social events depend in part on my own positive input. When it comes to relating to God, however, given God's and nature's independence and unknowability, then restraint and non-behaviors seem to predominate: "*Don't* vow," and so forth.

Qohelet's deeper point, though, is that *all* our judgments are quotations, impressions, and expressions of what we feel at the moment, and this applies even and especially to self-quotations. Since judgments and evaluations are good and bad only relatively (this is the only absolute truth here), then why get upset when things do not go your way? They are beyond your control! Calm down, go with the breath.

To review, the world's axiological indifference (neither positive nor negative) is presented as an enigma; no absolute notions of good and bad, there are only *yapeh*, and that is God's point of view, not ours. That does *not* mean that humans need be indifferent. Our choice, however, is always between what is good for my ego development and enjoyment, on the one hand, and what is good or bad for the Other. When the world's intrinsic indifference becomes a human philosophical choice, the modalities become problematic to the "normal" ways of community thinking. One example would be Camus's Meursault (*The Stranger*), whose indifference is tenderized, so to speak, and transferred to the world itself as *la tendre indifférence du monde*. Another literary example would be Bartleby, whose ego desires are vaporized into mere "preferences" and thus out of reach of "normal" human assertions. It seems to me that Qohelet's *hebel* litany, even when initially read as ranting and raving, arrives at a point of emotional stasis through the mere pulverizing force of repetition.

4. *The Literary Genre of Qohelet*

A crucial and as yet unresolved literary question regarding Qohelet is its generic definition: is it treatise, diatribe, sermon, satire, reflection, autobiography, confession, poetry,[56] essay, wisdom collection, and if so what kind? While our search would ideally be for a single generic definition that encompasses the entire received text and accounts for its literary unity, we remind ourselves that to date the most accurate description of the work's literary genre may still be Roland Murphy's, who declared Qohelet to be *sui generis*. It seems to me that "wisdom collection" may be a workable solution. The book is, after all, the work of a Qohelet or collector, and one who sets out on a quest for wisdom (1:12, 16, 18). Moreover, this designation may also serve as a meta-concept, seeing Qohelet as pursuing multiple generic directions. Thus, just as figures of speech are often figures of thought as well, a rich and expanded literary sense of "collection" may itself develop and expand the work's ideology. I do not suggest, of course, that such a collector's pursuit is systematic, mainly out of respect for the fragmentation and messiness of daily experience.

Qohelet Is a Wisdom and Maxim Collection
Perhaps we can begin where for centuries interpretation has taken greatest interest and delight, in Qohelet's putative pessimism – all, of course, focused on his spirituality or lack thereof. By viewing Qohelet's discontent from the perspective of maxim collections and modern practitioners of the genre, we may further reflect on the strengths and weaknesses of this approach, in particular how he recovers from his philosophical immobility and attempts to return to the world. Let us scan some generic similarities and divergences between Qohelet and other types of collections. Take the following works: the biblical Book of Proverbs, LaRochefoucauld's *Maximes*, and any of Cioran's gnomic writings (e.g., *Syllogismes de l'amertume*), Marcus Aurelius's *Thoughts*, and Montaigne's *Essais*. All are wisdom collections, but the differences will bring Qohelet's into sharper relief.

A collection involves gathering certain things together that are related by similarity of style and purpose, such as a stamp or doll collection. Common examples of word-thing collections would be dictionaries and phone books. Wisdom collections have as a purpose to teach a way of living, and among their distinguishing features are the length of each

---

[56] Although Qohelet is not predominantly a poetic work, roughly one-third of it is presented in some kind of poetic style. Its most outstanding poetic feature is perhaps polysemy, such as allows the rich development of the *hebel* concept. For further thoughts, see Chapter 9 and Conclusions. The best study of the effect of sound repetition remains Scott B. Noegel, "Word Play in Qohelet," *Journal of Hebrew Scriptures* 7 (2007): 2–28.

individual item and the connections among the items. What seems to me most pervasive, stylistically speaking, are the following:

1) that Qohelet offers a large number of wisdom sayings or aphorisms or proverbs;
2) that these proverbs are strung together in some kind of collection, not always sequential, but more so than traditional collections such as the Book of Proverbs – exception taken, of course, to chapters 1–9.

First of all, what is being collected? The Book of Proverbs is a collection of proverbs, brief and end-stopped sayings hardly related to one another except in casual ways. In the other works thoughts and reflections are collected. Stylistically speaking, maxims are closest to proverbs in their brevity, yet they tend to expand to prose, still succinct but less so than epigrams, say. Thus, although proverbs and maxims both often survive in collections, strings of pearls of wisdom that constitute their own subgenre of wisdom literature, proverb collections often gather sayings helter-skelter. And since maxims are generally stylistically longer than proverbs, they tend to string themselves more easily together, constituting units of sustained narrative. In the case of maxims, such extended narratives tend to be pessimistic, though not always so.

Now, whereas the Book of Proverbs is more truly a collection, Qohelet's personal, autobiographical persona, especially in chapter 2, imposes a pervasive tone of confession and complaint, a pessimism that colors many of its parts, a methodological reflection that could be compared to Montaigne's *Essays*, were it not for Qohelet's moodiness and predictably (to some) negative twist, declaring that "this too is *hebel.*" Maxims are typically referred to the personality of their speaker, as reflecting a consistent or at least recognizable global point of view. I therefore propose that Qohelet is less a proverb collection than a book of maxims on life's meaning, as all such books are. Rather than both the straight valuations and metaphors common to proverbs, Qohelet's reflective style simply recounts the facts of daily experience (as he sees them) and especially the overall meaning that they collectively seem to have. Thus, Qohelet the writer of maxims or maximizer (it would be more appropriate, of course, to call him the minimizer) does not set out to solve particular problems but rather to state and characterize the general problem of human existence itself.

Let us try to state this differently. Like proverbs, maxims project the presumption of authority. Through rhetorical tricks such as generalizations and pithiness they attempt to persuade us that their observations are general truths of universal application. Unlike proverbs, the projected anonymity of their origin is betrayed in every instance, for rather than proverbs' voice of age-old, popular consent, maxims couch their generalizations in the discourse of personal reflection. Literature thus distinguishes two voices of universal truth, similar only at the surface. The one advances experiential observations as general truths such as "Haste makes waste." The other hypothesizes general truths from personal observations – for instance, LaRochefoucauld's relentless rehash of his comment that "our virtues are only vices in disguise." So that at the heart of the former there is a democratic tyranny; behind the other a wounded pride but also a scientific modesty.

In wisdom contexts such as the Book of Proverbs and Qohelet, this scenario has to be slightly adjusted. Proverbs such as are found in the Book of Proverbs invite to action and critical thinking; the mood induced by maxim narratives such as Qohelet – at least according to most pessimistic readings – is one of (often morose) meditation. It may thus be appropriate to call Qohelet a maxim collection – that is, a sustained *and realistic* reflection on life's meaning and value. It may address particular circumstances and issues, but each unit is steeped in a more general sense. Nothing is more eloquent in this regard than LaRochefoucauld's decision to set the tone of his entire collection of maxims by an epigraph. The parallel with Qohelet seems clear: "breath of breaths," a coloration that runs through the entire maxim collection and that has succeeded in imposing a particular bias upon generations of readers. Thus, Michael V. Fox speaks repeatedly of Qohelet's literary cohesiveness as constituted by the framework of perception of a "single brooding consciousness."[57]

For those who would maximize Qohelet's pessimism, maxims become a way of maximizing the void. At least the opening chapters of Qohelet are a disavowal, a renouncement of past pleasures and efforts. It is less repentance in the classical sense that I am sorry I did it than in the sense that I would never do it again: "What profit to humans?"[58]

It is not helpful to minimize or limit Qohelet's radical and blanket brooding over existence, the superlative and totalizing "breath of breath, repeat, all is breath." Anyone who has lived a full human life senses the deep relevance of these words, but our commentaries do not always go

---

[57] Michael V. Fox. *Qohelet and His Contradictions* (Sheffield: Almond, 1989), 159; *A Time to Tear Down*, 151.

[58] See, for example, the Cioran text quoted above, p. 50.

to the heart of the issue. I mean that this central term *hebel,* what we have
agreed to call "breath," has come to have several senses:

> without knowability, not questioning the existence of absolute truths but
> claiming, rather, that we have no access to them
> without meaning (*Sinnlos*)
> without permanent or extra value or *yitron*

One should be more critical of such totalizations, however. Even the interpretation "vanity" suggests "nothing," and "nothing" is neither positive
nor negative, it simply denotes the leveling of values or, better yet, their
absence. Humans try to rectify this nothingness by creating value, and
this is here described as a *re'ut ruakh,* a chasing after or herding the wind,
perhaps, but also and especially an "afflictio spiritus," a human intensity
and passionate effort that, given universal "breath," is simply inappropriate. What *is* appropriate in such a universe is certainly not anger or disappointment but rather withdrawal (chronicled in Qohelet chapter 2),
resignation, deep indifference, what some are tempted to call quietism.

Although we have used a rather refined and restricted religious concept to characterize a neglected area of Qohelet's spirituality, it seems to
me that his quietism is both limited and of the practical sort, and this in
several senses. First of all, Qohelet does not present a treatise, a systematic proof of the necessity of quietism, since that would undermine his
general point of knowledge's insufficiency and, more dangerously, further its enormous pretense. Secondly, a usual quietism based on a radical trust in only God in the abstract would be but another occasion for
pretense, for a secret feeling of supremacy over the spiritual approaches
of others. No, his general sense is that things must be worked out prac-
tically, must be consistent in every detail with the quotidian character of
our personal existence and reflection.

Autobiography and Pseudo-Authorship: The Collector's Presence
How these bits of personal and traditional wisdom sayings are strung
together to form an identity – both personal and, as we shall see later,
social – points to a profound connection between collection and authorship. In this case a very interesting one, given a double modesty that
conditions the narrative: that of a merely *pseudo*-authorship, and the tentative nature of fragmentary experience that he gathers in.[59]

---

[59] For an outstanding instance of the method of stringing proverbs into an autobiography,
see T. A. Perry, *The Moral Proverbs of Santob de Carrión* (Princeton, NJ: Princeton University
Press, 1987).

I begin with Roland Barthes, who, while declaring the death of the author, reclaimed the need for one.[60] In the case of Qohelet, Barthes's imaginative need is more than a critic's fantasy. Inscribed in the text as the author's pseudonym Qohelet, it becomes the focus of the work's interpretation. For no ancient text poses more (in)directly the enigma of authorship than the biblical book of Ecclesiastes. Directly because its purported author, King Solomon, is hardly concealed by the *nom de plume*, since it is attached by the specification "son of David, and King in Jerusalem."[61] Directly because this author's "name," as the narrative unfolds, encodes the entire plot and must be unpacked if the pedagogical message is to be grasped. It is thus a deliberate and purposeful enigma, a challenge and a tease to provoke and formulate questions of authorship. Indeed, from the very start, what could have been a benign self-introduction ("[These are the] words of Solomon"), it is the author function that both sets the discourse in motion and dominates/directs the work's plot and themes. Since the author himself (or herself) self-deconstructs by a partial rather than a full self-concealment, both of Barthes's wishes are accommodated: his grand denial of authorial existence and his need for some kind of real literary presence. Thus, in both worlds – that of literary structure and historical reality – the author's pseudo-name "Qohelet" becomes the focus of the work's interpretation.

Between Scylla and Charybdis, as we used to say. On the one hand, Barthes's famous claim that the author is dead; on the other hand, Foucault:

> Since literary anonymity is not tolerable, we can accept it only in the form of an enigma.[62]

Since authorial anonymity is intolerable and direct or full authorship impossible, what of Qohelet? I shall suggest that such a navigation between opposing negatives constitutes a kind of *partial* enigma, a meta-enigma, if you will, in that it focuses on the underlying nature or aspect of enigmas that stand out, revealing the pedagogical intent of wisdom literature while projecting an ironic escape route. A parallel

---

[60] Roland Barthes, "The Death of the Author" (1969): http://artsites.ucsc.edu/faculty/Gustafson/FILM%20162.W10/readings/barthes.death.pdf.

[61] The word "and" does not appear but needs to be added to avoid the appellation "King" to David, who of course was king, but everyone knows that. It is v. 1:12 that confirms this, when Qohelet says, "I was king." Since there is no known son of David named Qohelet who was ever king, it is assumed that Solomon is alluded to, especially in view of his grandiose experiments and experiences in both kingship and wisdom, as developed in 1 Kings.

[62] Michel Foucault, "What is an Author?" *Truth and Method*, 109–10.

example of such an authorial ambivalence might be Levinas's desire to play both sides of the coin, asserting that his philosophical research can appear as either purely ethical *or* edifying and theological.[63] By that he means to square the circle, of course, meaning that *both* are the case. So too Qohelet, the most philosophical of our biblical books, still managing to squeak into the canon. By a closing polite bow to orthodoxy, as some claim (fear God and keep the commandments), or, as I argue, by a redefinition of both philosophical ethics and theology so as to accommodate one another, indeed to be aspects of a single spirituality.

Autobiography and Confession: The Quotational Imperative

Let us go directly to Derrida's own [Cir]Confession, which quotes Augustine abundantly, who quotes Scripture abundantly as well, and this quotational trope, as Jill Robbins has pointed out, has typological significance.[64] I think this is true of Derrida as well, although one could argue here that the resemblances are mostly circumstantial (their common geographical origin in North Africa, the death of their mothers). Although Derrida may also be mimicking Augustine's style of presentation, this fact in itself has typological significance in that both Derrida and Augustine seek to expose and perhaps also effect their transformations through writing.[65] In fact, the act of writing becomes a figure (in the spirit, as it were) of Derrida's original circumcision undergone at the age of eight days.

I propose that, like many of Franklin's anonymous proverbs, Qohelet's entire collection is built out of proverbs that he (and perhaps his colleagues) collected – all anonymous, some undoubtedly from the people and others from unnamed sages – as per the program of chapter 12 and quoted for retention and further study. His method is to listen well, to polish them up, straighten them out, and make sure they are true. My point is that collections like Qohelet's are essentially quotational. This is hardly surprising, since wisdom writing is not interested in originality; rather, it is specular, and typology is one of its major figures of thought. It refers to earlier texts as strengthening knowledge, using resemblance in order to establish real personal identity by showing continuity with significant past events and ultimately eschatological hopes. In terms of the overall structure and genre of the Book of Qohelet, then, we may call it a confession,

[63] Emmanuel Levinas, *De Dieu qui vient à l'idée* (Paris: Vrin, 2004), 130.
[64] Jill Robbins, "Circumcising Confession: Derrida, Autobiography, Judaism," *Diacritics* 25 (1995): 25.
[65] Ibid., 24.

understanding this term not in the theological sense of self-exposure (to anyone else including God) but that of a semi-anonymous author/collector of anonymous fragments and quotations that he then himself quotes as possible subjects of study. Confession is thus, very much in Derrida's sense, a circumfession, an ongoing turning around (like the cosmos) of words. The enigma is compounded when we reflect that the purpose of traditional attribution is to establish the author as an *authority figure*, authorship and authority being etymological derivatives of the same word *auctor* and *auctoritas*.[66] In this regard, the pseudonym seems to imply an abandonment of authorial and authoritative appropriation, thus a specular aspect to the renouncement of kingship.

Qohelet goes in a different direction from Barthes but also arrives at the conclusion that we don't need authors. At least not in scientific literature and not in the Bible either. Strangely, the orthodox insistence that the Bible was dictated by God has the same effect, if understood not historically but as "out of the box" and beyond the limited range of human experience, ever open to the infinite (Levinas's favorite word) possibilities of interpretation and human development.

5. *Miscellaneous*

Is All *Vanity?*
In an earlier book I floated an alternative translation of the Book's first and enduring question, usually read as an assertion. I wondered whether the focus was not rather in fact on a matter to be discussed, namely whether that pessimists' beloved thesis could be universalized. Or challenged. Thus, "All is *hebel*" becomes, revocalized,

"Is All *hebel?*"

As the book progresses and, indeed, at least some things are not entirely vanity (food, love, some forms of wisdom, etc.), at least retroactively the opening *question* becomes a matter of investigation rather than an authoritative assertion of world- and God-hatred.

The Qal Form of the Name Qohelet
The fact that the name Qohelet is derived only from the *pi'el* and the *hif'il* conjugations in other instances in the Hebrew Bible has raised concerns. Such attempts, however plausible, seem farfetched, based on the

---

[66] Foucault, "What is an Author," 110.

assumption that the author knew Hebrew imperfectly or even, with H. L. Ginsberg, that the book was translated from an Aramaic original. My own suspicion, based on literary considerations, connects the *qal* form with that word that concludes the entire autobiographical section, transforming it into a confession: the collector QOHEL(et) is a KHOTE', a sinner (2:26). The words that open and conclude the entire argument thus form an echo chamber, an auditory and grammatical *inclusio* that brings further emphasis to Qohelet's personal transformation.

Slanting the Truth; Ac(counting) for an Absence: Qoh 1:15

> What is slanted cannot be made straight;
> And what is lacking cannot be numbered.
>
> Qoh 1:15

There is a well-known tradition, at least in Jewish ethics, of parsing negativity. For example, to the complaint that Jews are a stiff-necked people, the retort is: Thank God, otherwise they would not have survived. So too the habit of thinking in clichés, which gets good comeuppance in Qohelet's leisure moments. As against the Bible's central wisdom category of righteousness, Qohelet advises:

> Don't be such a great Tsaddiq, and don't be too wise either.
>
> 8:16

So too the Bible's abundant praise of "straightness" as a moral category, as mirrored in

> God has made mankind straight (*yashar*).
>
> 7:29

The second part of the verse is connected by the word *waw*, usually understood here as a disjunctive:

> *But* they have invented many stratagems.

A proper come-uppance, however, would be to read *waw* as a connective: *And* they have invented many stratagems.

The point would then be one of divine testing, like the unexplained exile of an entire people into Egyptian slavery and which – like Genesis 22, the Akedah – pushes interpretative ingenuity to its breaking point.

Note, however, that *yashar* is often a divine attribute (as is Tsaddiq, Deut 32:4), and although humans were created in the divine image, Qohelet often stresses that they are not divine in either knowledge or power. It is perhaps in recognition of this state of affairs that for humans, access to God has to take different paths, one appropriate to their status and capacities:

> Consider God's doing, for who can straighten what he has made crooked?
>
> 7:13

The poet has penetrated God's own strategy in how humans are to be dealt with:

> Tell all the truth but tell it slant/ Success in circuit lies,
> Too bright for our infirm delight/ The truth's superb surprise;
> As lightning to the children eased/ With explanation kind,
> The truth must dazzle gradually/ Or every man be blind.
>
> Emily Dickinson

As with straightness, so too with numbering. Noteworthy here is Qohelet's addiction to quantity and excess in his early career, whereupon he transformed his pursuits from counting possessions to accounting for his life. And who better than Einstein can speak of numbers and their limitations?

> Not everything that can be counted counts,
> and not everything that counts can be counted.
>
> Einstein

Love of quantity, typically at the expense of quality, has the ironic tic of imploding at both levels, the higher as well as the lower. Recall God's promise to Abraham:

> I will make your offspring as the dust of the earth, so that if one can count the dust of the earth, then your offspring too can be counted.
>
> Gen 13:16

For, as Einstein suggests, those beyond counting count, can be counted on.

Praising the Not-Yet Born (Qoh 4:2–3)

I once heard this anecdote from a person in Maine and pass it along:

Not Yet

Huck had three grandchildren from his daughter Bertha: Harold, the oldest, Josh, and Sam. Sam died of crib death when he was only one year old.

When Josh started school, the teacher asked him if he had any brothers and sisters.

"Yup. I got two brothers," Josh replied. "Sam, who died last year, and Harold, who is not dead yet."

This anecdote shows how the concept of not yet can convey premonitions of the saddest variety. A puzzling and even mysterious passage in Qohelet presents a positive or flip side of the same notion:

4:2 I praise[67] the dead who are already dead

more than the living who are still alive.

4:3 But better than both of them is he who has not yet been....

Qohelet goes on to give a reason for this form of un-living (the first being, of course, someone who has already died): an unborn person has not yet seen the evil that humans do. Praise hardly seems a possible reaction to such passivity as being dead (or alive, for that matter). Would there then be a more active and praiseworthy sense of not yet being born?

If both our texts give instances of the not-yet, the first deals concretely with a real (if dreaded) eventuality: Harold is both surely alive and, from that very fact, as sure to die at some point. However, Qohelet's advantageous position of the not-yet existent human may be mere theory if there is no guarantee that that person will ever be born in the first place! It is clear, therefore, that the person in question is, while *not yet* born, standing in line to be born. But how can you possibly know that?! Wouldn't that be a perfect example of Qohelet's "an absence that cannot be counted" (1:15)? How can you possibly count an absence, or count on its being eventually a presence?

A literalist reading relies on such an impossibility, viewing the relative happiness of the unborn as not an option for humans, "inasmuch as they already are living."[68] The only way out of such a reading is a perceived irony of human existence, since, stating the super-obvious, "what is 'better' in this regard is not within the grasp of mortals" (ibid.).[69]

Two alternatives are possible. On the one hand, the reference may presuppose a situation of reincarnation wherein souls or angelic beings may indeed float around for eternity without ever becoming incarnated

---

[67] I stress the literal meaning of *shabeakh* rather than the popular rendering "count as happy, fortunate."

[68] Choon-Leong Seow, *Ecclesiastes: A New Translation with Introduction and Commentary* (AB 18C, New York: Doubleday, 1997), 187.

[69] Krüger, *Qoheleth: A Commentary*, 96 ascribes such irony to the author, seeing the two verses as a progressive *reductio ad absurdum*, which would presumably read as follows: a) unhappy enough are the living; b) less unhappy are the dead; c) the least unhappy of all are the unborn. Note that there are two levels of not-alive: the already dead (a) and the not-yet born (c). Since (b) is already absurd (for why would the dead be better than the living?!), (c) would be a further *reductio ad absurdum*. Furthermore, Krüger's illustration works in the wrong direction to prove his point: "A living dog is better than a dead lion" (on v. 9:4). For Roland Murphy, *Ecclesiastes: Word Biblical Commentary* 23A (Dallas: Word Books, 1992), 38, irony is conveyed by the word "praise."

in this life under the sun. Such characters in fact do make appearances in the Bible, making earthly stopovers only to deliver messages and not really attached to local conditions such as eating or earning a living or filing a tax return in time.

A different solution is suggested in the language of the text itself, in Qohelet's phrase "a dead person who is already dead." His intention, of course, is to refer to two forms of non-living: those who have already died and those that precede life, the yet unborn. But, until these two possibilities are outlined, a reader is likely to exclaim: "*a dead person who is already dead*!? What? Are there then dead persons who are somehow still alive?!"[70] Or, reversing the formulation through a *renversement de langage*, are there already-born persons who are somehow "dead"? Levinas presents such a scenario, one in which the "non-living" or unborn person is, in a metaphorical or wisdom sense, already alive:

> This is the situation of consciousness. To have consciousness is to have time, it is to be on this side of nature, in a certain sense to be not yet born. Such an uprooting is not a lesser form of being but rather the *manner* of the [human] subject. It is the power of rupture, a refusal of neuter and impersonal principles, a refusal of Hegelian totality and politics, a refusal of the bewitching rhythms of art. It is the power to speak, the liberty of words … Whence the power to judge history instead of waiting upon its impersonal verdict.[71]

Levinas' "not yet born" thus expresses, metaphorically, the status of humans who, through detachment and the power of words, uproot themselves, in Qohelet's phrase, from the conditions of life "under the sun." Born perhaps, but not yet. The paradox is extreme: to be un-born to the world and its history is to be truly born. Or, in Qohelet's formulation, to be dead (to the world, through detachment) is to be, as a free human being, not dead yet, and yet "dead" and truly alive.

"Finding" a Good Woman (Qoh 7:28)
The drama of counting is pursued by Qohelet at even deeper levels, that of numbering human beings:

---

[70] I am assuming that for Qohelet "life after death" in the current religious sense – including resurrection of the dead – is not within the parameters of this discussion.

[71] Emmanuel Levinas, *Difficile liberté* (Paris: Albin Michel, 1976), 407–08. He continues: "But time and language and subjectivity presuppose not only a being capable of uprooting itself from the totality but also a being which does not englobe that totality. Time, language, and subjectivity outline a pluralism and consequently, in the strongest sense of the term, an experience: one being's reception of an absolutely other being."

I have found [*matsa'ti*] one man in a thousand,

but I did not find [*matsa'ti*] a single woman in the same number.

Qoh 7:28

This so-called antifeminist declaration harks back to pre-confessional Qohelet, for whom number and quantity and ownership were prime values, and the number of a thousand may not be random, since Solomon's women were of that same number.[72]

Numerical rarity is not the only point, however, as the repetition of *matsa'* may suggest. So too the possible doublet in the further exploration of the verb:

That which is, is far off and deep, very deep:
Who can [*yimtsa'ennu*] find?

Qoh 7:24

Two domains are presented here: the spatial (far off) and the intellectual (very deep). The verb does double duty here, active in the domains of both extended and intellectual substances. These doublets are based on the ambiguity of *matsa'*, meaning both "find" and "understand," as Ceresko has shown.[73] Qohelet's point is that he has tried to understand women his entire life and has not yet succeeded even once, despite the harems at his disposal – or perhaps *because* of them. Here the thought arises not from misogyny but rather incomprehension bordering on mystery, two of Qohelet's favorite topics.

The situation is exquisitely captured by Grace Paley:[74]

I wanted to have been married forever to one person, my ex-husband or my present one. Either has enough character for a whole life, which as it turns out is really not such a long time. You couldn't exhaust either man's qualities or get under the rock of his reasons in one short life.

As Grace Paley puts it, the human complexity of even one can occupy an entire life.

---

[72] See 1 Kgs 11:3. I argue that Solomon's love of women is parodied in Cant 8:12. See T. A. Perry, "Love's Philosophy in Canticles: The King and the Pastoral Setting," ed. J. Harold Ellens. *Bethsaida in Archeology. A Festschrift in Honor of John T. Greene* (Newcastle: Cambridge Scholars, 2014), 318–29.

[73] Anthony R. Ceresko, "The Function of *Antanaclasis* (*mts'* "to find" // *mts'* "to reach, overtake, grasp") in Hebrew Poetry, Especially in the Book of Qoheleth," *CBQ* 44 (1982):551–69.

[74] Grace Paley, "Wants," *The Collected Stories* (New York: Farrar, Straus and Giroux, 1994), 131.

Solomon's having "too much," even "of a good thing" may also be an issue, as we have seen:

> A woman of valor who can find (*matsa'*),
> Her price is far above rubies.
>
> Prov 30:10

The ambiguity persists in this praise of woman, at least in its performance in Jewish liturgy, it being recited by the husband to his wife at the Sabbath meal. For one might immediately ask, in shock: "What do you mean 'who can find'?! She is right in front of you!" I would argue that the denial of her existence can be removed, again, only by resorting to the double meaning: "I don't mean 'who can find' but rather 'who can understand?'" again in Grace Paley's sense of human mystery and complexity, as it is compounded by the erotic relationship.

Building Communities
In the book's grand finale to enjoyment, a sage full of wisdom addresses a youth in a series of imperatives:

> "Young man, rejoice in your youth
> and let your heart cheer you in the days of your youth."
>
> 11:9

In a fine comment, Eunny P. Lee evokes the sage/youth pedagogical figure wherein "a community of learning is thereby evoked, in which the wisdom of one generation is passed down to the next."[75] This social environment is quite naturally extended in the institution of houses of learning that conclude the work in 12:10–11. There is also a moving evocation in the Elegy on Death in chapter 12, where death applies to the entire human family but where also the individual is still socialized by the company of mourners who gather together as a community.[76]

6. Figures of Speech as Figures of Thought

The Transcendence of Words and Hope for the Future
As an indicator of Qohelet's resilient optimism, consider his advice about planting one's garden. Or perhaps one's seed:

---

[75] Lee, *The Vitality of Enjoyment*, 74.
[76] See my commentary in *Wisdom in the Hebrew Bible: God's Twilight Zone*, 151.

In the morning plant your seed

And in the evening do not rest your hand,

For you know not which will succeed, this one or that one.

And perhaps they will *both* succeed as one.

11:6

I like the positive use of a skepticism ("for you do not know") that opens the mind and heart to a broad range of possibility: since we don't know, why foreclose? There is a spirit of adventure here, a wish and project to take possession of the entire day and by extension an entire life – "all the days of my breath-life" – as a unified pursuit and exploration. And the ending of the verse further expands the triumph, since until then the optimism was open – for it may not occur to the average reader that *neither* planting will succeed – but perhaps limited: this one *or* that one. But after unifying the entire day from morning to evening in all of its endeavors, a single pursuit to the end bears the surprising possibility of fructification: why settle for only one success when *both* are possible? Who knows? Who can tell?[77]

I also admire the organic *peshat* of planting a garden (shades of Candide), which easily takes on metaphorical extension such as the planting of one's human seed, a move already programmed in the preceding verse:

> Just as you do not know how the lifebreath [*ruakh*] passes into the womb of the pregnant woman, so you cannot foresee the actions of God, who causes all things to happen.

11:5 JPS

Insemination is also hinted by the addition of "in the evening," not the usual time for literal planting, as well as by "your hand," easily understood as "your strength or power," as in God's "hand" (Ps 19:2). And the strength of this *peshat*-metaphor is ultimately referred – as in so much of Qohelet and traditional thinking – to the human being's positive interaction with the natural cosmos. Thus and as we have seen, the opening Cosmology (1:4–7) is read doubly and the four elements themselves behave as doublets, each traveling in its own direction and then returning upon itself after spanning the entire interim space, ready to start anew. Their cosmological being gradually reveals human characteristics, serving as an image and pattern to earthly creatures. Thus, the

---

[77] Cf. 7:14b, referring to the future; 8:7; 10:14. Qohelet here is giving the upbeat side of the implied negativity of such texts as 6:12; Prov 27:1: "for you do not know what the day may bring forth, to what it may give birth."

element *'erets*, earth, is also by metonymy the people or inhabitants of the earth. *Both* are to be read as part of the wisdom argument of the close and positive relationship between the macrocosm and the microcosm, a single living and interactive world for all creatures. Especially notable in this regard is the perfect ambivalence of *ruakh*, referring *both* to the life-breath *and also* to the wind, as many translate. The point of the literary figure of comparison is meant to stress the ontology of universal life in its eternal movement of return and renewal.[78] For this passage to be the climax that it is, we must note the reference to the Creator of everything, as well as the immediate sequel:

> How sweet is the light, and what a delight for the eyes to enjoy the sun!
>
> 11:7

In addition to the concrete and immediate experience of light, mention of its source extends this enjoyment to cyclical and thus renewable dimensions as the solar day and year. Perhaps the context of 11:5–7 in its broadest dimensions may have been on Qohelet's mind as well: that the sun is a figure for the Creator and the light a figure for life itself. Could this not deepen our understanding of Qohelet's bold metaphor, at the very start of the book, of the sun's breath-panting to renew life (1:5)?[79]

Doublets

To access theological interpretations of Scripture, I proceed here by way of literary analysis, with the reminder that *figures of speech typically program figures of thought*. The rhetorical figure of choice for decoding the Book of Qohelet I have called doublet, a single word that goes in two different and often opposite directions; or, in Rabbinic language, where "one thing is said and two are meant." Noteworthy examples include the Latin *hospes* (French *hôte*), meaning both guest and host; also, French *conscience*, meaning both consciousness and moral conscience. Above, I argued this approach for the Book of Qohelet, where the opening word *debarim*, "words," also projects a second meaning, "things," and

---

[78] Lee (*The Vitality of Enjoyment, 137*) convincingly sees verse 11:6 as part of the unit 11:1–6, thus suggesting Qohelet's notion of the "double agency in enjoyment" that is also her pet theme: "God's work, precisely because of its mystery and unknowability, may be liberating rather than debilitating for the human agent" in its life-giving potential.

[79] For the sun as a figure for the Creator El, see Ps 19:5–7 and my forthcoming study, *Psalm 19, Hymn of Unification.*

that the book's plot is indeed a progress from one meaning to its delayed doublet.[80]

To review the argument, the book's opening presentation – "the *words* of Qohelet" – are taken as announcing words of Solomonic wisdom, including, especially for some readers, the vanity complaints about the world and God. Most notably in the royal autobiography, which opens the book, however, Qohelet's words have no apparent wisdom intent or focus, they merely recount the king's deeds, and the first surprise is that those deeds have neither wisdom nor grandeur in them, they recount no mighty achievements of war or administration. Rather, they boastingly list, almost as a litany, the numerous and cumulative deeds of acquisition and pursuits of pleasure and power, also listed as *debarim*, as Qohelet's actions (Gen 24:66) and, more generally perhaps, his usual course of action (Gen 20:10).

The important point here is that the book's opening word *dabar* (*dibrei*, in the plural) is bipolar, what I have called here a doublet, a dual reference centered in a single word:

– The words of wisdom of Solomon the sage
– The acts or deeds or history of Solomon (1 Kgs 11:41), the business of the king (1 Sam 21:9).

If this enigma[81] – or patent irony – is not grasped, at least retroactively, then we have missed the book's plot, which tells of a navigation between

---

[80] Qohelet's opening doublet *dabar* has meta-value for Henri Meschonnic, who views the duality of *dabar* as paradigmatic of all such double metaphors: "At the start comes the divine Word, that traces the Latin *verbum*, which traces the Greek *logos*, which traces the Hebrew *dabar*, whose dual value as language and event, of word-action, has split in two in passing to Christian theology" (*La Rime et la vie* [Paris: Verdier, 2006], 32, italics added). Curiously, Michel Foucault ascribes compressions such as doublets – which abound in Greek and Latin – to the material rarity of words, proposing that there are just not enough of them to go around, so to speak, and attaches their use to the sophist, "who uses the same word, noun, expression to say two different things, so that he ends up saying two things in the very identity of the thing said." Michel Foucault, *Leçons sur la volonté de savoir: Cours au Collège de France, 1970–71* (Paris: Gallimard/Seuil, 2011), 43.

[81] If "in my end is my beginning," that is because, through a *renversement de langage*, "in my beginning is my end." Since readers/interpreters see the double reference (to things as well as to words) only in retrospect if at all, this doublet functions as a kind of weak enigma which, once recognized, can henceforth act as a *blazon* for what follows, a grain of sand that summarizes and projects the work's message. An intriguing aspect of doublets is that their duality is at first unnoticed or covert, and that the second and perhaps more important reference is revealed only gradually. It is not until I get to the end that I understand the beginning, awaken to the realization that the conclusion was already foreshadowed. Had I only suspected, paid more attention. Delayed disclosure is also a feature of *Antanaclasis* (q. v.), repeating a word in close proximity and changed context,

the one and the other. For, as we advance through the autobiography (1:12–2:26), we find that the opening *debarim* now focuses on different – indeed, opposite – directions as well.[82] Here the focus is repetitively on the second main meaning of *debarim*, the "things" or objects or personal projects of the world that we desire and pursue and collect, for purposes of maintenance but also for pleasure and power. Is this dual use of the term not made official in the career of Qohelet's shadow figure?

> And the rest of the *debarim* of Solomon, *all that he did and his wisdom*, are they not written in the book of the *debarim* [acts, actions] of Solomon?
>
> 1Kgs 11:41; also 14:29

A primary example in our text is Qoh 1:8:

> SO MANY *things/words* [*debarim*] in ceaseless activity!
> Even a great person cannot express them all:
> The eye is never satisfied with seeing
> Nor the ear filled with hearing.[83]

Scott Noegel lists this as an instance of Janus parallelism, since *ha-debarim* both points back to the natural phenomena in the previous stich and forward to the words that one is unable to speak.[84] Noegel also captures this phenomenon in 2:25–26, where the verb *yakhush* is illustrated, in its opposite meanings of feeling pain and feeling pleasure, by two

except that this repetition is unanticipated and often provokes comical surprise rather than unifying insight. As such, the effect of this double reading is immediately perceived; in doublets, the second and enigmatic meaning emerges only gradually and can be incorporated into the original program only in a meditative re-reading. A further parallel example of a term expressing alternatively opposite valences may well be the term *mah*, "what, how," used both as an exclamation of awe and admiration, and alternatively as expressing contempt. See Nahum M. Sarna, *Songs of the Heart* (New York: Schocken, 1993), 53.

[82] For the possible meaning of *dabar* as "event," both personal and cosmic, see R. N. Whybray, *Ecclesiastes* (The New Century Bible Commentary; Grand Rapids, MI: Eerdmans, 1989), on vv. 1:8, 10. More generally, the reference is to the products of *'amal* (labor) that Qohelet pursues and collects and now calls into question. For further uses of the nonverbal meaning of *dabar* in Qohelet, see 1:10; 7:8; 8:3, 5; 12:13. *Debarim* in 6:11 seems to apply to both levels of meaning. For the meaning "evil thing" (incitement to idolatry), see Deut 13:12; Esther 1:17 (evil deed); customary behavior (Esther 1:13); deeds or works = *ma'aseh* (Ps 145:5). Whether the term *dabar* came to mean literally "things" such as the things Qohelet collected (pools, buildings), would be related to the dating of the text. It is well known, for example, that with time many such terms navigated from the activity of their pursuit or causative sense to the actual thing pursued: *'amal* from "labor" to the riches obtained; *khepets*, from the desire for things to the desired things themselves. Qohelet may occupy a point of transition.

[83] For a discussion see above, p. 75.

[84] "Word Play in Qoheleth," *Journal of Hebrew Scriptures* 7 (2007): 2–28 at 16.

separate and adjacent examples (p. 17). Doublets function in a similar way, except that here a single polysemic word points in a forward direction.

Doublets or double reading, *amphibologie,* occurs rather frequently in all types of guises. A common example would be typographical, using either parenthesis such as (s)he, or oblique stroke as in sexual/textual. In Hebrew Scripture as well, there is the distinction between the *kri,* the spoken version, and the *ketiv* or written form of the same word. One might say that such devices assist in *navigating to a conceptual opposite* while retaining its original meaning as an organic point of reference. Setting out to describe how ideas associate in literary texts, Levinas reviews Leiris's theory to explain how *bifurs*

> invite thought to separate itself from the direction it seems to have taken and to travel unexpected paths; *biffures* [erasures], for the single meaning of these elements is at every moment corrected, overburdened. Except that in these *bifurs* or *biffures* [bifurcations or erasures] the point is less to travel the new roads that open up or to attach one's self to the corrected meaning, than to seize thought at the privileged moment where it swerves into something other than itself. It is because of this fundamental equivocation of bifur-cation that the very phenomenon of the association of ideas becomes possible.[85]

Levinas continues by noting that "with the notion of bifur[cation] the process of the association of ideas loses its fundamental role. Thinking is originally *biffure* [erasure], that is to say symbol. And because thought is symbolic, ideas can attach themselves to others and form a network of associations. However, this network is important not because it enables one to pass from one idea to another but rather because it guarantees the presence of an idea *in* another."[86]

Polysemy

> When you come to a fork in the road, take it.
>
> Yogi Berra

Whenever the contextual meaning of a word is in doubt, the automatic assumption and application of a default either/or rule – Occam's razor principle triumphant – spells the death of polysemy, which is both the

---

[85] Emmanuel Levinas, *Hors sujet* (Paris: Fata Morgana, 1987), "On the Transcendence of words: Concerning Biffures," pp. 197–203 at 198.

[86] Ibid., 199.

soul of poetry and the transcendence of language.[87] Rather, let the competing reaction prevail, so that when you come to a word that can mean two things, believe it and let both/and become the default. Such doublets are of course but one stepping-out ceremony of polysemy, the prime doublet in Qohelet being of course *hebel* itself, a virtual "nothing" that, in the course of the book and through its repetitive insistence, navigates from a nothing to a no-thing to an every-thing, life itself. I think that the concreteness of association is less of ideas than word-things, of a polysemic universe in words that surface unexpectedly toward the symbolic once the erasure occurs.[88]

André Neher locates this figure of speech at the very start of human history:

> When the Bible says "hebel" (i.e., Abel), there is an *amphibologie*... This seems to me very important because it allows a first meaning to emerge in the philosophical research of Qohelet. It attaches human destiny to the myth of a being who was invested with a role in history at the origins of humanity.[89]

The text thus designates both breath and its human incarnation, both doomed to evanescence. In a moving resurrection of such biblical figures, Rachel in particular, Betty Rojtman writes as follows: "Abel had his task of silence to accomplish."[90] Like Joseph, in Abel there is "the truth of failure, an insistence of that nothing which makes of evanescence the *raison d'être*, the subterranean victory of the human."[91]

To be open to polysemy is to accept the risks of surprise and expansion of consciousness. One of its glories in world literature is Qohelet's polysemic *hebel*, read in its *peshat* as "breath," then extended metaphorically (thus a *peshat*-metaphor) as breath-wind and spirit, the figure that expresses the vitality and unity of life in All domains. This would illustrate the transcendence of metaphor at its highest, as a "miraculeux surplus."[92]

---

[87] Polysemy or multivalence is in need of further study in Qohelet. For an excellent review of the problem see Eunny P. Lee's thoughtful discussion, *The Vitality of Enjoyment*, 25–26.

[88] For an interesting application of the doublet figure to metaphysical discourse, see Gaston Bachelard, "La philosophie scientifique de Léon Brunschvicg," *Revue de métaphysique et de morale*, Jan.–Apr. 1945, 77–84, in particular p. 81, where Brunschvicg focuses on dialectical pairs such as "le mesurant et le mesuré – le nombrant et le nombré -le déterminant et le déterminé – l'instrument et l'instrumenté." I thank Professor Andrew Kelley for this reference.

[89] *Notes sur Qohélét* (Paris: Les Éditions de Minuit, 1951), 74.

[90] See Betty Rojtman's extraordinary *Le pardon à la lune: Essai sur le tragique biblique* (Paris: Gallimard, 2001), 11.

[91] Ibid., p. 69.

[92] The expression is Levinas's, PS 325.

Antanaclasis *and the Ethics of False Identities (Qoh 3:15–17; 4:1)*

> In thy youth learn some *craft*, that in thy old age thou mayest get thy living without *craft*.
>
> Samuel Johnson

> If you are not *fired with enthusiasm*, you will be *fired with enthusiasm*.
>
> Vince Lombardi[93]

The rhetorical figure called *antanaclasis* argues that the same word repeated means different things, and it does so with panache, flaunting the false impression of their identity by placing them in close proximity. The opposite of this type of polyvalence would be strict synonymy, the reduction of two or more words to the same meaning. Neither possibility would be allowed in a post-1984 Huxleyan universe, which permits but one meaning per word. In the first case, any extra meanings would be declared null and void; in the second case, one of the two words would be declared extinct and withdrawn from use. In a limited literary context, biblical scholars might still wish to argue an exception for the latter, on the basis of modest esthetic criteria such as "stylistic" nicety, and they might even be permitted to continue referring to such redundancy as "parallelism." *Antanaclasis* would of course continue its undercover existence, unnoticed and thus of little consequence for their kind of reductive interpretation.

My main purpose here, through the exegesis of sample word repetitions in the Hebrew Bible that have resisted interpretation and that may be susceptible to antanaclastic readings, is to clarify key passages in Qohelet. Such verbatim repetitions are often seen as embarrassments, as evidence of inferior literary prowess or as tiresome repetitions of a possibly corrupt text. Other than outright emending the Hebrew text or simply deleting the troublesome element because of a presumed dittography, current solutions, as we shall see, have resorted to two stratagems: 1) decide that the repetitions in fact mean the same thing and translate them literally and thus meaninglessly; or 2) regard them as in need of esthetic and affective embellishments that conceal the repetition but also obscure their intended purpose. In a more positive vein, *antanaclasis* has been studied both as a linguistic term and as a rhetorical

---

[93] Samuel Johnson is quoted in the *Oxford English Dictionary* (Clarendon, 1933), 353. For the Vince Lombardi quote see Gideon O. Burton, "Silva Rhetoricae," n.p. [cited 8 May 2006]. Online: http://rhetoric.byu.edu/figures/A/antanaclasis.htm.

figure. In such cases scholars, stressing the semantic and phonological echoes of the repeated words, speak of its functions both in giving esthetic pleasure and in providing connections among various parts, what biblical scholars like to call *Leitwörter* or catch-phrases.

In this study sample illustrations of *antanaclasis* from the Hebrew Bible form the basis both for alternative interpretations and for a reflection on some of its exegetical and theoretical features. In particular, we shall raise the possibility of viewing this figure as a deliberate (wisdom?) attempt to teach an ethics of reading and linguistic analysis. For it is very much the case, especially in complex literary works such as the Bible, that figures of speech are doubled as figures of thought. The time may thus be ripe for further strategies, for we must inevitably probe the truth of Thoreau's conviction, that our classical books "must be read as deliberately and reservedly as they were written."

Examples from the Hebrew Bible

EXOD 14:8–31. Polyvalence is a given in literary discourse. Rashi states the case well:

> And Israel saw the great work (*yad*, literally "hand") that the Lord did upon Egypt.
>
> > (Exod 14:31)
>
> The "great hand" denotes the great *power* which the *hand* of the Holy One, blessed be He, exercised. There are many meanings appropriate to the language of *yad*, and all of them are related in some way to an actual hand. But exegetes must adapt their language according to the subject matter.[94]

If Rashi is certainly not arguing that God does literally have a hand, why then assert the common denominator "hand"? Because the exegete is referring not to the physical organ but rather to the polyvalent concept "hand" (e.g., "the hand of fate"), and he chooses precisely this place to make his provocative comment because it is the final and culminating repetition of "hand" (*yad*) in a series of seven, four of which refer to Moses's actual raised hand (Exod 14:15–16, 21, 26, 27), whereas the others depart from the literal sense: "raised hand" (Exod 14:8), rendered as "defiantly" (NJPS); and the others as some kind of "power" (14:30, 31).

---

[94] Rashi is cited in *Torat Hayyim: Chumash* [The Five Books of Moses], with Classical Commentaries, ed. Mordechai Breuer et al.; 7 vols. (Jerusalem: Mossad Harav Kook, 1986–93), 2:180.

JONAH 4:5. Whereas Exodus 14 has long been domesticated by translators – would it occur to anyone to translate all occurrences of *yad* as "hand" there? – such literalist monovalence is still practiced, for example in a crucial passage in the book of Jonah:

> [Jonah] went out from the city and sat down (*wa-yesheb*, NRSV) to the east of the city and made a booth there and sat (*wa-yesheb*) under its shade.
>
> Jonah 4:5 (NRSV)

Did he in fact only "sit" east of the city, as he surely did "sit" in his booth? Well, consider the close antanaclastic parallel, where the same verb is repeated with different meanings within the same verse:

> Moses settled (*wa-yesheb*) in Midian and sat down (*wa-yesheb*) next to the well.
>
> Exod 2:15

As most interpreters beginning with the Vulgate acknowledge, this "sitting" in Midian is actually a settling down, as subsequent events confirm. In Jonah also, the repetition of "sitting" is hardly superfluous, a reverse parallelism, if you will. Rather, it portrays two different actions: a *sitting* in the booth and a *settling down* and *dwelling* east of Nineveh. Thus,

> Now Jonah left the city and *settled* to the east of the city and made a booth there and *sat* under its shade.
>
> Jonah 4:5

Such a reading, in its assertion of an extended rather than a fleeting stay in the desert, has importance implications for interpretation.[95] *Antanaclasis* brings this possibility to our attention, and it also prompts the question: why didn't the text, to avoid the current misunderstanding and confusion with "sit," simply use another term for "settle," *gur* perhaps? Put differently, what is the point in pointedly (in close proximity) expressing different concepts with the same word?[96]

1 SAM 1:24

And the boy [was] a boy (*we-ha-na'ar na'ar*).[97]

---

[95] See T. A. Perry, *Jonah's Arguments with God: The Honeymoon Is Over!* (Peabody, MA: Hendrickson, 2014), 180.

[96] See "Pedagogical Reasons for *Antanaclasis*," p. 235.

[97] P. Kyle McCarter (*I Samuel* AB 8 [Garden City, NY: Doubleday, 1980], 57) finds the text "unintelligible" and follows the Septuagint, along with the École biblique de Jérusalem (*La Sainte Bible* [Paris: Editions du Cerf, 1956], 280): "l'enfant était avec eux."

Robert Alter's translation captures the pure identity of the repeated words but weakens the oppositional sense implied by *antanaclasis*:

> And the lad was but a lad.[98]

Of course he was a lad, what would one expect? But, in fact, one would expect a great deal more from the future Samuel, a mere lad at that age but destined to lead the nation. Whence the speculative but suggestive reading:

> And though the boy was still very young, she brought him to the House of the Lord at Shiloh. (NJPS).

Yehudah Keil also goes part way, but in the opposite direction:

> And the lad was a servant.[99]

Here the same word does indeed produce a different meaning, but the oppositional sense is again weakened by what sounds like a simple report of the lad's occupation.

I think that the stronger and intended sense can be reached by reversing this solution:

> And the servant [of God and Eli] was still but a lad.[100]

We would then have a biblical precursor of the famous medieval topos of *puer-senex*, of a lad who precociously behaves like a venerable sage.[101]

QOH 3:15–17. We now come to our Qohelet text. Qoh 3:1–17 is an integrated theological discourse on God's relationship with the world and especially the world of humans "under the sun."[102] The unity of this section is established both by the unnoticed *inclusio* "a time for all things" at the start and end (vv. 3:1, 17), as well as by the bipartite structure of its three movements: each presents a different order of events under the sun, followed by God's relationship to that order.

---

[98] Robert Alter, *The David Story: A Translation with Commentary of 1 and 2 Samuel* (New York: Norton, 1999), 7.

[99] Yehudah Keil, *1 Samuel* (Jerusalem: Mossad Harav Kook, 1981), 13 n. 3 [Hebrew].

[100] And, in fact, Keil (ibid.) gives this as an alternative interpretation. "It is possible that the first *na'ar* has the meaning 'servant' and the second *na'ar* has the meaning of 'youngster.' That is to say, Samuel, set apart by his mother to become a 'servant in the house of the Lord,' entered into his service while still a small child."

[101] See the classic discussion in Ernst Robert Curtius, *European Literature and the Latin Middle Ages* (trans. Willard R. Trask; New York and Boston: Harper, 1953), 98–105.

[102] Douglas B. Miller makes passing reference to *antanaclasis* in Qohelet, "Qohelet's Symbolic Use of Hebel," *JBL* 117 (1998): 444.

1) 3:1–11

The famous Catalog of the Times (3:1–8) describes the oppositions that, cyclically experienced, make up the ebb and flow of human life. The theological conclusion is that, despite their contradictions and negative aspects, all things are part of the total universe and thus appropriate: "He [God] made everything beautiful in its time" (3:11), suggesting that there is some kind of harmony of opposites.

2) 3:12–13

Humans' purpose is to enjoy life and to extend that enjoyment to others as well (3:12). Theologically, it must be remembered that everything is a gift of God (3:13).

3:14 This verse, asserting that God is to be respected or feared, is to be read Janus-like, both above and below, forming a transition between them. The verb *yr'* allows both: God is to be respected as a giver (v. 13) and feared as a judge (vv. 15–17).

3) 3:15–17

Although things are subject to flux (vv. 2–8) and their larger purpose is hidden (v. 11), they remain essentially the same (v. 15), and God will search out what needs to be pursued – that is, justice. The human and divine domains are thus clearly delineated. God gives, and humans enjoy and share that enjoyment. God has established a stable universe with fixed laws that humans must respect. Humans have maximum freedom, yet God will pursue infringements.

While the first two movements of this chapter have received ample discussion and commentary, the meaning of the third remains unclear:

> What has been, already is; and what will be has already been. But God will investigate the pursued (*nirdaf*). So, when I saw under the sun that [in][103] the place of justice (*mishpat*) wickedness is there, and [in] the place of righteousness (*tsedeq*) wickedness is there, I thought in my heart: "God will judge the righteous and the wicked." For there is a time for every thing and upon every deed there.
>
> Qoh 3:15–17

Three problems stand out in particular:

a) the meaning of (*nirdaf*), "the pursued" (v. 15)
b) the curious repetitions in v. 16:

---

[103] This is a case where the preposition *b–* is swallowed up by a following labial, as in "the money which was left [in] the House of the Lord" (2 Sam 12:11).

> *the place of* judgment, *wickedness is there*
> *the place of* righteousness, *wickedness is there.*

c) the concluding reference to "there" (v. 17).

By focusing on the second of these, I hope to clarify the entire passage.

Typical interpretations are reductive in their attempts to deal with the repetitions, viewing "judgment" and "righteousness" as either near or complementary synonyms (hendiadys) and their phrases as parallelistic. The two words are thus collapsed into the conceptual repetition "righteous judgment" that blurs rather than clarifies distinctions.[104] Secondly, the real and meaningful repetition "the place of … there wickedness" is seen as either emphatic or, worse, esthetically inept, and thus rejected in favor of solutions that wish to beautify at the expense of the fuller meaning.

The problem can be dislodged by noting that at the very start Qohelet stresses the importance of *maqom*, that in this universe things have their proper and necessary place.[105] One is therefore prompted to ask: If each thing, as exemplified by two of the world's original elements (fire and water), has its own distinctive place, where is the place of judgment and where of righteousness? There is broad and correct agreement on seeing the place of *mishpat* as a concrete place – that is, where justices sit and justice is rendered, courts of law. But the *place* of righteousness is distinct, because (*tsedeq*) or righteousness is. First of all, *tsedeq* is something to pursue (cf. Deut 16:20), as in a court of law when judges judge:

> You shall judge righteously.[106]
>
> Deut 1:16

> Justice shall return to righteousness, and all the upright of heart will follow it.
>
> Ps 94:15

What they pursue is righteousness in its place. Here the concept of place becomes more abstract (thus not a mechanical repetition!), as in Job's

[104] For example, Fox, *A Time to Tear Down*, 214: "These are the same… 'Judgment'/'righteousness' is a distributed word-pair equivalent to *mishpat tsedeq*, 'righteous judgment.'" While it is quite true that the phrase "mishpat tsedeq" does exist (Deut 16:18), the components are hardly always the same, as I am sure Fox would agree.

[105] "The sun shines forth and sets and yearns towards its *place*, where it shines again" (1:5). So too the rivers: "To the *place* where the rivers go, from there they return in order to go forth again" (1:7).

[106] Reading *be-tsedeq*; see n. 112.

question on the "place of understanding."[107] I would therefore propose that here *tsedeq* means *law*, the law that should be codified and institutionalized in courts of law, that judges should pursue in their courts, and that citizens should obey. In the language of Ps 94, justice will again return when judges follow the law. This is confirmed by the affirmation that "God will judge the righteous (*tsaddiq*) and the wicked" (3:17), meaning that God too will judge according to the (Toranic) law.[108]

So far so good. We have now identified not one but two levels of place and two of wickedness: the first relates to courts of justice, and the second to the law itself, particularly to the rule of equity upon which it is founded. Wickedness would thus also be two-tiered: breaking the law and corrupting the laws. These two themes do not exhaust the discussion, however, because there is yet a more pervasive "repetition" to be brought into the picture. It is now appropriate to notice – as most translations do not – that the "place of wickedness" is embedded in a broader *antanaclasis* that unites all verses in the passage (and thus also a *Leitwort*), the three-fold occurrence of "there":

> What has been, already is; and what will be has already been. But God will investigate the [case of the] pursued.[109]
> So, when I saw under the sun that [in] the place of justice wickedness is THERE (*shammah*) and [in] the place of righteousness wickedness is THERE (*shammah*), I thought in my heart: "God will judge the righteous and the wicked." For there is a time [of justice] for every thing and upon every deed THERE (*sham*).

> Qoh 3:15–17[110]

Wickedness is everywhere in the world under the sun: *there* in the courts of law intended to correct them, and even *there* in the laws themselves,

---

[107] Job 28:12, 20. In Jewish theology the word *maqom* achieves the highest level of abstraction: "Why is God called 'Maqom'? Because He is the Place of the world, and the world is not His place" (Bereshit Rabba 68: X). HALOT, 1004, makes an important distinction between *tsedeq*, "which has a collective [i.e., more general and abstract] meaning," and *tsedaqah*, which "denotes a single proof of uprightness, an act of justice," thus closer to what Qohelet calls *mishpat*.

[108] The rabbinic concept of *tsaddiq*, "righteous person," as one *mutsdaq ba-din*, cleared of guilt in judgment, may also apply here. For further on this subject see Moshe Weinfeld, *Justice and Righteousness in Israel and the Nations*.

[109] Alternatively, "what is to be pursued," which is *tsedeq*; see below.

[110] Anton Schoors, *The Preacher Sought to Find Pleasing Words* (Leuven: Peeters, 1992), 101, discusses the possibility of relating the final *sham* to the previous *shammah* in v. 16, wherein both would "indicate a court of justice." To this correct reading of identity, *antanaclasis* would add the complementary reference to two different levels or kinds of courts of law, the human and the divine.

which have become debased. But it is not *there*, in the place where God will judge.[111] This concluding antithesis has led many commentators to postulate a reference to the final judgment. Such a suggestion would certainly give a unified reading to a passage that begins by asserting that God will "search out the pursued" (v. 15), and what is pursued by both the divine Judge and human judges is *tsedeq*.

> Righteousness righteousness you shall pursue.
>
> Deut 16:20[112]

The unity of this passage is now clear. As 3:1–8 argued, there is a time and a place for every thing, justice as well as its miscarriage, wickedness as well as righteousness. As Krüger so beautifully observes, this very fluctuation "not only allows wickedness but also limits its duration." Coincident with this is the concept of divine judgment, which is "integrated into the understanding of God's activity that is developed in 3:1–15 and at the same time thereby relativized: if everything that God makes is beautiful and appropriate in its time (v. 11), this is true both for his tolerance of wickedness and for his intervention against it."[113]

QOH 4:1

> I again considered all the oppressed who have become so under the sun: Behold the tears of the oppressed, *and there is no comforter for them.* And behold [...] power from the hand of their oppressors, *and there is no comforter for them.*

It is important to note that this verse refers to the subject just studied in 3:15–17, and in three ways: it again refers to oppressions;[114] it does so with repetitions, here italicized, that also require *antanaclasis* for their correct interpretation; and it again asserts the presence of

---

[111] The reference is not necessarily to a final judgment, since, as Michael V. Fox points out (*Proverbs 1–9.* [AB 18A; New York: Doubleday, 2000], 284, citing Prov 8:27), "it is doubtful that *sham* ever has a simple temporal sense, 'at that time,' 'then'." Its likely meaning here is a "situation or set of events" (ibid., citing Isa 48:16b), thus "in God's judging," whether at some future time or right now.

[112] Here too *antanaclasis* seems preferable to the simple argument of emphasis: "You shall pursue righteousness righteously" (Deut 16:20). That is to say, one of the repeated nouns "righteousness" is read adverbially, *be-tsedeq* (e.g., Ps 9:9) with the preposition suppressed, as in Deut 1:16. And what might be an example of unrighteous righteousness? One where evil means are used to promote righteous ends.

[113] Krüger, *Qoheleth: A Commentary*, 91.

[114] See T. A. Perry, *Dialogues with Qohelet: The Book of Ecclesiastes: Translation and Commentary* (University Park: Penn State University Press, 1993), 96. Fox (*A Time to Tear Down*, 219) thinks otherwise and thus translates it as introducing a new subject; as does Seow, *Ecclesiastes*, 177.

justice in the universe.[115] This verse has raised interesting commentary. One strain, combating what is perceived as its weak esthetic impact, refers to its "litany style" (Lohfink), while others stress affective impact such as "deep feeling" (Murphy), "emotional intensity" (Whybray); or, combining the two: humane emphasis (Fox), poignancy and emphasis (Crenshaw).[116]

Since such effusiveness is "rare" in Qohelet, however, as even Whybray admits, an alternate solution, already suggested by a number of scholars, may be worthy of consideration.[117] To make *antanaclasis* work in this context, however, a number of textual emendations have been introduced, which, in my opinion, distort the meaning and, further, are not essential to prove the theory. The first issue, unrelated to the larger *antanaclasis* ("and there is no comforter for them"), is the repetition of the noun "oppressed," usually seen as awkward and thus a candidate for reinterpretation. Following Targum Jonathan, some read *'ashuqim* as an abstract noun meaning "oppression," a solution that makes contextual sense and also makes a nice stylistic point of allowing different levels of "oppression" in this passage. The plain sense, however, is "the oppressed," as later in the same verse, except that here too different kinds of oppressed are intended. Thus, while both indeed refer to persons oppressed, the first group is more inclusive: "*all* the oppressed." This may seem curious, as if to suggest that Qohelet might otherwise withhold sympathy from some of the oppressed, but in fact he will go on to do just that. The matter is further clarified by the otherwise clumsy reference to those who "*become* oppressed," and these include the additional group to be triumphantly specified at the end of the verse: those who will become oppressed because, measure for measure, they have oppressed others.[118]

[115] This last item challenges those who see this verse as cynically resigned, as a testimony to Qohelet's enduring pessimism. See the discussion and bibliography in Krüger, *Qoheleth: A Commentary*, 95.

[116] Norbert Lohfink, *Qoheleth*, 68; Murphy, *Ecclesiastes*, 37; Whybray, *Ecclesiastes*, 81; Fox, *A Time to Tear Down*, 218. James L. Crenshaw, *Ecclesiastes: A Commentary*, 105.

[117] See the seminal discussion in Ceresko, "The Function of *Antanaclasis* (*mts'* "to find" // *mts'* "to reach, overtake, grasp") 551–52. See also Noegel, "Word Play in Qoheleth," 2–28 at 21, citing Jack Sasson.

[118] This reading shifts the meaning of "all," typically understood emphatically as an exclamatory ("ALL, a very great number, however many!") to another meaning in Qohelet: "both," referring to the two groups that are seen as oppressed. See also 7:18, 2:14, 3:19 and especially Perry on Qoh 7:15 (*Dialogues with Qohelet*, 127–28), where the important point is made that in such cases the complementary binaries are viewed as opposites.

The view of "and there is no comforter for them" as mere repetition must be questioned. Ogden's grammatical approach, while agreeing that the referent is also to the "oppressed," does not rely on the explanation of stylistic or affective repetition of the entire phrase but identifies the antecedent as the grammatical suffix of "*their* oppressors" (*'oshqehem*).[119] This proper grammatical focus does not require this conclusion, however, since the antecedent may be not the suffix but rather the participle itself, the oppressors: (*'oshqehem*), their *oppressors*. This solution retains the identical meaning of "comfort," while noticing that the usual referent "to them" has changed:

> Behold the tears of the oppressed, and there is no comforter for them.
> And behold ... their oppressors, ... and there is no comforter for them [their oppressors].

This reading will surely appeal to those many interpreters who have sensed in this passage a desire for revenge, who have harbored the suspicion of at least partial redress and revenge against the oppressors.[120] An *antanaclastic* reading both focuses on the revenge theme and avoids emendation:

> I again considered all those who become oppressed under the sun: Behold the tears of the oppressed, and there is no comforter for them (*la-hem*, for the oppressed). But [He will remove][121] power from the hand[122] of their

---

[119] "In the second of the reiterated phrases, the word 'them' refers back to the suffix of the passive participle *'oshqeihem*, 'those who oppress them.' In other words, the reiterated *'ein lahem menakhem* refers to the one group, the oppressed" Graham Ogden, *Qoheleth* (Sheffield: JSOT Press, 1987), 66.

[120] Their reading has been succinctly summarized, but rejected, by Seow (*Ecclesiastes*, 178).

[121] The point is made more explicitly in Ps 103:6: "The Lord executes righteousness and judgment for all that are oppressed (*'ashuqim*)." Here a subject and verb need to be supplied in order to specify who will remove – not "derive," as is usually assumed – the power of the oppressors. That the subject "God" remains implicit is often the case, especially in wisdom texts. Perry (*Dialogues with Qohelet*, 97) postulates that the verb is implied in the preposition *min* of *miyyad*. Alternatively, the subject would be not God but rather the shepherd king (Qohelet 12:11) in charge of administering divine justice. In view of Qohelet's revised status as a *deposed* monarch, however ("I *was* king"), the pathos would be extreme; or perhaps stressing that there is no longer a single judge but rather a council of sages/judges, which gives a judicial setting of Qohelet's conclusion and specificity to their words or judgments as "goads and nails."

[122] One popular emendation is *b-* ("*in* the hand") instead of MT *m-* ("*from* the hand"), which is seen as having little meaning. Only Robert Gordis (*Koheleth – The Man and His World* [New York: Schocken, 1968], 238) seems to retain the preposition *min* "and behold power out of the hands of their oppressors." NJPS, disregarding *mi-yad* altogether," is intelligible and would even be correct if it were able to stress, perhaps by italics, that those without comfort are the oppressors themselves: "and the power of their oppressors – with none to comfort them (i.e., *them*)".

oppressors, and there will be no comforter for them (*la-hem*, for the oppressors) either!

In sum, in Qoh 4:1 the *antanaclasis* theory works fine *without* the textual emendations. The oppositional twist that gives this figure its pungency does not occur in the word (*menakhem*), which means "comforter" in both cases, but rather in the referent "them," which refers to the oppressed in the first instance and to their oppressors in the second. Of course, "comforter" may also have a dual reference: to humans in the first case, and to God in the second.

An alternative reading would focus the *antanaclasis* possibility in a different direction, whereby we would continue to read both occurrences of *la-hem* ("to them") as referring to the oppressed, but understand the repeated phrase as an exclamatory pious question:

> I again considered all those who become oppressed under the sun: Behold the tears of the oppressed, *and there is no comforter for them.* But God will remove power from their hand. And will there [then] be no comforter for them!?

This would not be the first time a question mark is inserted at a critical point into a biblical text, one without any formal indication but required or at least allowed by the sense. Such an ambivalence would then offer available comfort to optimists as well as pessimists.

Theoretical Considerations

A brief consideration of theoretical underpinnings may be helpful at this point. The standard definition that underlies our discussion will do nicely: *antanaclasis* is the rhetorical figure that repeats the same word or words with a different meaning, usually in close juxtaposition. Here are two examples that, in my view, exemplify its quintessential form.

CHEAP IS CHEAP

This statement, taken as an equivalence, has no greater interest than "red is red." However, at least in its current or received proverbial usage, it surely does not assert an equivalence or identity. Just the opposite, something cheap – financially speaking, that costs little – will end up costing a lot, perhaps because of its "cheap" quality. The lack of synonymy is highlighted even grammatically, since the first "cheap" is really a noun [an inexpensive thing] and the second an adjective ["of little value"]. Thus, the meaning here is oppositional rather than equivalent: "cheap is only apparently or deceptively so, but it is in reality expensive."[123] Identity is therefore denied, and the point is made stronger by first asserting a false identity. This point is central to Derrida's famous quip:

"TOUT AUTRE EST TOUT AUTRE"

The literal equivalence, whereby "every other is every other," is of no greater interest than "John is John," meaning that he is only another John like all the others. Oppositionally, however, the point could be that "John is indeed John and not Harold," and this is in fact Derrida's point at the deeper level: that John can be only John and not any other person. Now the noun "other" meaning "another, a similar one," is repeated, but as an adjective meaning "different." Further, the opposition is accentuated by a second *antanaclasis* on the word "tout," which was an adjective modifying the noun "autre" and is now an adverb modifying the adjective, also "autre."[124] The focus of attack here is the principle of identity itself, the supposition that every *autre* or "other" is only *an*other version of the same. Quite the opposite, says Derrida,

> Tout autre est [*tout à fait*, entirely] autre.

Every repetition is in fact totally different, unique.

These two examples model the characteristics of *antanaclasis* in especially clear and concise ways:

a) they repeat the same word, thus creating the impression of identity of meaning

b) This (false) impression is accentuated by having the repeated word proximate in the extreme, separated only by the sign of equivalence or identity "is," and even this is only implicit in such texts as 1 Sam 1:24 ("And the boy was a boy").

c) the repeated (identical) word has a different meaning, revealing that the "obvious" simplified semantic equivalence is false. Or the opposite, as the repetition of *ruakh* in Qoh 8:8 stresses the positive equivalence of wind and breath.

[123] See T. A. Perry, *Wisdom Literature and the Structure of Proverbs* (University Park: Penn State, 1993), 37–40.

[124] Jacques Derrida, *The Gift of Death* (trans. David Willis; Chicago and London: University of Chicago Press, 1996), 82–114.

Pedagogical Reasons for Antanaclasis

Pedagogically speaking, it may be useful, following Quintilian (*Institutes of Oratory* 9.3, 68), to ruminate on why one would use such a figure of speech. In the Vince Lombardi example cited above, *antanaclasis* was explained as a desire to "impress the listener with a sense of the intelligence and wisdom of the speaker"; to "leave the hearer thinking you are very smart" and thus more able to persuade him.[125] To this may be added the entertainment factor, the desire to seem humorous by clever punning, often at someone's expense. Spoonerisms may also qualify here, since the original word is implicit and visible in its deformation (otherwise it would not be funny). And the repetition need not even be verbal. Richard A. Lanham cites the phrase "Law Suits Our Specialty" placed as an advertisement next to men's clothing.[126] It is to be noted that such uses of *antanaclasis* occur in dialogue situations, as noted by Dupriez, even when, as in the last example, the dialogue (with potential buyers) is only implied.[127]

By contrast and at a deeper or pedagogical level, in the biblical and wisdom texts examined above the opposite is closer to the truth: *antanaclasis* is a pedagogical method for suggesting to the student not that you are smart or clever or humorous but rather that the student is, that speech and thought and reality can reflect one another but not always, and that a rhetorical figure can jolt and awaken one's awareness of the danger both of easy but false identities and of the soothing supposition that language has performed its full task if it has either entertained or asserted a comforting (but false) identity. Of course, beyond the pedagogical advantages of such rhetorical practicums, crucial ideological lessons are also conveyed. Dupriez refers to this deeper function as a form of diaphora, citing Pascal's probing "the heart has reasons unknown to reason."[128] This *antanaclasis* teaches two lessons: the practical one of language's complexity, and Pascal's ideological notion of a higher reason that resembles but also transcends normal rationality.

I close with three further examples, these quite unnoticed. The point is, even in such minimalist cases, to illustrate how the figure of *antanaclasis*,

---

[125] See Bill Long, also commenting on the Vince Lombardi quote: "Rhetorical Devices I," n.p. (cited May 23, 2004). Online: http://www.willamette.edu/~blong/MoreWords/RhetDevI.html.

[126] Richard A. Lanham, *A Handlist of Rhetorical Terms* (Berkeley: University of California Press, 1991), 12.

[127] Bernard Dupriez, *A Dictionary of Literary Devices* (trans. Albert W. Halsall; Toronto: University of Toronto Press, 1991), 43–44.

[128] Ibid., 133.

while configuring important points of biblical ideology, also advances the cause of biblical exegesis and wisdom's practice of language.

GEN 49:1

> Now Jacob called (*yiqra'*) to his sons and said: "Gather together so that I may tell you what will happen (*yiqra'*) to you in the end of days."
>
> Gen 49:1

The purpose here is to address the relationship between prophetic consciousness and secular activity.[129] At least in the prophetic perspective projected in traditional Jewish exegesis, the intent is to explain chance happenings by prophetic knowledge or even causality. The message: When things "happen" to you in the future, remember that I have already "called" or announced them and that they are therefore not happenstance but rather expressions of the divine will. For it is the prophetic word or "calling" that is seen to regulate and define the "happenings," that calls the shots and "names" things according to their real natures. This example shows how, as often, the identity principle inherent in *antanaclasis* comes full circle: the (false) identity of expression (the repetition) is first compromised by its oppositional sense, and then reasserted within the realm of discourse by a causality that reconciles the opposites.

PS 51:1–2

> A Psalm of David. When Nathan the prophet came to (*ba' 'el*) him after he had come to (*ba' 'el*) Bathsheba.
>
> Ps 51:1–2

Anyone familiar with the background story in 2 Sam 11 is aware of the striking contrast between Nathan's "coming to" David and the latter's "coming *into*" (NRSV) Bathsheba.[130] Indeed, Nathan's mission of reproof has as its purpose to redress David's "coming into" Bathsheba: (harsh) discourse in response to (illicit) intercourse, one might put it, to phonically capture the ironic appropriateness of the prophetic response. Or,

---

[129] This problem was discussed in the beginning of Part IV as the interaction of dialectical discourse ("under the sun") and Outside perspectives. Strictly speaking, this example is antanaclastic only in its written form, since the final letter *'alef* is a substitution for the letter *heh*, thus *miqre'*, to call, and *miqreh*, to happen. This wordplay has the same effect, however.

[130] For *ba' 'el* meaning sexual intercourse, see Gen 6:4; 16:2. Fox (*Proverbs 1–9*, 122) points out that the expression has both meanings in Prov 2:19 and the same may be the case in 6:29 as well.

more prosaically, sin leads to reproof, its oppositional comeuppance. One might refer to this as retributive causality or measure for measure, as seen in the Qohelet passages above.

A second pedagogical principle, already seen in the previous text, illustrates a further and perhaps more radical way of dealing with opposites. Whereas the previous text reintegrated contradictions by showing their causal relations, here the focus is on a new and more difficult perception of opposites as modeled in the Qohelet "Catalog of the Times" (3:1–8): as contradictions that cannot be reduced or even related but that nevertheless form part of the whole. In wisdom literature the starkest possible opposition is that between life and death, the first item of the Catalog. Yet one recalls Montaigne who, wishing to comfort a dying person, explained that "you do not die from being sick, you die from being alive."[131] The ground principle here is not the pantheistic coincidence of opposites but rather their harmonization, so that the final perception is not of a regained equivalence but rather a wider unity that requires both aspects of the contradiction to remain viable.[132] Such thinking, I believe, underlies the wild attempt surely not to justify David's vicious adultery and subsequent murder of Uriah, but rather to bring them within the universe of prophetic reproof and repentance. Three oppositional forms of "coming to": David's to Bathsheba, Nathan's to David, and, at least in the modern English idiom, David's "coming to."

PROV 6:30–32

> People will not despise a thief who steals only to satisfy his desire (*nafsho*) when he is hungry.
>
> – [To be sure,] if caught he will pay sevenfold, will forfeit all the wealth of his house.[133]
>
> But he who commits adultery with a woman has no brains. He who does this kills his own self (*nafsho*).[134]

---

[131] Michel de Montaigne, *Les Essais de Michel de Montaigne*, ed. Pierre Villey (Paris: Presses Universitaires de France, 1965), 1091 (III:13).

[132] On the harmony of opposites see Curtius, *European Literature*, 202.

[133] The severity of the punishment (sevenfold) is however problematic, unless it is taken as a mere figure for full compensation (e.g., Bruce K. Waltke, *The Book of Proverbs chapters 1–15* [NICOT; Grand Rapids, MI: Eerdmans, 2004], 358). R. N. Whybray (*Proverbs* [The New Century Bible Commentary; Grand Rapids, MI: Eerdmans, 1994], 107) strangely sees a contradiction between not being despised and yet punished. More puzzling, however, is the question raised by Keil (*Proverbs*, 35 n. 21): if he stole because of poverty, how do we understand the reference to the wealth and house that he will lose?

[134] One should not be deceived by the apparent simplicity of this text, which compares and contrasts adultery and its consequence with theft, for, as Whybray points out, "the

This occurrence of *antanaclasis* is apt to pass unnoticed, not only because the distance between key words is longer than usual but also because the project "to satisfy *nafsho*" is easily rendered, contextually and with some latitude. Thus, the thief will seek to stuff his throat, fill his belly (Fox), appease his hunger (NJPS), satisfy their/his appetite (NRSV, Waltke) or desire.[135] As for the adulterer, again going from the concrete to the more abstract, he kills or destroys himself (NRSV, NJPS, he is "a self-destroyer" Fox), he takes his own life (Waltke).

Waltke, sensing an intended opposition here, distinguishes between satisfying one's nutritional hunger and one's sexual hunger.[136] Thus, for example and as the popular *a fortiori* argument would have it, if the famished person still receives full punishment (v. 31), how much more so the adulterer, perhaps, as the narrator goes on to show, because of the intense revenge awakened in the cuckolded husband.

It is also the case, however, that the thief and the adulterer have a great deal in common. Elsewhere in Proverbs the comparison is made between the pleasures of eating and sexuality, thus pointing to the commonality of their strong appetites.[137] Whence Whybray's brilliant perception:

> There is probably a hidden allusion here to the adulterer in the words *to satisfy his appetite when he is hungry*: this is precisely the motive of the adulterer who "steals" someone else's wife because he cannot control his sexual appetite.[138]

What the adulterer has in common with the thief is that he too is a thief, but of persons and reputations rather than simply food property. Why the thief, even acting out of urgent motives, still receives full punishment is because, like the adulterer, he has not controlled his appetites and thus has opened the way for further (and perhaps less justified) infringements. *Antanaclasis* helps us see both the contrasts – between throat/belly hunger and self-annihilation – and also the common denominator

> nature of the argument is obscure, and no commentator has succeeded in elucidating it satisfactorily" (Whybray, *Proverbs*, 107).

[135] For the meaning "throat" see HALOT, 712. Fox, *Proverbs 1–9*, 228. Waltke, *The Book of Proverbs chapters 1–15*, 349.

[136] Waltke, ibid., 357.

[137] Pace Waltke, *The Book of Proverbs chapters 1–15*, 356. See Prov 9:17; 20:17; 30:20. In classical Jewish exegesis (see Rashi ad loc) "eating bread" was understood as a euphemism for sexual intercourse, as in Gen 39:6, 8–9. In Exod 2:20 it is said to refer to marriage. See my recent study, "Sexual Metaphors of Field (*sadeh*) and Food as Keys to Interpretation in the Hebrew Bible," in *A Life in Parables and Poetry: Mishael Maswari Caspi*, ed. John T. Greene (Berlin: Klaus Schwarz Verlag, 2014).

[138] Whybray, *Proverbs*, 108.

of both cases: that they are all functions of appetites that must be filled
or killed, and that overindulgence at any level will lead to the destruction
of the ultimate appetite, that of the self. Like greed for gain, "it takes
away the life of its possessors" (1:19). Translators must commit to one
of these, of course, but it is the repeated polyvalent *nafsho* that expresses
their common denominator.

This brings us back to our previous question as to the value of such
puns as *yesheb* to express both "settling down" and "sitting" in Exodus
and Jonah. Rather than the complaint of stylistic poverty, one might be
brought to reflect on the importance of one's *place*, on how where one
chooses to dwell conditions one's opportunities for growth and even for
revelation. Or, conversely, where I choose to "sit" leads to what I become
willing to settle for.

7. *A (Somewhat Polemical) Postface*

This manuscript has benefited from a number of outside readings and
reviews, some less than positive but all well-intentioned. Since these issues
are bound to come up in future critical readings, I would like to make
things easier and clear my own ground so that meaningful discussion
can ensue. This may be harder than it sounds, since the centuries-old
dogma of Qohelet's pessimism, rooted in Jerome's choice of translating
hebel as "vanity" and promoted as prime Scriptural backing for all kinds
of dualisms and world-hatreds, brings a joyous philosophy to its negation and poor Qohelet – except as purportedly managed by canonical
interests – to the status of fall-guy.

Noting my use of modern philosophers, some have suggested that
I pitch my essay to some postmodern or Derridean or whatever intellectual style, which could in fact amount to my saying about Qohelet
whatever I damned please. If I do make a big deal of Blanchot and
Jankélévitch and Levinas in particular, this is because Qohelet is a philosophical text begging to be explained philosophically, because these
scholars are indeed prominent philosophers, because they also have
an exquisite sense of just how literature can function in this area, and
especially because they raise issues and propose readings that seem to
me particularly relevant to Qohelet and that remain unexplored. In
other words, I propose that Levinas et Cie. can translate Qohelet into
concepts that make sense both to the text and to modern readers, and
this is because, far from eisegesis, such formulations can help us recover
and understand what has been there all along. This is quite different

from a certain postmodernist agenda that should indeed be viewed with suspicion.

Rather than argue the philosophical approach here, let me turn to philology, both its dialectical opposite and also partner in arms. For I propose that philosophy alone cannot carry the burden, nor can philology; but my notion of the latter differs from that of some of my colleagues. A personal notation may clarify my high regard for philology, which was the area of my Yale Ph. D. at a time when the term referred to rigorous linguistic expertise coupled with a broad literary and cultural approach (the names of Leo Spitzer and Erich Auerbach come to mind). We studied language both synchronically and diachronically, as for example the evolution of the Romance languages from Vulgar Latin. The goal was always, however, to situate philology, as narrowly understood, within literary and philosophical/theological contexts that made sense of texts as expressions of a people and a culture. I hold to these ideals in my work to this day. In dealing with Qohelet, this means, first of all, pursuing what meaning that text could have had in its day and within the cultural ideals it projects. (That the author of Qohelet did everything she could to enigmaticize historical and cultural underpinnings is significant in its own right, of course).

Let me focus on a single critic as emblematic of a problem in Qohelet criticism. H. L. Ginsberg's work is well known to me, and although he is less frequently cited nowadays, his work continues to be of interest. I leave aside his theory of an Aramaic original of Qohelet, a path that even some of his disciples are reluctant to tread. My main divergence here is on what an old colleague and friend of his told me, that "H. L. never missed an occasion to emend a received text." In Qohelet I find this impulse misguided. To take only the most egregious example (regrettably followed by Michael V. Fox), why reject *'olam* ("eternity") in 3:11, which opens the door to expanded thoughts on time – the real context of chapter 3 – in favor of the overworked *'amal* ("labor, or the results thereof"), which requires little effort in philosophical speculation. Or why disregard the clear grammatical reading of "there is a time *to give birth* and a time to die' (3:1, see "Giving Birth vs. Being Born") when a reading both philosophical and grammatically faithful to the received text taps deeper levels of meditation?

And, while we are on the subject of emendation, what of all the tricks applied to the concluding chapter of Qohelet in order to "make it look kosher," as many critics are pleased to believe? Although one reader waxes rather poetic on "Perry's heroic efforts of exegesis" in this area,

Perry is really undeserving on this count. Rather, the opposite is the case, since I explain the received text without alteration, whereas it is others who bring in unnecessary alterations, designed to read the text according to their own (im)pieties. As an aside, I wish to report that I read this paper (my Chapter 11) as it stands at the International SBL Conference in Rome, where it was well received by leading scholars, who expressed their agreement with my restored and *un*-revised reading.

One final general point, if I may be allowed, regarding the validity of what is "widely regarded" by critics. I stand in agreement, but with the awareness that readings do change like the weather and according to dominant ideological and social moods. I would imagine, for example, that before Copernicus the world was "widely regarded" as flat. Closer to our task here, I stand alone – but with Hugo Grotius: what a companion! – on the issue of Qohelet's confessional perspective, although the point is beginning to be discussed in some European publications. I also project that, although it has not yet emerged into full discussion, Qohelet's bipolar perspective offered here and as navigated by his confessional autobiography will soon become a standard point of reference.

I continue to be amused by the projection, by critics and countless others including rabbis, that Qohelet's place in canonical Scripture was salvaged by the importation of the final chapter in a desperate attempt to render the entire book "kosher" ("and it worked!" one reader exclaims). The Book of Qohelet does at some point make an about-face and reject (in part) the monologic vanity argument, but this transformation is not a rabbinic sleight of hand imported from outside and serving canonical interests. For then we would have a hybrid Book, whereas what we in fact have is a hybrid world and its readers, recognized as such by the hybrid author/protagonist Qohelet, who undergoes this dual awareness and narrates his own transformation through what I describe as a confessional perspective.

8. *Qohelet from the Geniza*

As the saying would have it, wisdom's proof is in the…
putting it all down in words.
Here are a few that I fancy Qohelet might have allowed into the original collection:

1. Qohelet to a religious person:
    You wish to bask in the divine presence
    and cannot enjoy even a simple glass of water?!

2. Qohelet on experience:
    The fool is one who gets burned twice.
    The worse fool is one who never gets burned.

3. Qohelet's adage on quietism:
    Don't just do something: stand there!

4. Qohelet's Jobean encounter with pleasure:
    Shall we receive evil from the Lord and not also good?

5. Getting on with it:
    O. k., all is vanity/breath. Now what's for supper?
    Alternatively:
    The living pray for another year; the dying ask for another breath.

6. Dealing with the infinite details of everyday life:
    Don't sweat the small stuff, and it's all small stuff.
    Alternatively:
    Sweat the small stuff. It may be small, but it's your stuff.

7. Qohelet's own justification for writing the book:
    "I have written this book in order to assess my fellow humans' favorite pastime: complaining."

Bibliography

Álvarez, Julia, in *You've Got to Read This*. Edited by Ron Hansen. New York: HarperCollins, 2000.

Alter, Robert. *The David Story: A Translation with Commentary of 1 and 2 Samuel*. New York: Norton, 1999.

Apollinaire, Guillaume. *Oeuvres Poétiques: "Calligrammes."* Paris: Gallimard, Bibliothèque de la Pléiade, 1956.

Appelfeld, Aharon. *The Conversion*. Translated by Jeffrey M. Green. New York: Schocken, 1998.

Aurelius, Marcus. *Thoughts*. Loeb Classical Library, 2 vols. Cambridge, MA: Harvard University Press, 1970.

Auster, Paul, ed. *The Random House Book of Twentieth Century French Poetry*. New York: Vintage, 1984

Bachelard, Gaston. "La philosophie scientifique de Léon Brunschvicg." *Revue de métaphysique et de morale*, Jan.–Apr. 1945, 77–84.

Barthes, Roland. "The Death of the Author." 1969 http://artsites.ucsc.edu/faculty/Gustafson/FILM%20162.W10/readings/barthes.death.pdf

Barucq, André. *Ecclésiaste*. Paris: Beauchesne, 1968.

Bechtel, Lyn M. "Rethinking the Interpretation of Genesis 2.4B-3.24," in *A Feminist Companion to Genesis*. Edited by Athalya Brenner. Sheffield: Sheffield Academic Press, 1993, 1–18.

Bergo, Bettina. "The Face in Levinas." *Angelaki* 16 (2011): 17–38.

Blanchot, Maurice. *L'Attente l'oubli*. Paris: Gallimard, 1962.

    L'Écriture du désastre. Paris: Gallimard, 1980.

    L'Espace littéraire. Paris: Gallimard, 1955.

Bolin, Thomas. "Rivalry and Resignation: Girard and Qoheleth on the Divine-Human Relationship." *Biblica* 86 (2005): 245–59.

Breuer, Mordechai et al., eds. *Torat Hayyim: Chumash* [The Five Books of Moses], with Classical Commentaries. 7 vols.; Jerusalem: Mossad Harav Kook, 1986–93.

Buell, Lawrence. *The Environmental Imagination: Thoreau, Nature Writing, and the Formation of American Culture*. Cambridge, MA: Harvard University Press, 1995.

Camus, Albert. *L'Étranger*. Paris: Gallimard, 1942.

    Le Mythe de Sisyphe. Paris: Gallimard, 1942.

    L'Exil et le royaume. Paris: Gallimard, 1957.

Caputo, John D. *The Weakness of God*. Bloomington: Indiana University Press, 2006.

Ceresko, Anthony R. "The Function of *Antanaclasis* (*mts'* "to find" // *mts'* "to reach, overtake, grasp") in Hebrew Poetry, Especially in the Book of Qoheleth." *CBQ* 44 (1982): 551–69.

Char, René. "Conversation avec une grappe, en hommage à Maurice Blanchot." *Critique*, June 1966, 483.

Christianson, Eric S. *Ecclesiastes through the Centuries*. Oxford: Blackwell, 2007.

Cioran, E. M. *La Tentation d'exister*. Paris: Gallimard, 1956.

Crenshaw, James L. *Ecclesiastes, a Commentary*. Old Testament Library. Philadelphia: Westminster, 1987.

    Joel: A New Translation with Introduction and Commentary. AB 24C; Garden City, NY: Doubleday, 1995, 60.

Curtius, Ernst Robert. *European Literature and the Latin Middle Ages*. Translated by Willard R. Trask; New York and Boston: Harper, 1953.

De Fontenay, Elisabeth. *Actes de naissance*. Paris: Seuil, 2011.

Dell, Katharine. *The Book of Proverbs in Social and Theological Context*. Cambridge: Cambridge University Press, 2009.

Derrida, Jacques. *The Gift of Death*. Translated by David Willis. Chicago and London: University of Chicago Press, 1996, 82–114.

Di Lella, Alexander A., trans. Ben Sira. AB 39.

Dillard, Annie. *For the Time Being*. New York: Alfred A. Knopf, 1999.

Diogenes Laertius. *Lives of Eminent Philosophers*, "Diogenes." Translated by R. D. Hicks. Loeb Classical Library, 2 vols. Cambridge, MA: Harvard University Press, 1970.

Dor-Shav, Ethan. "Ecclesiastes, Fleeting and Timeless." *Azure* 18 (2004): 67–87.

Dupriez. Bernard. *A Dictionary of Literary Devices*. Translated by Albert W. Halsall. Toronto: University of Toronto Press, 1991.

Emerson, Ralph Waldo. "Experience," in *The Portable Emerson*. Edited by Carl Bode. New York: Penguin Books, 1981.

Farmer, Kathleen A. *Who Knows What Is Good? Proverbs and Ecclesiastes*. Grand Rapids, MI: Eerdmans, 1991.

Fisch, Harold. *The Holy Scriptures: English Text Revised and Edited*. Jerusalem: Koren, 1992.

    Poetry with a Purpose. Bloomington: Indiana University Press, 1990.

Foucault, Michel. *Foucault's Legacy*. Edited by C. G. Prado. New York and London: Continuum, 2009.

    Leçons sur la volonté de savoir: Cours au Collège de France, 1970–71. Paris: Gallimard/ Seuil, 2011.

    "What is an Author?" *Truth and Method*, 113–38, n.d. http://artsites.ucsc.edu/ faculty/Gustafson/FILM%20162.W10/readings/foucault.author.pdf

Fox, Michael V. *Ecclesiastes: The JPS Biblical Commentary*. Philadelphia: JPS, 2004.

    "The Epistemology of the Book of Proverbs." *JBL* 126 (2007), 669–84.

    "The Identification of Quotations in Biblical Literature." *ZAW* 92 (1980), 416–30.

Proverbs 1–9. AB18A; New York: Doubleday, 2000.

Proverbs 1–9: A Commentary. http://www.bibleinterp.com/articles/proverbs .htm

Qohelet and His Contradictions. Sheffield: Almond Press, 1989.

A Time to Tear Down and a Time to Build Up: A Rereading of Ecclesiastes. Grand Rapids, MI: Eerdmans, 1999

Hartman, Geoffrey. *A Scholar's Tale.* New York: Fordham University Press, 2007.

Ginsberg, H. L. *Koheleth.* Tel Aviv-Jerusalem: Newman, 1961, 1977 [Hebrew].

"The Quintessence of Koheleth," in *Biblical and Other Studies.* Edited by A. Altmann. Cambridge, MA: Harvard University Press, 1963, 47–59.

Studies in Koheleth. Jerusalem: Newman, 1961.

Goethe. *Faust.* Translated by Walter Kaufmann. New York: Anchor, 1990.

Gordis, Robert. *Koheleth – The Man and His World.* New York: Schocken, 1968.

Ha-Meiri, Menahem. *Commentary on the Book of Psalms.* Edited by Menachem Mendel Zahav. Jerusalem: Otsar ha-Poskim, 1971 [Hebrew].

Hacham, Amos. *The Book of Psalms,* 2 vols. Jerusalem: Mossad harav Kook, n. d. [Hebrew].

Heschel, Abraham Joshua. *The Sabbath.* New York: Noonday, 1951.

The Sabbath. New York: Farrar, Straus and Giroux, 2005.

Hölderlin. *Poems.* Translated by Michael Hamburger. New York: Pantheon, 1942.

Jabès, Edmond. *Le Livre des questions.* Paris: Gallimard, 1963.

Jankélévitch, Vladimir. *Le Sérieux de l'intention: Traité des vertus I.* Paris: Flammarion, 1983.

Jankélévitch, Vladimir and Berlowitz, Béatrice. *Quelque part dans l'inachevé.* Paris: Gallimard, 1978.

Japhet, Sara and Salters, Robert B. *The Commentary of R. Samuel Ben Meir Rashbam on Qoheleth.* Jerusalem: Magnes, 1985.

Johnston, Robert K. "'Confessions of a Workaholic': A Reappraisal." *CBQ* 38 (1976): 14–28.

Josephus, Flavius. *The Life. Against Apion.* Cambridge, MA: Loeb Classical Library, Harvard University Press, 1976.

Kaplan, Robert. *The Nothing that Is: A Natural History of Zero.* New York: Oxford University Press, 1999

Katz, Claire Elise. *Levinas, Judaism, and the Feminine: The Silent Footsteps of Rebecca.* Bloomington: Indiana University Press, 2003.

Kazin, Alfred. *Writing Was Everything.* Cambridge, MA: Harvard University Press, 1995.

Keil, Yehudah. *1 Samuel.* Jerusalem: Mossad Harav Kook, 1981 [Hebrew].

Proverbs. Jerusalem: Mossad Harav Kook, 1983 [Hebrew].

Krüger, Thomas. *Qoheleth: A Commentary.* Minneapolis: Fortress Press, 2004.

The Ladino Bible of Ferrara [1553] Edited by Moshe Lazar. Culver City, CA: Labirinthos, 1992.

The Ladino Five Scrolls Edited by Moshe Lazar. Culver City, CA: Labirinthos, 1992.

Lange, Gershon. *Sefer Kohelet: übersetz und erklärt.* Frankfurt am Main, 1910. Translated and annotated by Yosef B. Fagin. Lakewood, NJ: Gilayon, 2007.

Lanham, Richard A. *A Handlist of Rhetorical Terms.* Translated by Albert W. Halsall. Berkeley: University of California Press, 1991.

Lee, Eunny P. *The Vitality of Enjoyment in Qohelet's Theological Rhetoric.* Berlin/ New York: Walter de Gruyter, 2005.

Levinas, Emmanuel. *L'Au delà du verset.* Paris: Les Éditions de Minuit, 1982.

Carnets de captivité et autres inédits. Paris: Grasset, 2009.

Dieu, la mort et le temps. Paris: Grasset, 1993.

De Dieu qui vient à l'idée. Paris: Vrin, 2004.

Difficile liberté. Paris: Albin Michel, 1976.

Éthique comme philosophie première. Préface par Jacques Rolland. Paris: Payot et Rivages, 1998.

Hors sujet. Paris: Fata Morgana, 1987.

L'Intrigue de l'infini. Paris: Flammarion, 1994.

Parole et silence et autres conférences inédites. Paris: Grasset, 2009.

Le Temps et l'autre. Paris: Arthaud, 1947.

Totalité et infini. Paris: Kluwer, 1987.

Totality and Infinity. Translated by Alphonso Lingis. Pittsburgh: Duquesne University Press, 1969.

Limburg, James. *Encountering Ecclesiastes: A Book for Our Time.* Grand Rapids, MI: Eerdmans, 2006, 19.

Lo, Alison. "Death in Qohelet." *Journal of the Ancient Near Eastern Society* 31 (2009): 85–98.

Lohfink, Norbert. "Koh 1,2 'Alles ist Windhauch' – universale oder anthropologishe Aussage?," in *Der Weg zum Menschen.* Edited by R. Mosis and L. Ruppert. Freiburg: Herder, 1989, 201–16.

Qoheleth: A Continental Commentary. Minneapolis: Fortress, 2003.

Longman III, Tremper. *The Book of Ecclesiastes.* Grand Rapids, MI: Eerdmans, 1998.

Machinist, Peter. "Fate, *miqreh*, and Reason: Some Reflection of Qohelet and Biblical Thought," in *Solving Riddles and Untying Knots.* Edited by Z. Zevit et al.. Festschrift for Shemaryahu Talmon. Winnona Lake, IN: Eisenbrauns, 1995, 159–75.

Maimonides, Moses. "Laws of Repentance." In *Book of Knowledge* [*Mishneh Torah, Book I*]. Translated by Moses Hyamson. New York: Bloch, 1937.

Mattila, Sharon Lea. "Ben Sira and the Stoics: A Reexamination of the Evidence." *JBL* 119 (2000): 480–84.

Maussion, Marie. *Le mal, le bien et le jugement de Dieu dans le livre de Qohélet.* Orbis Biblicus et Orientalis 190; Göttingen/Fribourg: Vandenhoeck & Ruprecht, 2003.

McCarter, P. Kyle. *1 Samuel.* AB 8, Garden City, NY: Doubleday, 1980.

Meschonnic, Henri. *La Rime et la vie.* Paris: Verdier, 2006.

Miller, Douglas B. "Qohelet's Symbolic Use of Hebel." *JBL* 117 (1998): 437–54.

Montaigne, Michel de. *Les Essais de Michel de Montaigne.* Edited by Pierre Villey. Paris: Presses Universitaires de France, 1965.

The Complete Essays of Montaigne. Translated by Donald Frame. Palo Alto, CA: Stanford University Press, 1976.

Mopsik, Charles. *La Sagesse de ben Sira.* Paris: Verdier, 2003.

Morgan, Michael L. *The Cambridge Introduction to Emmanuel Levinas.* New York: Cambridge University Press, 2011.

Murphy, Roland E. *Ecclesiastes*. Word Biblical Commentary 23A. Dallas: Word Books, 1992.

The Tree of Life. An Exploration of Biblical Wisdom Literature. New York: Doubleday, 1990.

Neher, André. *Jérémie*. Paris: Seuil, 1998.

Notes sur Qohélét. Paris: Les Éditions de Minuit, 1951.

Noegel, Scott B. "Word Play in Qoheleth." *Journal of Hebrew Scriptures* 7 (2007): 2–28.

Ogden, Graham. *Qoheleth*. Sheffield: JSOT Press, 1987.

Paley, Grace. *The Collected Stories*. New York: Farrar, Straus and Giroux, 1994.

Paul, Sherman. *The Shores of America: Thoreau's Inward Exploration*. Urbana: Illinois University Press, 1958), ch. 7. Quoted in Robert Sayre, ed. *New Essays on "Walden."* New York: Cambridge University Press, 1992.

Paulhan, Jean. *L'Expérience du proverbe*. Paris: L'Echoppe, 1993.

Perry, T. A. *Dialogues with Kohelet: The Book of Ecclesiastes: Translation and Commentary*. University Park: Penn State University Press, 1993.

Erotic Spirituality: The Integrative Tradition from Leone Ebreo to John Donne. Tuscaloosa: University of Alabama Press, 1980.

Jonah's Arguments with God: The Honeymoon Is Over! Peabody, MA: Hendrickson, 2014.

"Just Say No: Montaigne's Negative Ethics," in *Approaches to Teaching Montaigne's Essays*. Edited by Patrick Henry. New York: MLA, 1993.

"Love's Philosophy in Canticles: The King and the Pastoral Setting," in *Bethsaida in Archeology. A Festschrift in Honor of John T. Greene*. Edited by J. Harold Ellens. Newcastle: Cambridge Scholars, 2014, 318–29.

The Moral Proverbs of Santob de Carrión: Jewish Wisdom in Christian Spain. Princeton, NJ: Princeton University Press, 1987.

"A Poetics of Absence: The Structure and Meaning of Chaos in Genesis 1:2." *JSOT* 58 (1993): 3–11.

"Sexual Metaphors of Field (*sadeh*) and Food as Keys to Interpretation in the Hebrew Bible," in *A Life in Parables and Poetry: Mishael Maswari Caspi*. Edited by John T. Greene. Berlin: Klaus Schwarz Verlag, 2014.

Wisdom in the Hebrew Bible: God's Twilight Zone. Peabody, MA: Hendrickson, 2014.

Poulet, Georges. "Maurice Blanchot, Critique et romancier." *Critique*, June 1966: 494–97.

Provan, Iain. *Ecclesiastes/Song of Songs*. Application Commentary. Grand Rapids, MI: Zondervan, 2001.

Rilke, Rainer Maria. *Sonnets to Orpheus*. Translated by C. F. MacIntyre. Berkeley: University of California Press, 1960.

Robbins, Jill. "Circumcising Confession: Derrida, Autobiography, Judaism." *Diacritics* 25 (1995): 25.

Roubaud, Jacques. *Cent cinquantes poemes (1991–98)* Paris: Gallimard, 1966.

Rousseau, Jean-Jacques. *Rêveries du promeneur solitaire*. Genève: Droz, 1967.

Sarna, Nahum M. *Genesis: The Traditional Hebrew Text with the JPS Translation*. Philadelphia: JPS, 1991.

Songs of the Heart. New York: Schocken, 1993.

Sartre, Jean Paul. *La Nausée*. Paris: Gallimard, 1938.

Sauer, Georg. *Jesus Sirach/Ben Sira*. Göttingen: Vandenhoeck & Ruprecht, 2000.

Scheindlin, Raymond P. *The Gazelle.* Philadelphia: Jewish Publication Society, 1991.

Schifferdecker, Kathryn. *Out of the Whirlwind: Creation Theology in the Book of Job.* Cambridge, MA: Harvard Theological Studies, 2008.

Schoors, Anton. *The Preacher Sought to Find Pleasing Words.* Leuven: Peeters, 1992.

Scott, R. B. Y. *Proverbs, Ecclesiastes,* AB 18. New York: Doubleday, 1965.

Seneca, *Ad Lucilium Epistulae Morales,* 3 vols. Translated by Richard M. Gummere. Cambridge, MA: Loeb Classical Library, Harvard University Press, 1971.

Seow, Choon-Leong. *Ecclesiastes: A New Translation with Introduction and Commentary.* AB 18C. New York: Doubleday, 1997.

Shapiro, Rami. *The Way of Solomon: Finding Joy and Contentment in the Wisdom of Ecclesiastes.* San Francisco: Harper, 2000.

Ecclesiastes Annotated and Explained. Woodstock, VT: Skylight Paths, 2011.

Shuster, Martin. "Being as Breath, Vapor as Joy: Using Martin Heidegger to Re-Read the Book of Ecclesiastes." *JSOT* 33 (2008): 219–44.

Sibony, Daniel. *Entre-deux.* Paris: Seuil, 1991.

Lectures bibliques. Paris: Odile Jacob, 2006.

Smelik, Klaas. "God in the Book of Qoheleth," in *The Language of Qohelet in Its Context: Essays in Honour of Prof. A. Schoors on the Occasion of His Seventieth Birthday.* Edited by A. Berlejung and P. Van Hecke; Leuven: Peeters, 2007, 177–81.

Sneed, Mark R. *The Politics of Pessimism in Ecclesiastes: A Social-Science Perspective.* Atlanta: Society of Biblical Literature, 2012.

Stevens, Wallace. *The Collected Poems of Wallace Stevens.* New York: Alfred A. Knopf, 1954, 1982.

The Palm at the End of the Mind: Selected Poems and a Play. New York: Alfred A. Knopf, 1971.

Tanenbaum, Adena. *The Contemplative Soul: Hebrew Poetry and Philosophical Theory in Medieval Spain.* Leiden: Brill, 2002.

Thoreau, Henry David. *Walden, or Life in the Woods.* New York: New American Library, 1999.

Tilliette, Xavier. "Gabriel Marcel et l'autre royaume," in *Jean Wahl et Gabriel Marcel.* Paris: Beauchesne, 1976.

Waltke, Bruce K. *The Book of Proverbs: Chapters 1–15.* NICOT. Grand Rapids, MI: Eerdmans, 2004.

Whybray, R. N. *Ecclesiastes.* New Century Bible Commentary. Grand Rapids, MI: Eerdmans, 1989.

Whybray, R. N. (*Proverbs* [The New Century Bible Commentary; Grand Rapids, MI: Eerdmans, 1994], 107.

Wolff, Hans Walter. *Anthropology of the Old Testament.* Mifflintown, PA: Sigler, 1996.

Index

Printed in the USA
CPSIA information can be obtained
at www.ICGtesting.com
LVHW091653300124
770329LV00001B/116